A Personal Chronicle of an Epoch

IMPRESARIO

Grace Denton Esser

Foreword by Merle Armitage

MANZANITA PRESS
YUCCA VALLEY
CALIF.

**Dedication
For my husband
Maurice H. Esser**

CONTENTS

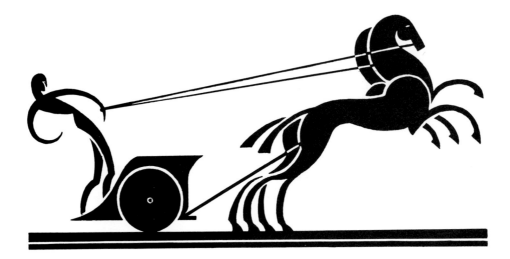

FOREWORD

It was an amazing epoch. The turn of the century was an era of expansion in America in every dimension. We had built several transcontinental railways, and our cities were not only growing at an unprecedented rate, but were pushing up high-rise buildings that became known in Europe as skyscrapers.

Soon the Wright brothers would fly the first plane, and in the meantime, in addition to telegraph, telephones were becoming universal, even in rural districts. Soon there would be radio, followed by television.

All the arts were fast cutting the umbilical cord that had for so long bound us to Europe. Painters appeared that offered universal quality, and Rockwell Kent, George Bellows, Robert Henri and especially John Marin were respected in a world sense. Everything was burgeoning.

Soon everyone in the civilized world was reading Hemingway, Faulkner, Steinbeck and that American in Paris, Gertrude Stein. And who but America could have produced the giant of architecture, Frank Lloyd Wright! And a new art form, that of the camera, became extremely important through the work of Steichen, Steiglitz, Strand and particularly Edward Weston.

In performers, too, we produced some of the best. After all, the Barrymores, the Lunts, and a dozen other bright stars such as Helen Hayes received plaudits on both sides of the Atlantic. And that new type of ram-

1

bunctious music, known as Jazz, came to a brilliant head with the advent of George Gershwin.

Even the hardest nut of all to crack, Grand Opera, had to make room for the Americans, Geraldine Farrar and Lawrence Tibbett at the Metropolitan, and Mary Garden and Charles Hackett at the Chicago Opera.

It was an exciting, heady time. Margaret Anderson with her *Little Review*, and *The Dial*, not to mention the *Smart Set*, spawned by George Jean Nathan and Henry Mencken, gave us avant-garde magazines that set the pace.

Into this lively, dynamic and lusty milieu came a young woman with a burning desire to put her shoulder, even a slender one, to the wheel. Grace Denton had a very solid background in music, and she not only wanted to belong to that enthusiastic national tide that had given us more symphony orchestras than there were in all of Europe, but she wanted to make a contribution.

As I have gone over her manuscript, I have been very much impressed with her modesty. She plunged into things in which she believed, and nothing, be it said, was too big for her. She of course had some failures, but her successes were all on the right side of the ledger.

She never pats herself on the back, but the discerning reader, who in these pages will likely relive some of his or her personal experiences, will read between the lines and discover a very stalwart, a very shrewd, and a very dedicated worker in the vineyard of music. *Madame Impresario* takes us gently through some of the most brilliant pages of our musical, operatic and theatrical history of the past fifty years.

MERLE ARMITAGE

The Glory of Max Reinhardt

For many years after the turn of the century, Max Reinhardt dominated the theatrical life of Europe. There was indeed a Reinhardt fever which engulfed the entire western world, for his influence was everywhere.

Based on Salzberg, his power ranged from London to New York and his influence penetrated every theatrical project from Piccadilly to Broadway, and to every little theatre movement in England and America. Even chauvinistic France paid heed.

Books and magazines were avidly scanned as I sought to know more about this masterful, magnetic man, who infused new blood and powerful ideas into the then moribund theatre.

Not only was he master of pageantry in its largest and most inspiring forms, but he created a synthesis, returning painting, sculpture and music to the theatre.

My first encounter with this history-making dedicated man was in connection with his Cleveland production of "The Miracle," which brought deep inspiration to uncountable thousands in the capitals of Europe. From 1922 to 1926 "The Miracle" was produced in leading American cities. The printed program stated: "The most stupendous production in the history of the world." The performances in the United States, staged by Reinhardt, were designed by Norman Bel Geddes with F. Ray Comstock and Morris Gest, the producers.

3

From New York it was next brought to the Public Auditorium in Cleveland, seating 6,000. This was transformed into the interior of a Cathedral as were the Century Theatre in New York and the largest Auditoriums and Opera houses in Philadelphia, Cincinnati, Chicago, St. Louis, Kansas City, Los Angeles, San Francisco, Detroit, an unprecedented stage setting for a performance having a cast of 600.

The performance in Cleveland attracted 150,000 spectators from a radius of hundreds of miles. This is where *Madame Impresario* became involved as the representative in Toledo for "The Miracle" in 1923, managing the sale of tickets there and arranging for special New York Central trains to transport the ticket buyers to Cleveland.

Who could remain unmoved with the entrancing beauty of Lady Diana Manners as the motionless statue of the Madonna. Before her the maimed, halt, blind knelt in order to become healed. While the production of the legend was largely in pantomime, music was an integral factor — chants, choruses, orchestra.

Another role, impeccably enacted by Rosamond Pinchot was that of the Nun who followed the call of the Knight into the world, placing her raiment, veil and keys at the feet of the Madonna before she departed through the gates. In gradual poetry of motion the Madonna comes to life, dons the garments of the Nun and takes over her duties.

The populace was aghast at the disappearance of the beloved Madonna not realizing that she had assumed the life of the Nun. Then came the depiction of turbulent experiences of the Nun. After seven years she returns to the Cathedral. The Madonna ascends her pedestal and the Nun resumes her duties. Lights come up, the awed spectators depart in silence — a tribute to the inspired creativity of Max Reinhardt.

Years later, 1935 to be exact, Fate came along in a grandiose mood, when I was requested to present the Reinhardt Hollywood Bowl production of "A Midsummer Night's Dream" in Chicago. The entire cast and production came direct to the Auditorium Theatre from Hollywood, even the forest trees were transported on railroad flat cars. A glade was built on stage as a slanting hill ascending from the orchestra pit to the rear of the stage. As the mist arose in the trees came the Corps de Ballet with premiere ballerina, Nini Theilade, and the music of Mendelssohn. It was an enchanting scene.

In the cast were Olivia de Havilland as Hermia and Mickey Rooney as Puck. A mere stripling in his first major role, he proved a sensational success.

4

Reinhardt, of course, was there in person. An announcement read:

CRACE DENTON *has the honor to present...*

MAX REINHARDT

PERSONALLY DIRECTING HIS PRODUCTION OF SHAKESPEARE'S COMEDY

"A Midsummer Night's Dream"

MUSIC BY MENDELSSOHN

Two weeks only • OPENING THURSDAY, NOVEMBER FIFTEENTH

CLOSING THANKSGIVING DAY

AUDITORIUM THEATRE

My final contact with Reinhardt was in 1938, when we envisioned that Santa Barbara, California, might be the locale for an American Salzberg. The County of Santa Barbara had built a gem of an outdoor Bowl of field stone in the hills overlooking the Pacific. This seemed an ideal setting for a Reinhardt Festival. It was arranged for Reinhardt to come to Santa Barbara which he did, journeying from Los Angeles by motor with his wife, Helene Thimig. I made the trip with Reinhardt's attorney, Ronald Button, in his private plane. Reinhardt was enthusiastic about the locale and wrote an outline of plans.

The Santa Barbara *News Press* gave a banner-headline to the occasion, and stated: "Miss Grace Denton accompanied Max Reinhardt, world-famous producer of musical pageants, on an inspection tour of Santa Barbara's Bowl. Reinhardt was considering one of his spectacular presentations here and expressed pleasure at the facilities offered by the local Bowl."

Reinhardt Festivals are costly affairs — it didn't happen. There was a Festival in the Bowl, however, of which more later in these pages.

The Lure of "Music under the Stars"

My interest in Festival performances "Under the Stars" had become whetted through doing promotion and publicity for the reopening of Ravinia Park in suburban Chicago with Mrs. Edward Moore, wife of the Music Editor of the Chicago *Tribune,* my assistant. This was a shrine of music, which for years had Grand Opera in the grand manner sponsored by Louis Eckstein until his death.

Regretfully closed for a few years, Mrs. Eckstein gave her consent in 1936 for its reopening for a Festival of concerts by the Chicago Symphony. This brought real joy to thousands of music lovers.

From the days when I was located in Toledo and presented George Gershwin on his famous tour with Paul Whiteman's orchestra, introducing "Rhapsody in Blue," I later rejoiced in managing several concert appearances by the magnetic George. To open the Ravinia season I enlisted him to appear in this first Ravinia Festival. He came and performed "An American in Paris" and "Concerto in F" with the Chicago Symphony. The night was balmy and beautiful. The Ravinia pavilion was jammed to the last seat. Hundreds sat on the surrounding grass and others literally hung in the trees. Back stage George kissed me and said he "would always play concerts for me" but alas this was the final one. The last time I saw him was when I was a guest in his box at a performance of the first production of "Porgy and Bess" in New York. He lamentably succumbed in 1937.

Another outdoor Bowl — the Hollywood Bowl — is a cultural monument to the Twentieth Century. Not only Hollywood but the entire nation can boast of its accomplishments. So many great events in music, dance and productions of magnitude have occurred on its spacious stage, it exudes grandeur and inspiration. Its Reinhardt production of "A Midsummer Night's Dream" was my only personal connection with the Bowl except for the unmatchable friendship with its revered Founder, Artie Mason Carter.

It was she who came upon the lovely site in the Hollywood hills and who envisioned its future for "Symphonies Under the Stars." Although she

6

enlisted the cooperation of many, it was she, beset with the many vicissitudes of the early days, who never gave up. She remained dedicated throughout her life, subscribed for a season box, regaling her friends with invitations to attend concerts. How fortunate was I to be among those invited. It was stimulating to witness the enthusiasm of this zealot for music. She aided financially many a young American composer for she believed mightily in American music.

Artie Mason Carter organized the first Easter Sunrise service in the Hollywood Bowl, which has continued through the years. It all began in 1922, when make shift wooden benches were used for seats. Making it possible for untold thousands, through the Bowl's capacity of 20,000, to hear great music "under the stars" was Artie Mason Carter's dream and she made her dream come true.

Laguna Beach has a charming outdoor Bowl and there in 1963 I presented Victor Borge in one of his inimitable programs of "Comedy in Music." The weather cooperated, stars shone, the Bowl could not have held another person and laughter echoed through the hills. Jim Killingsworth and his publications, *"The Newporter"* and *"Orange County Illustrated,"* sponsored the occasion as a benefit for a Cultural Center Fund. I had instigated a Council of Arts for this objective which now is building a Cultural Center for Orange County on Irvine Ranch property in Newport Beach.

Motivation — From Whence Does It Come?

How did I become propelled into the sophisticated melange of concerts, opera, ballet, super theatrical productions? Could it be that the first seeds of these exotic interests began in childhood? How well I remember my mother singing to me when I was beset with children's ailments. These songs struck a responsive chord which made a deep impression. Was it these deeply felt emotions that propelled me into a career that became the chief motivation of my life?

Life is surrounded with song — the lullaby at the beginning, the dirge at the end. War, peace, love — every facet of existence is chronicled with song.

The former Professor of Chemistry at Johns Hopkins University, Dr. Donald Hatch Andrews in an address given in 1951 stated in effect: the atom reveals that the vibrations constituting all life really pertain to music rather than matter. How strong a creating force music obtains in all life is beyond fathoming.

7

Setting for the unparalleled pageant, "The Miracle," an epic of human struggle to overcome evil, restoring peace and happiness. It was the power and magic of Max Reinhardt's genius that resulted in the performances given in leading cities in Europe and the United States which were witnessed by millions.

Max Reinhardt, who brought a whole new concept to the theatre which demonstrated the universality of the arts.

In the chapel of his castle in Austria, Max Reinhardt instructs Lady Diana Manners in the role of the Madonna, who as a statue comes to life and takes over the duties of the Nun when the Nun departs into the world.

10

The populace beseeches
the Madonna for healing.
The piper is healed.

The statue of the Madonna
comes to life as Lady Diana
Manners emerges in poetry
of motion.

Before laying aside her robes as the Nun and returning to her pedestal, the Madonna prays.

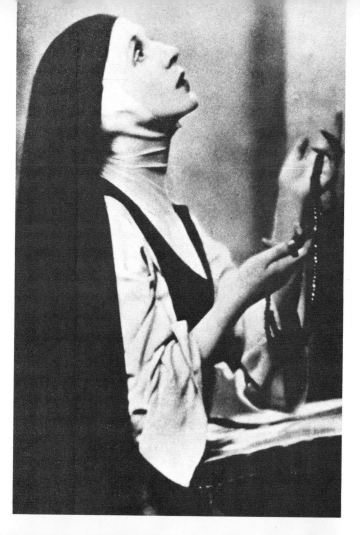

The Knight lures the Nun into the world.

Lady Diana Manners as the Nun.

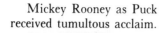

Mickey Rooney as Puck
received tumultous acclaim.

Olivia de Havilland was a beautiful Hermia.

Nini Theilade, Premiere Danseuse in Max Reinhardt
production of "A Midsummer Night's Dream."

Artie Mason Carter, beloved founder of the Hollywood Bowl, rises in her box to accept an homage of roses.

The Hollywood Bowl has become the home of one of the most important of the world's summer music festivals.

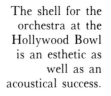

The shell for the orchestra at the Hollywood Bowl is an esthetic as well as an acoustical success.

The Wallensteins, Virginia and Wally. Wallenstein began his career as a cellist, holding first chair position with the Chicago Symphony, later with Toscanini and the New York Philharmonic Orchestra. He conducted for radio at WOR and N.B.C. in New York then spent thirteen years as Music Director of the Los Angeles Philharmonic. He now is in demand as guest conductor with major Symphony Orchestras.

Celebrated musicians in early Hollywood Bowl days lend distinction to the theme of "Music Under the Stars." From left: Iturbi, Klemperer, Lert, Svedrosky, Cimini, Molinari, Schoenberg, Monteux.

George Gershwin brought his scintillating music and captivating personality to Ravinia Park outdoor theatre near Chicago.

Ernest Ansermet conducts Chicago Symphony at **Ravinia Park**.

Ansermet was a native of Switzerland but in his orchestra conducting an international citizen. He led the majority of great orchestras of the world. Shortly before his demise he conducted a Festival at Stanford University in California

Karen Margreta Wood, (left) John Scott Trotter, (formerly Music Director for Bing Crosby) and Grace Denton confer on details concerning the organization of a Council of Arts for sponsoring a Cultural Center in Newport Beach.

"THE FUNNIEST ENTERTAINER IN THE WORLD"
— Atkinson, N. Y.

VICTOR BORGE

WITH
LEONID HAMBRO

Sponsored by NEWPORTER Magazine
for Benefit of Cultural Center Fund

Box Office
Karen Margreta Imperia
2625 East Coast Hwy, Corona Del Mar

IRVINE BOWL
650 Broadway - Laguna Beach
SUNDAY SEPTEMBER 8 at 8:30 P.M.
Tickets: $2.75, 3.30, 4.40, 5.50 tax incl
Boxes (4 seats each) $10.50 per seat including $5.00 donation
Mail Orders to Newporter, P.O Box 2117, Newport Beach

Borge caricature.

After the performance smiles! Victor Borge extends handclasp of friendship to Jim Killingsworth (left) publisher of "Orange County Illustrated" and "The Newporter," which sponsored the concert as a benefit for the Cultural Center Fund, and to Grace Denton who managed the "Comedy in Music" event. Spontaneous laughter echoed and re-echoed as never before in the Irvine Bowl hills.

the early years

How wonderful to have been born in the horse and buggy age as I was! What joy for the child I was, to be allowed by an indulgent grandfather to hold the reins, slapping them on patient "Old Black Joe's" back as we jogged from the house in town to the family farm three miles distant over a dusty, sometimes muddy, country road of hills and dales, chirping birds, animals grazing in lush fields, a myriad of charms that gripped the soul.

At the foot of the big hill leading out of town was the village blacksmith shop with its robust smells of the forge, hot horse shoes shaped with clanging on the anvil and of horse flesh, the sum total exuding something of drama in the life of a horse. Near it was a mossy drinking trough, fed by a spring, where horses could have a refreshing drink.

We passed neat farms with big red barns; the one-room country school. In season there were high elderberry bushes by the roadside dripping with glossy sprays of fruit, and how delicious when made into juicy pies. And there was the little cheese factory. One knew it was near by the aroma wafted on the breezes from the shelves of large rounds of cheese, also the numerous piglets fed on the whey.

Pulling up, grandfather would sample slivers of cheese, then choose a cut of several pounds to take home — cost fifteen cents.

The farm was one hundred and sixty acres of undiluted delight — the orchard, the pond fed by a gushing spring, the woods of towering maples which in Spring yielded golden maple syrup, and where wild blackberries grew along with chestnuts, hickory nuts, black walnuts and varieties of ferns and wild flowers.

This smiling country, which my forebears had carved from the wilderness some hundred and fifty years before, was in the Western Reserve — Mantua, Ohio, thirty miles southeast of Cleveland, and there in 1890 I was fortunate to have been born.

Grandfather's Dutch parents came to Clayton, Michigan, from

19

Rome, New York, as pioneers in 1838. He was three years old and twelve years later he came to Mantua where he lived an active life until age 95. "It is the adventurers who make things move, I reckon," grandfather remarked in an interview at age 94. He continued, "While there are no longer big forests to be subjugated, no log cabins to be built and no empires of pioneer homes to be established in these parts, the urge to keep going is as strong now as then. But it has to be done in other ways and so we find people gadding about in automobiles and airplanes instead of oxcarts and buggies."

Grandfather, Reuben Oliver Halstead, a direct descendent of Aneke Jahn Bogardus, who once owned the land where Wall Street and Trinity Church now are located, reminisced that he knew Mantua when there were only two houses in it. Now there are several thousand school children. His first job was driving cattle on foot. He spent one entire summer driving cattle to New York City, walking the entire distance from Mantua. His education consisted of the district school, but this proved abundantly sufficient for the practical affairs of his business. Boy students had to cut a cord of wood to pay for tuition. He married his cattle-drover employer's daughter, Maria Frost, on New Year's Eve, just before the advent of 1858. "Aunt Tip," as she was known throughout the countryside, and "Uncle Rube" celebrated their 68th wedding anniversary on December 31, 1925. There were two boys and two girls in their family, my mother, Gertrude, being one of them.

"Aunt Tip" was born in Mantua, daughter of pioneers John and Elvira Kellogg Frost, whose forebears migrated through the wilderness from Massachusetts. Elvira's mother was the first white child born in Portage County. They prospered, owned first sewing machine and mowing machine in the township. The Halsteads purchased the old Frost homestead and lived there until 1893, when they moved to the village of Mantua. Their daughter, Almira (she was called "Mide") and her husband, Russell Trowbridge, became the keepers of the farm which brought so much joy to my youth.

The house was rambling, surrounded by a city block of lawn which was kept like a park with many beautiful trees. Grandfather believed in trees. For a half mile approaching the house he had planted maple trees on each side of the road. These grew until there was a majestic avenue of shade, the branches meeting overhead. In the Spring, there were soft light green buds expanding into a full bower of green, changing in Autumn to russets and flame, and in winter to dark angular forms except when laden with a blanket of glittering snow or of ice, if rain froze on the branches. Grandfather watched these trees grow from saplings, and how he rebelled when the telephone company insisted that branches had to be chopped off to make way for telephone wires. The phones, all party lines, were wooden boxes on the wall with a little crank for calling "Central." Each party had a special ring — 2 short, 1 long, 3 short, etc. — which rang in all homes on the party line. It was a sure way to catch up on the neighborhood goings on to just lift the receiver and listen in.

Aunt Mide shared grandmother's love of flowers and each summer they surrounded the farm house in abundance. There were never off limits for picking flowers, so my sister, Georgia, and I filled the house with bouquets and more bouquets. First in Spring were the jonquils and daffodils. Long after our family moved from the little village, every Spring Aunt Mide would wrap the stems of these lovely blooms in wet cotton and strips of muslin and mail a box full to us. We would bury our noses in them to enjoy their lovely fragrance and reveled in their rich yellor color.

There was a special row of sweetpeas along the fence by the asparagus bed. There was a pansy bed on the north side of the house where they grew more lush in the shade. There were climbing nasturtiums growing to the roof of the outhouse, gladiolas, dahlias, a bed of spotted calla lilies, and large clumps of maidenhair fern to embellish the bouquets. Between the two sets of stone steps leading to the large veranda, there was a bed of queenly lilies-of-the-valley, the plants and blossoms returning each year in the same place.

Also, Aunt Mide had a great many house plants; geraniums, various cacti which flowered in miraculous color. There was a rubber tree that grew to the ceiling and was considered very special. Aunt Mide took great pride in her house plants, indeed her entire house was a pattern of neatness, even though her duties included helping milk by hand the barn full of registered cows before daybreak, in order to get the milk hauled to the early milk train for Cleveland. She taught my sister and me to set a table properly, placing knives, forks, glassware; also to darn holes in stockings using a little wooden darner to stretch the hole over while darning.

She was an excellent cook and served her meals well that had been cooked on a wood-burning stove. Her cakes and cookies were models of delicious goodness. The cookie jars — for ginger and white — on the cellar shelf usually were well filled, and my sister and I had our hands in the jars often. That cellar — for winter its many bins were stocked with apples, winter pears, potatoes, onions, big green Hubbard squash, cabbage, turnips — foods they had sown and reaped from the good earth. There were hams that had been smoked in the stone smoke house, shelves of shining jars of canned fruits, pickles, too — what a place and way of life that these hard working, simple people made for themselves.

We loved to explore Aunt Mide's attic with its varied treasures, look at the old *Ladies' Home Journals,* which she had kept for years, and collect a few scraps for making doll clothes. I remember two of my dolls who claimed my special affection — one was a golden-haired beauty with movable legs, arms and head. She had a little wicker cradle, the wicker shaping into a little canopy at the head. It was lined with blue and had pillows edged with lace and a coverlet with tufts of blue yarn. Some years later, I recall, this beauty rolled off the table and was smashed. I unwisely had left her too near the edge in my dash to run after a fire engine that went whizzing by in the town where we lived. I was very sad indeed and cried. My other best loved doll was about six inches long, and I made her many garments, even a wedding gown. Perhaps I pictured that I would look quite that elegant myself someday.

In the Spring the orchard was a cloud of pink apple blossoms, which my sister and I picked to our heart's content. They usually came out for the first of May when we filled strawberry boxes with flowers, whereupon they became May baskets. These we would place on doorsteps in town, ring the doorbells and run. The recipient had to guess who the donor was.

At the farm it always seemed mysterious to go the short distance across the road to the orchard. There was a gate into the orchard but we usually climbed the fence. Perhaps some of the mystery was caused by Belle's grave. On the highest knoll there was Belle's grave, with a wire trellis covered with vines marking the head. There were thick beds of myrtle growing over the grave and spreading for several yards around. Also in the Spring there were jonquils and some double daffodils. We always felt justified in picking the flowers that grew about Belle's grave — she was a remote character as far as we were concerned. I never knew much about her history except that my grandmother loved her dearly and nursed her at the time she was ill with consumption. She died in early life, which we thought a great pity, and her wish was to be buried in the orchard. Now she is removed to the family plot in the village cemetery. Her name was Belle Silvernail, which seemed romantic to us. We pictured her as a beautiful creature as we played house near her grave.

There were fish in the pond and once upon a time a little row boat which sank, I surmise, before I ever had a ride in it. I loved to go to the pond and watch the dragon-flies, the lily pads, the bull-frogs and the water rippling in the sun, but I cared little for fishing. It was fun pulling the fish out of the water, but I did not like taking the little shining things off the hook, and mostly threw them back in the water after doing so.

Aunt Mide, who was adept at learning and reciting poetry, and Uncle Russ took great interest in caring for their stock which was of fine quality. The horses were the chief pride of Uncle Russ, particularly a glossy, handsome mare he had raised from a colt, named "Lady Belle," though we called her "Lady." There always was a little aura of danger about "Lady" because of her ability to travel fast.

How many trips were made from the farm to Grandfather's house in town, and vice versa! My sister and I had to be washed and combed. Then there were always filled baskets to carry to and from. Aunt Mide collected crocks of butter she had made, some for Grandmother, others to exchange at the grocery store for produce. Often I would help with the churning, working the wooden plunger up and down in the churn until the little globules of butter formed. Fresh eggs, too, were taken to the store. For Grandmother there were vegetables, baking, materials for sewing — the buggy would be packed fore and aft, but we would start off in style with the high-stepping "Lady."

Saturday night was a big night in the village. Sometimes the Country Band would play. The night could be pitch black in driving back to the farm. We might not even see the horse, let alone the road, but the horse seemed to know where the road was even if we didn't. There was somewhat of an apprehensive feeling as to whether we would land in the ditch. Some nights the stars would glisten and the heavens seemed very strange and mysterious.

The farm was something of a third home for there was our own parental home in town, next door to the maternal grandparents, Aunt Tip and Uncle Rube, who had an enchanting seven acres of land on a hill top. Here was another whole domain of memorable experience. The fact that grandfather had moved to town from the farm did not mean he was idle, far from this. He raised fruit for sale — long rows of cherry trees, peaches, pears, plums, then there were crops of strawberries, red and black raspberries, blackberries, currants, gooseberries. As children, my sister and I were paid two cents a quart for picking berries and we ate our fill. In my early teens, I again picked berries, the earnings being applied to coveted music lessons.

Views from the hill were enriching — rolling hills, valleys, the lazy Cuyahoga River. No mail delivery in those days, Grandfather walked down the hill taking a basket for garnering supplies from the country store as well as the mail, then spryly walked the mile and a half back up the hill. For delivering fruit, however, there was "Old Black Joe," getting gray in spots. The hill abounded in grandmother's flowers. Just name them, they were there — morning glories, sunflowers, roses, petunias, zinnias, hollyhocks, tiger lilies, on and on. This house, too, was brightened with bouquets. Grandfather watered the flowers by hand, but they were not neglected.

Grandmother was a stay-at-home. She seldom left the hill, but she practically kept an Inn so many people came to visit her and Uncle Rube. None was allowed to leave without partaking of her ample and tasty viands. Her hands, too, always were busy. There were rugs to make — hooked, looped and braided — and patch work quilts, mending, sewing.

In our own front yard there were flowers, too; a peony bush, lilac bushes, red roses, and a single-leafed yellow rose with many thorns but rich in perfume. One of my earliest cherished memories from perhaps age five was on awakening one morning to find a yellow rose, the first of the season, on my pillow, placed there by my mother. The joy and peace of this loving thought has remained through life.

My father, William Adrian Denton, had two white horses which were kept in the same barn as "Old Black Joe." With these he hauled logs from forest to mill — arduous work for both young man and beast. He was born in Fort Scott, Kansas, when Indians still roamed the prairies. One time when Indians were nearing, his father went for help and never returned, presumably a victim of the Indians. This left his mother with three boys to raise. She later married again and there were two charming half-sisters, Edna and Odessa Bordine, whom I came to know and admire.

There came the day, I was about seven, when my family moved to Perrysburg, Ohio, where a brother of my father lived. The back yard of our little house sloped down to the broad and glistening Maumee River. But we returned again and again to the farm and house in the town of Mantua until grandparents, uncles, aunts were all gone to another clime. I attended my grandfather's funeral. It was an occasion. He had been a member of the Masonic Lodge for some 70 years, attained the 32nd Degree, and had helped initiate James A. Garfield, when he was President of Hiram College, into the organization.

"It never occurred to me to grow old," said grandfather. "It is simply taking care of health given you. Play fair with nature and she will play fair with you and remain friend and protector to the end."

24

Grandfather Halstead, aged 94, with Granddaughter
Grace, aged 32.

Grandmother Halstead ("Aunt Tip") poses with flowers.
Grandfather Halstead ("Uncle Rube") with his newspaper.

Grandmother Denton
Bordine, a Kansan. A
stalwart—she had a little
Indian blood.

My father, William Adrian Denton. A kindly man, he had wonderful eyes.

My father was six feet, two inches, his daughter Grace almost six feet.

The Denton girls—
Georgia and Grace.

Enroute for Sunday
School arrayed in our
best.

Our favorite horse,
"Lady Belle," grows
older and so does
Grace.

Father with his white
horses, the vine
covered kitchen door,
the well (its handle let
a rope down which
pulled up a pail of
water)—the big apple
tree. Its crop of sweet
apples was large.

the study and teaching years

My father became a skilled engineer through study in the Scranton Correspondence School, and we found ourselves living in Sylvania, Ohio, nine miles from Toledo, where he was Chief Engineer for the Toledo and Western interurban streetcar powerhouse. My sister, Georgia, the bookish one, through Normal School study at Oxford, Ohio, became a teacher. Her first assignment was a country school having eight grades in one room. When she retired after 37 years of teaching, she had taught for 28 years in Arlington Public School in Toledo.

Music had become my beckoning muse. When our family doctor brought his musician bride to town, my sister and I, dressed in our best, went to call at the behest of our mother. Soon we were taking voice lessons of Myrtle DeMuth Armstrong. She also gave us fine training in church music as members of the Congregational Church Choir which she directed. The organist, Charles Wilkins, came from England and was steeped in the tradition of the "Abby" — Westminster. I sometimes sang solos.

At age fifteen, I went back to Mantua and a year's full scale serious study, piano, voice, theory, at a little school called Bartel's Musical College in Mantua. Back home, burning with ambition to continue studying music, but how could my modestly-funded parents assume a musical career for me as a means of my earning a living? This was a necessary aspect of life due to my father's precarious health. So I boarded a Toledo and Western streetcar and found my way to the Toledo Conservatory of

29

Music on Collingwood Avenue. On meeting the Director, personable Bradford Mills, I informed him that I wanted to study music but didn't have sufficient money. My quest succeeded — he gave me work in the school library and I was off to a concentrated year of study with able teachers, commuting daily from home leaving at 7:35 A.M. My progress found me playing in recital the Chopin Waltz, Op. 64, No. 1, with my father present to hear me. How could I know that in about ten years, I would be an adversary of this Bradford Mills, in the business of concert management? I didn't intend it to be that way.

What exciting things can happen in this life. One happening at this time was my father taking my sister and me to see Julia Marlowe and Edward Sothern in "Romeo and Juliet," at the beautiful Valentine Theatre in Toledo. This was our introduction to great theatre. We read Shakespeare aloud for weeks thereafter.

This was the year our town had its first automobile, and this was the year my parents presented us with a baby brother, sixteen years my junior. We did not realize his worth at first — the mixing of boy friends with a baby — but little William, Jr. soon won our hearts and holds them to this day.

My mother and Aunt Mide attended Hiram College briefly, so there went I next; intending to study public school music; however, the course there was limited, so I withdrew and became a student at Oberlin College Conservatory. This proved a thrilling experience, including singing in the Second Church (Congregational) Choir of more than a hundred voices with famous Dr. George Andrews, the organist. In June I walked out with my teacher's certificate in Public School Music from Dr. Karl Gherkins. My recital appearance here was the playing of MacDowell's Polonaise in E.

College rooms were gayly decorated with pennants, also mottos. One that I had framed: "Don't wait for the cow to back up to be milked. Get up and go after the cow." Another by Emerson: "Ever in the strife of your own thoughts, obey the nobler impulse."

The Teaching Years

Now that I had attained some ability and was 18 years of age, it was legal to sally forth in the world and hold a job. I was avid to find one. I had my Ohio State Teacher's Certificate and first applied to teach music in the public schools of Hiram, Ohio. I did not get the position and wept. My Oberlin College roommate wrote me, "Why not try the A.M.A.

(American Missionary Association)?" Result, I was on my way to Trinity College in Athens, Alabama, a Negro school. This was a rewarding experience. Most Negro children have music in their systems and some there were very talented. Outstanding, too, was the faculty, people of superior qualities.

For teaching positions, the Fiske Teacher's Agency was a key organization to contact. Fortune favored me for the next year at age 19, through Fiske I was engaged as a faculty member at Otterbein University in Westerville, Ohio. I taught piano, voice, also music in the public schools of the town. The latter entailed conducting high school students in chorus singing. I studied voice with the head of that department in the University and graduated, receiving a diploma in 1911.

The College enrollment at that time was around 600, with a student esprit de corps that was heartening. The tree-shaded campus exuded inspiration. There were rules, one that all residents of the women's dorm where I lived were to be in by 10:00 P.M. unless signed out for some special reason. As the youngest member of the faculty I was in demand as chaperon for parties. A chief recreation was walking in two-somes down the railroad track. The voice teacher had an automobile which went about 15 miles per hour. One felt privileged to be asked to go for a ride on a Sunday afternoon.

I played tennis and once my short and quick moving partner, Bryant Sando, and tall me with my long reach, won a doubles blue ribbon at a match at Ohio State University. Public dancing was not done, but I broke the rule when the tall, handsome football coach, Bill Gardner, a Carlisle Indian, asked me to go to an Ohio State University dance. Arriving home late, the voice teacher's wife took me in for the rest of the night — all very hush, hush.

When important concerts took place in Columbus, groups went by streetcar. Concerts by Lillian Nordica and David Bispham linger delightfully in the memory.

In my student days at the Toledo Conservatory, I played the orchestra parts of the Scharwenka Concerto, Op. 1, No. 32, on a second piano for a graduating student performing the solo. What a beautiful concerto it is, yet in all of my concert management experience as the years went by, I never heard an artist perform this Concerto, or found it on a phonograph record. But wonder of wonders, at my eightieth birthday party, I received a gift of the record — the Schwarenka Concerto, Earl Wild, the pianist, with the Boston Symphony, Leinsdorf conducting.

31

Teaching was not exactly my forte and I felt the urge for travel, so wrote to the Department of the Interior at Washington, D.C. applying for a position in the Government Schools of Porto Rico. I had practically forgotten about this when a year later I received an appointment, so after three years I left the significant and happy association at Otterbein, informed my family I was going to Porto Rico and with their blessing, I went. I was 22 when I sailed from New York.

The smell of the Atlantic, mixed with pungent odor of the hawsers holding ship to shore, the clanging of winches loading the hold, the scurrying of passengers boarding and looking for their staterooms and settling in for the voyage — this was a new world for a midwestern small town girl. The grandiose City of New York which in those days had air fresh from the sea — life was glowing with richness. Even though the boat was small, the "Caracas" of the Red D Line, the pier an obscure one in Brooklyn, it stirred the pulse. On arrival the first view of the semi-tropic island at dawn betokened romance.

What of Romance

I first saw him on the "Caracas," which required five days for the trip to Porto Rico, and pitched and rolled in all directions. I was to teach music and he science in the Government Schools. He was tall, dark and handsome and had a violin case under his arm as he boarded the "Caracas." Later he played good music in the salon. Though this was a magnet of interest for me I had little conversation with him. This was Maurice H. Esser, Phi Beta Kappa from Colgate University.

The passengers on the boat were mostly teachers, many having their first ocean voyage. The new teachers were not assigned to their locations until after an interview upon arrival so we found ourselves in the Government Schools headquarters awaiting our turn. Of course San Juan or its environs were the places most desired. While I was sitting there the man of the violin came out from the inner office and was heard to say that he was assigned to the San Juan High School. There goes my violin, I thought.

I was sent to the largest town on the East Coast, Humacao. We teachers first went to a little hostelry until living accommodations could be found. Here I had my first taste of Porto Rican food, palatable yet different, cooked on a charcoal stove. Before the days of airplanes, butter came in little yellow tin cans from Denmark.

Imagine my surprise when after a couple of days, my tall, dark and handsome violinist came walking in. He had been transferred! In due time we were enjoying Saturday morning sessions at the High School, where there was a piano — two people who loved music and were having a great time.

It was the custom in the area for swains to express interest in a maiden by serenading her. One bright moonlight night I was awakened by strains of Schubert's "Serenade" and other pieces played by that violinist and a flutist outside my window.

The next year Maurice became Principal of the Arecibo High School and teacher of Science. I was given the position of Supervisor of Music in the Government Schools throughout the Island and taught Normal Classes in the University of Porto Rico at Rio Piedras. Living in Santurce, suburb of San Juan, with six teachers in a cottage on a point jutting into the Carribean, the waves splashing over the rocks below, the enchanting blue of the water, our meals served on a sheltered corner of the veranda, the ride on the streetcar through swaying palms to the University, life was pleasant indeed. Romance entered with the occasional visits from the man from Arecibo. He would mix violin music on the veranda with the music of the waves. Are there any moonlight nights anywhere like those in Porto Rico? Of course, in those days the countryside was far more primitive than present-day Porto Rico.

Maurice had a project in Arecibo in addition to running a High School — raising pineapples on a finca and shipping them. But there was a war across the seas and we headed for the States. After a total of seven years, my teaching days were over. Maurice became involved in an experiment concerned with making potash, much needed in the war, from sugar beet refuse. As it turned out the sugar beet factory was ten miles from my home town of Sylvania, Ohio.

This was a stressful uncertain time — that of World War I. We did not marry, however romantically in 1937 I received this Valentine:

> Somebody cares, -
>   What a world of woe
> Lifts from our hearts
>   When we really know
> That Somebody really
>   And truly cares,
> And that we're in Somebody's
>   Thoughts and prayers.
> And I want you to know
>   And I feel that you do,

33

That Somebody always
        Is caring for you.

Another Valentine came in 1969 after we were married:

Within my heart
        I will always say
¹The very same thing
        That I do today -
The love we share
        Will always be
The dearest thing
        In the world to me.

There were poems, too, one entitled "To Grace."

I know not what, but when she
        lifts her hand
To point a flower's perfection with
        "But see! How exquisite!"
The blossom magically
Assumes a rare new fragrance
        As by wand,
And all the quickened sense is
        forthwith fann'd
With wave on wave of Eden fragrancy.
A subtlety - we may not understand -
Past painter's brush, past poet's
        minstrelsy.

And on "Debt."

My debt to you, Beloved,
Is one I cannot pay
In any coin of any realm
On any reckoning day;
For where is he who shall figure
The debt, when all is said,
To one who makes you dream again

When all the dreams are dead?
Or where is the appraiser
Who shall the claim compute
Of one who makes you sing again
When all the songs were mute?

We were married on November 22, 1968. We had known each other and the vicissitudes of life since 1912. For ten years he was director of the foreign department of Bausch and Lomb and traveled the world. Language was of great interest to him and he knew several fluently. Another ten years of action was spent in the civic affairs of Rochester, New York, particularly State and city taxation, through the Chamber of Commerce as General Secretary. He frequently worked with Franklin D. Roosevelt who was Governor of New York at that time. He spent the rest of his life in the field of metallurgy; however, he found time to translate mail from foreign countries for the University of Rochester. A brilliant man was Maurice Esser. We were married at the Bel Aire Hotel in West Los Angeles. Andrea Fulton sang the Schubert "Serenade!"

There was a period in America when great theatre meant Sothern and Marlowe. In the public mind, they WERE *Romeo and Juliet,* the roles in which they gave such superb performances. The memory of my experience in first seeing them is as fresh and romantic as yesterday. E.H. Sothern and Julia Marlowe are indeed among the immortals.

In my teenage years.

I graduate in voice in 1911 from
Otterbein University where I was on
the faculty for three years.

37

David Bispham, baritone, revered in his time for his allegiance to music by the American composer and his unsurpassed English diction in singing.

The beautiful soprano, Lillian Nordica, held the spotlight in the early 1900s at the Metropolitan Opera and in concert tours. The recollection of hearing her sing in a Columbus concert when I was teaching at Otterbein University, is a vivid one of greatness.

In Porto Rico I visit Maurice Esser in
Arecibo, where he was Principal of the
High School. He also managed a ranch
raising pineapples. Left, Grace Keefe,
High School teacher, Mr. Esser, Grace
Denton

Grace Denton enroute to Porto Rico

Tractors had not made their advent in
the early years of the 20th Century in
Porto Rico. Maurice Esser, High School
Principal, harvested pineapples with
oxcart.

My romance with Maurice H. Esser had a background of tropical moonlight, the soft murmuring of the sky blue Carribean surf as we walked on the beach, the gentle swish of coconut palm fronds glistening with rain from daily momentary showers—and the music of his lush-toned violin.

The NEW YORK YEARS

This was a time of World War I and all its stresses and worries. I went to New York City where several teacher friends from Porto Rico had embarked on doing Spanish censorship — war work. Four of us shared an apartment at 610 116th Street, between the Columbia University subway station and Riverside Drive. Music being my forte, I had not learned Spanish, so found a musical position working temporarily in the catalogue department of Schirmer's Music Publishing Co. When this ended I went to the *Musical Courier* magazine hoping to obtain information concerning an available job. To my surprise they hired me, first as sort of a receptionist but soon an editor became ill and I was asked to take over her desk — unequipped in this field I learned "hunt and peck" typing fast.

The *Musical Courier* chronicled news of artists and musical events nationally and internationally. Its chief revenue came from the advertising of artists, their tours and their quotes from reviews.

I edited news letters that were sent in by correspondents from all over the country. Also at my desk tickets were on file for all musical events that were to be "covered" and written about in the *Courier*. Certain members of the staff went to first performances of operas at the Metropolitan and to major events, but there were repeats of the operas and multiple other concerts. Going to concerts and writing reports turned out to be a part of my duties. For once I had my fill of music for I found myself attending a concert practically every night of the week, twice on Saturdays and Sundays.

41

What excitement, this being in the front door of the musical scene in New York. If I did not have the *Courier* tickets for something I wanted to hear, being on the *Courier* staff, doormen would pass me in. Standing was not to be frowned on for some special opera or artist, and often an empty seat could be found. There were thirty-five operas in the Met repertory during the season. I managed to see every opera and some of them more than once and this was the era of Caruso, Farrar, Ponselle, Scotti, Alda, Matzenauer, Martinelli, DeLuca. The distinguished Gatti Cazzasa was the Manager. What music poured forth!

Was there ever such a fabulous time in New York as the Fall of 1918? Uniforms of men involved in war met the eye on every side — the blue of the poilus of France, Canadians in gray, Aussies, the English Tommies, the "doughboy" in olive drab, the Navy blues, Air Corps men, Marines, the turbaned Sikh, Salvation Army lassies and Red Cross workers, whose blue capes had flaming red linings — a kaleidoscope that stirred the blood. Everyone believed this war was for the betterment of mankind. It was "to make the world safe for democracy" and everyone felt he must do his part if this meant only knitting sweaters. Young men yearned to be in the thick of the fray.

There were parades almost daily on Fifth Avenue of men and the machinery of war, bands playing, hearts quickening. The *Musical Courier* was on the corner of Fifth Avenue and 39th Street. We had a front row view of the excitement and trooped to the windows to watch the glory that passed by. Liberty Loan rallies on the steps of the Public Library at 42nd Street also were daily events and could be witnessed from our fourth floor windows — celebrities, celebrities, Mary Pickford, Charles Chaplin, Douglas Fairbanks, etc., etc.

For the Fifth Liberty Loan Parade, there was scarcely a window on the entire Avenue that did not have a flag of the Allies flying — color, color, such color, Fifth Avenue dripped with color. The parade began at 8:00 in the morning and was still continuing at 8:00 at night. One segment consisted of a solid mass of sailors from curb to curb that took a full hour to pass — ten thousand eager young "gobs."

In this parade President Woodrow Wilson — not rode but walked — down the middle of Fifth Avenue from 59th Street to Washington Square, tipping his tall silk hat to the countless thousands lining the streets.

Some of the parades included a variety of spectacles, such as Pearl White climbing a fire ladder several stories high as it meandered down Fifth Avenue. Then after November 11th, when the city went wild at Armistice (I joined the throng on Broadway), there were the homecoming Divisions parading on Fifth Avenue. One great moment in history, the homecoming of General Pershing on his unmatchable steed, leading his Division of all six-foot stalwarts — returned from VICTORY.

In the Spring I was sent to "cover" the annual May Festival of the University of Michigan at Ann Arbor, a musical event of signal importance. There was the Chicago Symphony, Frederick Stock, conducting, and soloists Tito Ruffo, Margaret Matzenauer, Edward Johnson (later to become Manager of the Metropolitan Opera), Leon Rothier, Lenora Sparkes, Caroline Lazzari, Joseph Lhevinne and others. There was much taking of photos and gathering of material to use for my three-page "story" in the *Musical Courier* of June 3, 1920. A bonus for me was visiting my family in nearby Sylvania.

During my second year on the *Courier* staff, I lived at 138 East 38th Street in a modern YWCA Hotel. Many interesting girls "in business," as was the expression, lived there, so I never lacked for someone to join me, using the second ticket of my pair. In order to hear opera at the Metropolitan, one opera "buff" managed to be on the list of "supers." If some notified "super" did not show up, an outsider could be gotten in, so I was pressed into going one night with this friend. We had to wait at the stage door until near curtain time to be sure there would be a vacancy, but Elsie, a teacher of anthropology at Hunter College, rolled her big brown eyes at the doorman and finally succeeded in getting me inside, but alas by this time most of the costumes had been taken. As I am nearly six feet tall, this posed a minor problem, the major one was shoes for my not small feet. The shortness of the shoes made me wonder if I would be a cripple thereafter.

The Opera was "La Juive" with Enrico Caruso and Rosa Ponselle in the leading roles. As the curtain went up we came out of a church and knelt on the stage. With my shoes it took courage to get up again. When the curtain went down, the scenery began moving in all directions in order to "set" the next act, and Caruso and Ponselle were taking curtain calls. We were not needed in the last acts so found our way into the opera house through a door leading into the top gallery, then proceeded to the main floor where with the cooperation of an usher, we found seats.

Some years later it was in "La Juive" that Caruso had a collapse, so this opera proved to be the final one in which he was heard.

What a gala era for music! So many events stand out like beacons. In some way I found myself in the tenth row for a benefit concert at the Metropolitan Opera House, which had on its program the Philadelphia

Orchestra with Leopold Stokowski, then at his zenith, conducting; Serge Rachmaninoff playing his Piano Concerto, No. 2, with Geraldine Farrar gliding on stage for solos. She wore a glittering gown with a cascade of varicolored morning glories from decolletage to the floor, her dark hair knotted sleekly in her neck. Audience enthusiasm brought applause like thunder.

Mary Garden

The Chicago Opera had a season at the Lexington Theatre during which I came, for the first time, under the spell of Mary Garden in "Thais." Listening to the "Meditation," I could but think of the days when I had played this lovely music with a certain violinist. Tears came. As it happened in years to come, I managed appearances by Mary Garden repeatedly.

Many times I have been asked, indeed, many times I have asked myself, who were the outstanding personalities among the host of celebrated persons whose paths crossed with mine. It is a very difficult and interesting question. There is the towering Chaliapin, the noble Kreisler, the vital Tibbett, the dignified Spalding, the gracious Rosa Raisa. Definitely outstanding were two reigning prima donna sopranos — the regal Geraldine Farrar of the Metropolitan Opera and the titian-haired, scintillating Mary Garden of the Chicago Civic Opera.

Garden had that quality possessed by but few performers . . . magnetism. Duse had it, as did Sarah Bernhardt and Chaliapin. It is something that cannot be learned, it is a native quality, you must be born with it. Whether as the mature temptress in "Carmen," the young girl innocent in "Resurrection," or the Juggler in "Le Jongleur de Notre Dame," Garden had only to make her entrance and one was conscious of nothing else. Chorus, scenery, supporting artists . . . all faded. Eyes were only for this great woman of the theatre — the glorious Mary Garden. She did not sing a role — she WAS the role, be it "Thais," "Sappho," "Salome," "Pelleas and Melisande" which Debussy composed expressly for her.

Her voice was not big, nor opulent as with Rosa Ponselle. But what she could do with it was remarkable. Her ability to color her tones gave her a place alone in operatic legends. Singing became an exercise in communication, with the utmost delicacy, with the most amazing nuances, she could delineate the content of a phrase, an aria and, in fact, an entire operatic role, and make it meaningful and rich, all stamped with the Garden personality.

Toward the end of her career, she gave some classes on opera in

44

Chicago. She told her auditors as she strode across the stage to a table and picked up an inanimate object, "Make this live as you pick it up." One would get shivers from the animation in her voice as she spoke. Mary Garden was the darling of Chicago. She made friends with the entire city.

Her mind diffused brilliance on many subjects. Interviewing newsmen were agog at her adroit replies to their questions.

Her final concert appearances in America were devoted to the music of Debussy, and in these she set aside a portion of the time to a most engrossing talk of the great composer, for she had enjoyed the friendship of Debussy as had no other artist.

Geraldine Farrar

During Garden's reign in Chicago, the dark beauty and glorious voice of Geraldine Farrar drew lines at the Metropolitan Opera box office like a magnet. Her following was immense. Farrar had had a remarkable career in Germany before her advent at the Met, where her first performances at age 24 established her as one of the real ornaments of the music drama, both in voice and in presence. Her voice was true, lush in quality and authoritative.

In 1907 she was chosen to portray "Madame Butterfly" in the first performance in this country of the favorite Puccini opera. The star-studded cast included Enrico Caruso, Antonio Scotti, Louise Homer. Puccini came from Italy to supervise the performance. He was demanding, yet in his final interview he said of Farrar: "Oh, she is delightful! I had to tell her very little. It is all herself that she puts into the role." By the time of her retirement Farrar had sung the role of "Butterfly" 95 times — a record that has not been duplicated.

The "in" group of young people during Farrar's reign was known as "Flappers." A special group called themselves "Gerryflappers." They were devoted to Geraldine Farrar, followed her every appearance and showered her with flowers.

The roles of "Manon Lescaut," "Carmen," "La Tosca," "Zaza" garnered resounding "bravos" for Farrar that no other Metropolitan star has surpassed.

The beauteous Farrar retired when in her prime. There were no repeat "final" performances. Her last appearance at the Metropolitan was a never-to-be-forgotten event. At its close, her stage-hands colleagues carried her out of the Opera House on their shoulders. She was cheered to the echo both inside and outside of the Opera House as she left for the last time.

45

Concerts at Metropolitan Museum of Art

The classic entrance hall of the Metropolitan Museum of Art proved an inspiring locale for the David Mannes Orchestra concerts. In one review I wrote in the *Courier:* "The second Mannes Orchestra Concert of the season, which took place at the Metropolitan Museum of Art, was attended by a large assemblage of music lovers, the number having grown from a few hundred present at the first concert to several thousand. These concerts are a triumphant success. They give to those who think we are an unmusical nation an opportunity to form a different opinion." The Mannes concerts at the Metropolitan Museum continued for twenty-five years. How little I could have dreamed that several decades in the future I would assist David Mannes at the Mannes School of Music in its drive to become the Mannes College of Music which it now is. David Mannes, a noble person, named his autobiography "Music in My Faith."

How many revered artists there were in those days whom I heard and wrote about. This was the era of concert going before the advent of radio, and enthusiasm abounded for the artists of the time who thrilled with their artistry — Violinists Maud Powell, Efrem Zimbalist, Albert Spalding. Jascha Heifetz was a teen-age lion. My report said: "The ravishing tones of Jascha Heifetz's violin subdued the throng that heard his second Carnegie Hall recital into a listening hush that was a far more eloquent tribute to his art than the outbursts of applause which followed each number."

There were pianists Harold Bauer, Mischa Levitzki, Percy Grainger, E. Robert Schmitz, Augusta Cottlow, Richard Buhlig, Edwin Hughes, to name a few; and Ossip Gabrilowitsch, poet of the piano as well as conductor of the Detroit Symphony, for which years later I was asked to become Assistant Manager.

And the plethora of singers — Florence Easton, Hulda Lashanska, Anna Case, Rafaelo Diaz, Louis Graveure, Sophie Braslau, Andres De Segurola and Anna Fitzhugh, a romantic twosome; Dan Beddoe, Alma Gluck.

A Beethoven Society Concert presented on one program the Flonzaley Quartet, Fannie Bloomfield-Zeisler and Pablo Casals. The intime atmosphere at the Sunday Evening concerts at the MacDowell Club always was enjoyable. One evening when Rosalie Miller was giving the program, I sat with her mother who was reserving a seat for a latecomer. (To inject an art note — at the Metropolitan Museum of Art I had become enamored with the sculpture of Daniel Chester French, particularly a

46

work entitled "Memory," a figure of a woman looking into a hand mirror. Her face held all that is memory.) When the latecomer arrived, Mrs. Miller introduced me to — Daniel French, the sculptor! He created so many wonderful sculptures, among them that of Lincoln at the Lincoln Memorial in Washington.

The palette of concerts was unlimited. Josef Stransky was conductor of the New York Philharmonic, Walter Damrosch of the New York Symphony, Bodanzky of the New Symphony. There were numerous Nationalist organizations presenting their special concerts, such as St. Erik Society (Swedish), Italian, Czechoslovak and others such as the Greenwich House Settlement Music School, The Humanitarian League, The People's Liberty Chorus. John Powell, the pianist, presided over an "Alien Music and Enemy Propaganda" event at St. Mark's-in-the-Bouwerie. He made a plea, according to my review for: "An annual season of Opera in English in Washington, with the finest Symphony in the world and with American singers ranking among the finest in the world, which could bring people from all over the United States to the National Capital with a new feeling of pride for the center of our Government as England feels for London, France for Paris, Italy for Rome."

Columbia University had a "Victory Festival," continuing for several days. During the summer the Philharmonic concerts at the Lewisohn Stadium attracted audiences of from ten to twenty thousand. There were the Edwin Franko Goldman Symphonic Band concerts, then performed on the Green at Columbia University. Morning Musicales were much in vogue and had elite following at the Waldorf, Plaza, Ritz-Carlton and other attractive ballrooms.

Sol Hurok burst upon the scene with some concerts at the Hippodrome. He was something of a law unto himself and at that time somewhat diffident in relation to tickets. Other managers sent tickets to the *Courier* promptly in advance. Hurok would say, "See me at the box office," and when you would arrive he was nowhere to be found. Since the *Courier* felt an obligation to the artist appearing, you would stand around and wait for word from Hurok. When the concert had begun, tickets that had not been sold would be handed out. "Music for the masses" was his theme. In his long and outstanding career as a manager, he provided countless masses in every nook and corner of the country with music.

With the war plays, theatre fare in New York during this period was lavish indeed. Some of the many plays I saw — "Three Faces East," "The Better 'Ole'," "Seventh Heaven," also "Lightnin'," "Dear Brutus,"

47

"Three Wise Fools," "Maytime," "The Royal Vagabond," "Friendly Enemies," "Clarence," "Greenwich Village Follies," and "John Ferguson" produced by the embryonic Theatre Guild. The success of this play launched the Guild on its brilliant career which has continued for decades. Who could have predicted then that the time would come when I would present seasons of Theatre Guild offerings in Toledo and Detroit?

The old Hippodrome, long since torn down, was in the heyday of its spectacle performances. Nothing like this has existed since. The line of dancers at the Radio City Music Hall in New York is famed for its aplomb, but the line of dancers at the Hippodrome descended the steps in formation into the enormous pool of water on the stage front and disappeared, leaving the audience to ponder how they ever got out. They must have for they were there for the next performance.

Friends came to New York from back in Ohio. I would pilot them from Grant's Tomb to the Battery Aquarium, the Statue of Liberty, the top of the then highest building, the Woolworth Tower, and always there was the ride on the Staten Island Ferry. One also saw the sights from the top of the Fifth Avenue bus. The Cathedral of St. John the Divine, the Little Church Around the Corner, Wall Street, and Trinity Church were points on the tour.

Dresses were ankle length, shoes — high-buttoned or laced — and we wore hats. I had a black, heavy velvet coat with large beaver collar extending to the waistline and beaver cuffs. The lining was brown satin. This my mother helped me buy. The top was bloused with a crushed sash belt, which looped over at the slightly left-hand closing. The skirt was plain and sleek. I wore a small, sort of brown derby felt hat and heavy meshed veil. If I wanted to be real elegant I pinned on a bunch of artificial violets. I've sometimes wondered if the coat did not have something to do with my being hired at the *Musical Courier*.

It was during this period that my long and beautiful brown hair was "bobbed," and I tried out lip-stick, and smoked my first cigarette — a Pall Mall — but I did not like this well enough to get the habit.

Life brings difficult pages. "Into each life some rain must fall" the poet wrote. On a February Friday, 1919, I felt a strong urge to journey home to see my father, whose health had been precarious ever since his "logging" days as a young man. Eventually he had to give up the powerhouse engineering, but so skilled was he that often he was sought to consult on the problems other streetcar powerhouses were having.

Yet my father was civic minded. He was on the School Board and aided in affairs of the town, attending meetings as needed. My mother called

48

him "Will." I loved him. Medical science now could have solved his problems, but then he suffered through with the constant and tender nursing of my mother, a valiant soul. She was camera shy. I have no picture of her.

As to my trip, obtaining leave, I arrived home Sunday morning after an overnight ride on the New York Central. Father was in good spirits, up and around as was the case on Monday. That evening he helped William, Jr., then in the eighth grade, with his arithmetic. As I retired I had a strong impression like a voice saying, "This is the last night." To myself I said, "Don't be silly," but in the night when I heard my mother phone the doctor, I knew. Hastily I went downstairs and had my arms around my beloved father, aged 56, as he left this plane. In such days, one moves as in a dream sustained by that Something that supports in times of trial. I went with the casket on the train to Mantua, where it was left. Then back to New York.

However, the world had changed in many ways. One was that my desk at the *Courier* had been moved. I had liked it where it was. Desks, except in the private offices, were in one long row next to the 39th Street windows. Mine was about fifth in the line, now it was first, and being against the wall at the back, the light hit me more in the face instead of over my left shoulder, which was annoying. In due time Fate intervened. An offer came from my former Toledo Conservatory benefactor, Bradford Mills, to work for him in connection with his concert management business.

THE "27TH" ON LEAVING New York's Own Boys photographed just before they sailed.

Enrico Caruso as Eleazar in "La Juive," taken
in his dressing room at Metropolitan Opera House
just before performance on December 24, 1921.
This was his last appearance.

In his sculpture "Memory" Daniel Chester
French has captured the essence of memory in
the face of the subject as she looks into the
mirror. Grace Denton went to the Metropolitan
Museum of Art several times especially to see
this sculpture.

David Mannes conducting an orchestra concert at
the Metropolitan Museum of Art. These concerts
attended by uncountable thousands continued for
twenty-five years. It was an inspiring experience
to hear great music in an atmosphere created
by the great art on all sides.

Soloists Margaret Matzenauer and Edward Johnson exchange greetings at the Ann Arbor May Festival in 1920.

Joseph Lhevinne, a pianist par excellence, was a soloist at the Ann Arbor May Festival.

Also participating in the Ann Arbor May Festival of 1920 were Titto Ruffo, bass-baritone (center) with his accompanist, Paul Longone, posed with Grace Denton, Musical Courier representative.

Edwin Franko Goldman who conducted the Goldman Band in concerts heard by thousands on the Columbia University Green and Central Park Mall. His programs listed symphonic music, favorite musical comedy tunes, his own and Sousa marches. For decades the Goldman Band was synonymous with summer in New York.

Mary Garden had great dignity.

Mary Garden demonstrated her versatility in her moving enaction of "Thais", her favorite among the operas in which she appeared. Here her deep religious feeling was manifested.

In the opera, "Resurrection," composed by Franco el Alfano, Garden first appears as a young girl. The audience was startled to see that this mature and sophisticated woman really *was* a young girl, in looks, in mannerisms and in every movement.

At almost the same period that Farrar was so successful in "Carmen" at the Metropolitan, Mary Garden was enjoying an equal but much different portrayal of the fiery Spanish gypsy at the Chicago Opera. It was amazing that this great artist, who could so color her tones in the operas of Debussy and Puccini, could also give a magnetic and thrilling performance in the tiger-like role of "Carmen."

After over a year of the most complimentary entreaties, Charles L. Wagner, then the most important concert manager of his time, finally persuaded Garden to do concert tours, Spring and Fall, after the opera season. Here is Mary Garden in the "gown of a thousand mirrors" which captivated the huge audiences that attended her first concerts.

Garden was such a striking and beautiful person that every role she portrayed took on a special sheen. Here is her elegant figure in "Sappho."

No singer or actor ever had a more magnetic
projection on stage than Garden had at her command.
Here she appears in the opera "Cleopatra,"
composed by Massenet.

Mary Garden introduced in America many operatic
works foreign to the United States, including
"Gismonda" composed by Henri Fevrier.

Garden had a great sense of style, which complemented her
lovely titian-hued hair and beauty of her flawless skin and
figure. She did not use these features alone to make an
impression but backed them up with her sparkling mentality
which served her well.

Mary Garden enjoyed a long friendship with the composer,
Debussy, and knew both his first and second wives. His selection
of her for the role of Melisande in his great opera, "Pelleas
and Melisande," was a brilliant stroke as no other singer has
ever approached her delineation of this role.

Farrar was one of the most dazzling personalities who ever
graced the stage of the Metropolitan Opera House when she
made her debut . . . coming direct from triumphs in Europe,
including persistent rumors of a romance with the Crown Prince
of Germany.

Farrar in the role of Madame Butterfly really created a tradition. Her flawless and appealing voice and her superb acting were seemingly meant for this favorite Puccini opera.

The Bettmann Archive, Inc. Photo

Giacomo Puccini is the most widely known Italian composer through his operas which have achieved success throughout the world. The popular "Madame Butterfly" had its premiere at the Metropolitan Opera in 1907 with Geraldine Farrar and Caruso the stars. "Madame Butterfly", "La Boheme," and "Tosca" are on the roster of opera repertoires permanently.

Whether on stage or in social gatherings, Geraldine Farrar was always the central attraction, for her beauty was only equalled by her vivaciousness and her contagious vitality.

Los Angeles Times Phot

The name Geraldine Farrar and the role of Carmen became synonymous at the Metropolitan. She left an impression as strong as had Calve in this colorful role.

At the Metropolitan Opera, Farrar held sway for a generation, and her great success singing with Caruso and other great artists is legendary.

Over six hundred officials, technicians and stage-hands greeted
Geraldine Farrar when she walked out the stage door of the
Metropolitan Opera House after her farewell performance on April
22, 1911. Hers had been a glorious career.

Harper's Bazaar—Louise Dahl Noyes Photo

After her retirement in
Connecticut, Farrar enjoyed
her leisure, wrote many
articles. She married the
adventurist and flamboyant
actor, Lou Tellegan, but
her career apparently came
first for the marriage did
not last.

BACK TO TOLEDO

Bradford Mills was the concert impresario in Toledo, presenting each season a series of artists — the Civic Concert Course. He was expanding his activities, offering a series of concerts in Indianapolis, Louisville, Fort Wayne, South Bend, and needed help. Fortunately he chose me. Merle Armitage, who later became famed in the impresario field, also was on the staff and I first worked under Merle's guidance on the series in Indianapolis. And who was the leading artist that year on the five series — beautiful, svelte Mary Garden. Her Indianapolis concert was on Sunday afternoon at the handsome Shubert-Marat Theatre. Garden chose a costume of soft rose colored velvet with clinging lines. On her head she wore a hat-like wreath of rose petals in all shades of red, which blended with her red hair in stunning effect. Back stage I heard her remarks to people who came to greet her. She never lacked for repartee, always charming, witty, scintillating. To one man she said, eyeing his stick-pin, "My dear man, aren't you superstitious about opals?" To a student, who was garnering some words of wisdom for his school paper, she advised: "Young man, make up your mind what you want to do and never turn to the right or to the left."

Garden always succeeded in acquiring headlines. In Louisville she wore the "gown of a thousand mirrors." It was fashioned with sequin-size crystals and others graduated to the size of a quarter, and it was backless. With her numerous bracelets on both arms, she made more than a rustle as she glided on stage, but she was ravishing to behold. Whether she sang well or not was not too important, just to see her walk across the stage with her enormous green feather fan was worth the price of admission.

Came the end of the season, work slackened, so Bradford loaned me to a firm that booked concert engagements for artists throughout the Northwest — Ellison-White of Portland, Oregon. I had never booked an artist but I was well versed as to the language of concerts. I had a portfolio of artists to sell to organizations, clubs, etc., in the State of Idaho. Trains did not have air-conditioning in those days. Train windows were opened when the weather was hot, and Idaho can really be hot in summer. Soot from the engine, sand, et cetera dirt blew in in bunches. I followed the Snake River the length of Idaho, but summertime was a doldrum time. I was not successful in enthusing prospects in purchasing artists to appear months ahead, and did not do well for Ellison-White. My metier in music was not "booking" engagements for artists.

The trip through the Northwest provided a pleasant summer for me. I managed four hours at Yellowstone — saw "Old Faithful" four times. Bradford wanted me back in Toledo by Labor Day without fail, so I was limited to twelve hours in San Francisco, twenty-four in Los Angeles. I had pictured sunny California a warm country so I was attired in summer clothes when I arrived in the early gray of morning, and crossed the Bay on the ferry to San Francisco — the chill of that morning, it makes me shiver just to think of it. For sight-seeing we rode in an open car with blankets over our laps — Golden Gate Park, Cliff House, Seal Rocks, then on the night train to Southern California. There some "Sunkist" people I had met in New York (they had a daughter studying piano) took me in tow and showed me the sights.

Back for the second year of concerts — Galli-Curci gave one of them. I was in charge of a concert in Louisville given by Tetrazzini, which took place in a Tabernacle having a sawdust floor but a large seating capacity!

When summer came along I said to Bradford, "Why not give me the summer off." "No," he said, he "preferred to keep me," and then left town on one of his frequent trips. He had a secretary who liked to feel that she was capable of steering things in general and Bradford in particular, so in a few days I received a letter from her that my services were no longer needed, not only for the summer but altogether. I did not question the matter but went to work for a Detroit concert manager on some special events — one of which was Isadora Duncan in her final tour. Her poet husband was with her, Serge Essenine, a Russian and very controversial. However Isadora was beautiful and all went well. I then had the urge to spread my wings and did.

Bradford's concerts in Toledo were given in a flat-floored "Coliseum," used for roller skating, anything but glamorous, the seats folding wooden chairs. Going to concerts belonged to the then way of life, but there was vociferous griping about the uncomfortable Coliseum.

There was a new moving picture theatre in Toledo, the Rivoli, seating 2600, main floor and one balcony, designed by Architect Crane, who also designed the new and handsome Orchestra Hall in Detroit. The two buildings were similar.

I knew I could have John McCormack, then the magnet of concert goers, as Bradford had had some misunderstanding with Charles L. Wagner, McCormack's manager. (Bradford was somewhat given to misunderstandings.) So one morning I stopped in to see the manager of the Rivoli, Howard Feigley by name, and asked to rent the Rivoli for a series of six concerts. What an unheard of idea — to turn away a paying moving picture audience (everyone went to movies in those days) — who could think of doing such a thing? I was told the owner of the theatre, by the romantic name of Mr. Sourbier, lived in Indianapolis, but the subject would be taken up with him. I left, not yet turned down, but I thought I had better write my proposition down on paper. Naively I went to the nearby department store, and in the waiting room where there were some desks I jotted down my proposition, then back to the theatre I went. Surprisingly the owner from Indianapolis had unexpectedly arrived, so I talked with him personally concerning my plans. His reply, "Come back tonight." Ah, not turned down as yet! I arrived promptly at 8:00 P.M., and the contract for six concerts was signed. To this day I wonder what sort of magic worked for me for I was totally unknown, had no references, and with not a sou to back up the deal — yet in one short day I rented that theatre, which had never been rented before. Madame Impresario was on her way!

61

Amelita Galli-Curci's spectacular coloratura voice brought her a spectacular career. For a concert date she had to be engaged a couple of years in advance. Her name was a magnet at the box office.

Luisa Tetrazzini sang in Louisville in a tabernacle with sawdust floor to accommodate the huge audience.

George M. Kesslere Photo

Bain News Service Photo

Giovanni Martinelli returns from Italy for another season at the Metropolitan Opera. He was a mainstay of the tenor segment for many a year, delighting untold thousands at the Opera and in concerts with the beauty of his resounding voice.

The most capricious, the most fascinating and certainly the most audacious artist in the realm of dance that America has produced, was also one of the most influential. She left her impression on all succeeding dancers. Isadora Duncan caused spirited young girls to throw off their physical as well as intellectual corsets, and run barefoot through the grass. Freedom was her banner.

'To dance is to live. What I want, is a school of life, for man's greatest riches are . . . in his imagination. There may be a life after this one, but I do not know what we shall have there. This I do know: our riches here on earth are in our will, our inner life.'

Isadora Duncan

One of the most gifted and certainly one of the most shocking characters to come from the American soil, Isadora Duncan was a moth intoxicated by the flame of life and its opportunities. She was not aware that she was opening the door to a new concept of the dance, which made possible the whole contemporary school, from Kreutzberg to Martha Graham.

Arnold Genthe, fashionable photographer of another era, took this picture of two of Isadora's adopted daughters, who, after the great one's death, toured in joint recital with the extraordinary pianist and American exotic, George Copeland.

Steichen took this picture of Isadora Duncan at the Parthenon in Greece, which satisfied her craving for immortality.

1923-1924

Bradford Mills threatened dire happenings like "running me out of town;" however, "The Rivoli City Concerts" continued in their glory for seven years before the wheel of fortune took me to Chicago. Should I report that the first year of Rivoli concerts was the last year of the Civic Music Course under Bradford Mills' management? I think he went on to greener fields, but I was so occupied with my own life I cannot recall. Years later when I saw him, he was as friendly as though we had not been friendly enemies, once upon a time.

Always I have been so involved with my own goings-on, I did not have time to even know I had competition. Surely I had plenty occupying me that first year, but it never crossed my mind that I would not succeed. I slept soundly. My family now lived in Toledo so I had a roof over my head.

Tax on admissions came into being and this was quite an item to add to the price of tickets. Bradford's series as a "Civic Music Course" was tax exempt. I had to do something about this. Lucky me, the University of the City of Toledo accepted my suggestion that it become a cooperating factor in the presentation of the concerts which were now called: "The Rivoli City Concerts," with the added line, "The University of the City of Toledo Music Series," and became tax exempt. With that hurdle leaped, I gleefully took off for New York to contract for artists.

I saved five hundred dollars at the start by obtaining Mme. Ernestine Schumann Heink of the Wolfsohn Bureau for September 28, two days before Hurok took over her management and upped her fee five hundred dollars.

Fortunately no managers from whom I was engaging artists asked me if I had money in the bank. If they had, I would have had to say, "No."

So the Rivoli City Concerts opened on September 28, 1923, with the illustrious Mme. Schumann Heink, the first musical event under the banner of: Management: Grace Denton. Others continued for over forty years.

For the first series I engaged Anna Pavlowa and her company of Hurok. It was the system with a concert series to have one key star who would aid in selling the whole series. Even with such greats as Schumann Heink and Pavlowa, John McCormack was the biggest drawing card. His singing of Irish songs, "Macushla" and "Kathleen Mavoureen" drew lines at the box office, though his programmed Handel ("O Sleep Why Dost Thou Leave Me?"), Schubert, Rachmaninoff, Elgar, exuded charm of a kind seldom seen or heard.

I opened an office at Grinnell's Music Store, had a pretty and capable secretary, Mary Curran, and with a telephone in hand advance subscriptions were being enrolled in the Spring. From Merle Armitage, skilled as he was in design, I learned the importance of good printing. Getting out my first announcement was exhilerating. On the cover I had three photos of the glamorous Rivoli, which initiated a new era of concerts in Toledo, the artist photos were on the inside pages. In addition to Schumann Heink, Pavlowa and Company of 80, and John McCormack, they included Frieda Hemple in her "Jenny Lind" concert. Costumed in a replica of a gown worn by Jenny Lind, wearing flowers in her hair, and singing songs Jenny Lind, "the Swedish Nightingale," had programmed, this was a pictorial as well as musical event. Also there was the Cleveland Symphony Orchestra, Nicolai Sokoloff conducting, and Charles Hackett, American tenor, in joint recital with Lionel Tertis, viola soloist. I listed Hackett on the announcement as "the sensation of the Paris Opera season," and Tertis, "the world's greatest viola virtuoso, first season in America." This attraction was booked from Charles L. Wagner who let me have the McCormack contract. I also announced: "Mme. Schumann Heink will sing 'The Rosary' with the Rivoli pipe organ accompaniment." Season prices ranged from $15.00 for box seats to "500 seats at $6.00." When the curtain went up the SRO sign was in evidence.

It was gloating but this I had to advertise. I spent one hundred dollars for the placard space on the front of streetcars announcing: "PAVLOWA,

SOLD OUT, Rivoli Theatre, November 30, 1923." I somehow wasn't in the concert business to make money — I was "hooked" on music.

On September 19, 1968, 45 years later, the Toledo *Blade* ran a story with the headline: "Urban Renewal Unit to Close Long Runs of Rivoli Theatre." In it was the line: "Anna Pavlowa once danced before standing room only crowds in the Rivoli." The memory of my Pavlowa performance lingered on in Toledo, Ohio, even though the theatre was torn down.

On the January 9th program by Hackett and Tertis, I printed: "NOTICE — Arrangements have been completed for the Rivoli City Concerts to continue at the Rivoli Theatre, during the season of 1924-1925. A course of six events will be presented to include an Opera, Symphony, and the finest artists. Reservations for subscriptions may be made immediately following the Hemple concert April 4."

One item that had to be solved before the doors opened for the first concert — ushers. I attacked this by phoning the YMCA. There I was put in touch with Herbert Arbogast, a resourceful young man who proved to be the ace of aces in the important business of getting people into seats with ease. The time came when I spread my wings to include Detroit, where I managed the opening concert at the super-beautiful new Masonic Auditorium, seating capacity 4,600. Herb Arbogast commuted to Detroit for me and organized a crew of ushers, requiring a total of 50 that functioned with clocklike perfection on this distinguished occasion. He later moved to Detroit and directed the corps of ushers at the Masonic Auditorium for some thirty years before retiring.

George W. Stark devoted his entire Detroit *News* Town Talk column to Herb in February 1946. A few of the paragraphs: "Herewith Town Talk presents one of the better-known faces in all Detroit. And your editor salutes its owner, whose name is Herbert S. Arbogast and who finds reason to celebrate Washington's Birthday next Friday with a fervor that is above and beyond the fact that it is Washington's Birthday. You see Mr. Arbogast is the usher-in-chief in the big Auditorium of the Masonic Temple and he has reveled in this assignment since the very first day the Auditorium was unveiled to the public, February 22, 1926, which turns out to be an even 20 years. What went on that eventful evening? The Detroit Symphony, Ossip Gabrilowitsch conducting, and Luella Melius, soprano soloist, under the management of Miss Grace Denton. This was a deluxe dedication. The cream of Detroit Society and naturally all of its music lovers who could find their way attended. Old Timers still remember that on that very first night the audience was seated without delay or confusion.

"Miss Grace Denton was the Masonic Temple's first impresario and I suspect one of her major achievements was bringing Arbogast to Detroit. In 1922 when she was combing the City of Toledo for experienced ushers she came across our hero. She was intrigued. She put him in charge of Toledo enterprises, and almost immediately realized that she had come across a jewel among ushers, a gentleman of tact and intelligence and the owner of a face that betokened almost a passionate interest in the well-being and comfort of the ticket holders." During the many years of the Ford Sunday Evening Hours on radio, which took place at the Masonic Auditorium, Herb was there to pilot to their seats the thousands upon thousands who attended those evenings; in fact, the statistics of his whole ushering activity over the 30 years are quite staggering.

Despite the exhilaration of my first year as an Impresario, sadness came to my door. An operation had prolonged my mother's life a year, but in January, five years after my father's death, she went to join him and at his same age, 56. I was by her side as she left, and again followed the trail to the little cemetery in Mantua. William, Jr. was a senior in high school. My sister had married. The home sold. I moved to an apartment, which was young William's home, too, and remained so during his years at Ohio State University where he graduated in Engineering Physics. During the summers he worked at Toledo's famous grocery-emporium— Tiedtke's.

The day after his graduation at Ohio State, he was accepted as Junior Physicist at B. F. Goodrich Tire Company, where he made a lifetime laudable career. When he retired at age 65 his title was "Manager — Research, Tire Construction and Design." After retirement he was sent twice to Korea as consultant with the Kankook Tire Manufacturing Company. He married Margaret Watts of Toledo, brought about by a college "blind date" when Margaret was attending Ohio Wesleyan. Now married for thirty five years, their life has been filled with good deeds and good friends.

At the time it was built, the Rivoli Theatre in Toledo was one of the most beautiful in America. This was where my Grace Denton concerts were held, to the vast enjoyment of my audiences.

The first concert presented under management of Grace Denton was the great Mme. Ernestine Schumann Heink, a legend in the annals of concerts.

Mme. Ernestine Schumann Heink wrote on the photo she gave me: "All the best for you dear Grace Denton! Mother Schumann Heink. Toledo 1923." Singing for thousands of United States soldiers in World War I, she made them feel they were all her boys, although she had sons on the German front.

John McCormack, the Irish tenor, captivated untold thousands with his golden tones. He was in such great demand he was booked for several years in advance.

Stanford Studio Photo

The Cleveland Orchestra, Nicolai Sokoloff, conductor, was heard on my first concert series in Toledo and returned several times in later years.

G. MAILLARD K

Charles Wagner, whose management of concert tours by John McCormack, Galli-Curci, Mary Garden and dozens of great artists, initiated a broad concept of concert going. It can be said that he gave me the impetus to become an Impresario by permitting me to have a contract for John McCormack.

72

This is a remarkable picture of Pavlowa because it shows her in repose, almost unique among Pavlowa photographs, and shows her Russian beauty of face.

Anna Pavlowa still remains the ideal ballet star in the hearts of those enthusiastic audiences which greeted her on her world tours. Here she is in her immortal "The Swan" by Saint-Saens.

The second event in the Rivoli Series was Anna Pavlowa and her Company. Few people realized that the snowflake-figure of Pavlowa which had such marvelous elevation covered muscles of which a wrestler would have been proud. She was a dynamo.

Bas relief of Pavlowa by Malvena Hoffman placed in Pavlowa's London home.

1924~1925

During the season 1924-1925 my concert activities pyramided. While Red Seal Records of the Victor Company proclaimed that phonograph records were here to stay, this still was before the days of radio, and going to concerts was of prime importance. It was true some men had to be coaxed to attend but with the years, how this has changed. Men, particularly young men, can now be considered leading supporters of classical music.

The Rivoli City Concerts offered Fortune Gallo's San Carlo Opera Company in "Martha;" an Opera Quartet — Frances Alda, Merle Alcock, Charles Hackett, and making his first tour, a young baritone, Lawrence Tibbett; the New York Symphony, Walter Damrosch, conductor; Reinald Werrenrath, baritone, and Renee Chemet, violinist; Louise Homer, contralto, and Mischa Levitzki, pianist; also Ruth St. Denis, Ted Shawn and the Denishawn Dancers.

In addition to this series, Zonta International of Toledo, the membership of which is composed of professional women, importuned me to manage a Zonta Series of Arts. My listing in the club was "Impresario." There were three events of varied interest — Thomas Wilfred with his remarkable invention of moving color as an art, the Clavilux; the Marmeins in their Dance Dramas; and Toledo's own Muriel La France in joint recital with the Flonzaley String Quartet. The latter two events were at the Rivoli, the Clavilux at the Coliseum. A permanent exhibit of the

75

Clavilux has been on view at the Museum of Modern Art in New York.

Lovely Muriel La France, a fairy story with a tragic ending. She was in voice and face a replica of Galli-Curci and became the world famous soprano's only protege. Galli-Curci took Muriel to New York and cared for her as if she were her daughter, but somehow the exigencies of a career did not appeal to gentle ethereal Muriel and after a couple of years she gave up her once-in-a-lifetime opportunity. She sang in radio with Morton Downey, then disappeared from the music scene.

Some forty years later, I was doing publicity in Palm Springs for an Art Gallery. The man to whom I gave the radio announcements asked me, "Where did you come from?" I replied Toledo, Ohio. He then said, "My wife knows you." His wife was Muriel LaFrance. We saw each other several times. Her husband became ill and died on Easter Sunday. Life seemed to be over for the beauty and grace that was Muriel. She wanted to make her will and did. I asked her to spend the summer with me, but when I went to pick her up, I found her reclining on a couch and life was gone. She had taken pills. Time went on — her estate was well over a hundred thousand dollars of which ten thousand came to me. Truth indeed can be stranger than fiction.

To Walter Damrosch goes the honor of introducing symphony concerts for young people. The Superintendent of Public Schools in Toledo, Charles Meek, gave his support for the first young people's symphony concert, Damrosch conducting, in Toledo. He and a group of young orchestra students went with me to meet Damrosch at the train when he arrived.

Ruth St. Denis

Memories, such rainbow-hued memories of Ruth St. Denis, who with Ted Shawn, flashed with great eclat upon the American dance scene. Their contribution to dance in America is legend. Their inimitable school — Denishawn — was where vital young dancers were instilled with the impetus to become creators in the Art of the Dance — Doris Humphrey, Charles Weidman, Martha Graham and more. Ted Shawn, in later years at Jacob's Pillow, Massachusetts, created a nationally famous school of the dance for men.

In her tours to the Orient, Miss Ruth, as she was known, became imbued with the color and inner meaning of Eastern dance forms which she incorporated in her programs. How she could manipulate yards upon yards of lavish fabrics in her glamorous dances! However her interpretations were not exclusively of the Orient. Another aspect was her dedication to

76

spiritual expression in dance, which graced programs given in churches, including the Riverside Church in New York.

I met Miss Ruth many times through the years. In New York she invited me to attend her "Philosophic Evenings." At these, robed in white like a Priestess, she would discuss subjects pertaining to life with a group of friends. In Los Angeles she took me to a Vedanta service. Her studio was a mecca for dozens who came for inspiration through Miss Ruth's zest for life. She was a meteor, flashing across this planet, until her demise at age 96.

When I was in New York obtaining contracts for the second season, I met a young Columbia University student of Journalism, Mildred Harrington. She asked me for lunch during which we talked of concerts. Shortly after I learned she had written a story about me as a class assignment and sold it to the *American* Magazine. The story was readable but not too much like me. Her caption was "She Rents Other Folks Throats," the theme being that I had lost my voice and therefore presented the voices of others in concerts. The "success story," so largely a figment of her imagination, won her a position as editor on the *American* magazine, which she held for many years. Since I still had as much voice as I ever had, I demurred about having the story published, but since her position was in prospect, Mildred wrote me vehemently — "she had misjudged my character" and more; whereupon I capitulated and the article appeared in the May, 1925, issue. I received numerous letters from all over the country and from people I had known in Porto Rico. There was a great divergence of comments. Among them I was asked to start a concert series in San Francisco; to aid in launching young talents; to advise clubs concerning money-making attractions; to collaborate with a New York Young People's Theatre; to locate a booking agent for a lecturer from Africa. A chiropractor from Detroit offered to bring back my voice gratis if I would make the trips to Detroit.

A former student of mine wrote: "The article about Grace Denton in the *American* recalled the time in 1910, sitting in the library in Cochran Hall at Otterbein trying not to be homesick, when I heard your voice singing a song about swallows and their flight I decided then I would try to follow in your footsteps. Later I had the pleasure of being one of your pupils and the instruction I received has been invaluable to me ever since." Martha Cassler Jones.

My picture was taken with a little old lady who came to every concert and this I liked, but the one used in the *American* was of me alone.

Booking agents began to seek me out to manage their wares. One event in Toledo, sponsored by the Boy Scouts, was a motion picture of Lieut. Jack Harding's "World Flight." Harding appeared in person, and Lowell Thomas, then at the beginning of his career, the official historian of the Flight, personally narrated.

It was an historic evening when Paul Whiteman and his concert orchestra introduced George Gershwin's "Rhapsody in Blue," with Gershwin as the piano soloist — the first time on tour. I am proud to have presented that one. As the years went by, I came to know Gershwin through several concert engagements. The next one was an all-Gershwin program in Detroit, performed by Gershwin himself and the glamorous Peruvian soprano, Marguerite D'Alvarez. Gershwin played his piano works and accompanied D'Alvarez in her singing of his songs. It was a memorable twosome. Backstage D'Alvarez took hold of Gershwin's coat lapels, and looking up at him, said, "Now, Georgie, don't ever let success spoil you," — and it never did. He was kind and courtly throughout his brief career. What a genius and what a man. His was a triumphant legacy for American music.

In 1934, the "Century of Progress" World's Fair was repeated, and I was asked to manage a series of concerts by The Chicago Symphony Orchestra. John Alden Carpenter and other Chicago leaders in music were back of this movement.

Time was short, I was speculating about possibilities for these concerts, and the Gershwin appearances were vivid in my mind.

Gershwin with the Chicago Symphony? Why not. I wired Gershwin, who agreed. I took the publicity to the Chicago *Tribune* and other papers. At this late date, the Committee changed its mind. They had decided it would be too expensive to have this program. Now what? I had to think fast for I couldn't countermand the publicity and I couldn't tell George we had changed our minds. I therefore made an offer to buy the Orchestra for this performance, guaranteeing the costs of the concert myself. I had faith in the ticket sales. The offer was accepted. When the box office opened there were lines of ticket buyers extending across the Auditorium Theatre lobby from morning until night, a sellout assured.

When the Committee realized that success was at hand, even though I had signed a contract which I assumed included the regulation rehearsal, I was informed that the rehearsal would be $500.00 extra. Now here was a dilemma. It wasn't in the cards to refuse. I took the subject up with George, and great person that he was, he payed half the amount and saved the day. The concert proceeded in glory, something akin to musical fireworks.

Another World's Fair attraction given long and arduous consideration by me and Giuseppe Castruccio, the Italian Consul General, was a gala Gala production of "Aida" in Soldier's Field. This was to be a part of the welcome festivities for Italo Balbo and his Flying Squadron of 100 flyers from Italy. Because of the uncertainty of his arrival caused by weather delays, the project had to be abandoned.

During his college years at Ohio State my brother, William, had his home with me. I missed him when he went on his own as Junior Physicist with Goodrich Rubber Company.

Lawrence Tibbett

Campbell Studios Photo

Charles Hackett

The Grand Opera Quartet, arranged by Charles Wagner, included opera soprano, Frances Alda; Merle Alcock, contralto; Charles Hackett, tenor, and introduced a new baritone, Lawrence Tibbett. It proved a great evening of music at the Rivoli.

Merle Alcock

Frances Alda

Walter Damrosch was a celebrated musician and had a noble face. The New York Symphony Orchestra, which he conducted, was an outstanding chapter in the annals of music in the United States.

Italian Fortune Gallo believed in Opera. For more than twenty years he organized, supported and toured the San Carlo Opera Company from Coast to Coast. "Martha" was given on the Rivoli Series. Many from his casts went on to outstanding careers with leading opera companies.

To Walter Damrosch goes acclaim as the first conductor of a major Symphony, the New York Symphony, to present his orchestra in concerts for youth. He had a rare gift in interesting his young audiences in symphonic classical music.

Charles Meek, superintendent of the Public Schools and Grace Denton meet Damrosch as he arrives to give the first symphonic concert for youth in Toledo prior to the evening concert on the Rivoli series.

Louise Homer, Metropolitan Opera
contralto, and famous American
personality, wife of Sidney Homer,
composer, gave a joint recital with the
young pianist, Mischa Levitzki.

A tall and handsome baritone, Reinald
Werrenrath, received rounds of applause
at his Rivoli concert.

Mischa Levitzki, young and talented, had
wide recognition for his fine artistry.

Kubey-Rembrant Studios Photo

Ruth St. Denis was a strong influence in creating a form of dance which had more freedom of motion than Russian Ballet. It was at the school, "Denishawn," which she developed with Ted Shawn, to whom she was married, that she nurtured dancers Martha Graham, Doris Humphrey, Charles Weidman and many other young dance aspirants.

Ruth St. Denis had a strong interest in Oriental dances which she incorporated in the programs of her touring company.

A St. Denis classic was her
famous dance, "Radha."

Ruth St. Denis, center, is kissed by husband Ted Shawn in 1960 at party given by dance pioneer
Martha Graham, left, a former Denishawn student.

It was momentous — Paul Whiteman presenting his Dance Band on the concert stage, the first time jazz and popular music had been elevated to this estate. He found a ready following particularly since this concert tour had as a feature, the pianist George Gershwin, who played his "Rhapsody in Blue" with the Band. This was a tour de force. Gershwin's status as a musician leaped and "Rhapsody in Blue" became a classic.

George Gershwin

Marguerite D'Alverez was a Peruvian and she was beautiful. Her contralto voice was rich and resonant. She essayed a repetoire covering many song forms, including featuring songs by George Gershwin on her programs with George as her accompanist.

Concert announcement in part.

HEAR —

MURIEL La FRANCE

"TOLEDO'S GALLI-CURCI"

GALLI-CURCI

MURIEL La FRANCE

IN FEATURE AND VOICE — THE REPLICA OF THE
WORLD'S MOST FAMOUS COLORATURA—AMELITA
GALLI-CURCI, WHO HAS TAKEN MISS La FRANCE
FOR HER ONLY PROTEGE AND PERSONALLY
COACHED HER FOR THE TOLEDO CONCERT.

This photo was used in the Grace Denton
success story published in the American
Magazine of May, 1925.

1925~1926

Wings — as I reached age 35, my flight encompassed a wider horizon. Aspirations zoomed. I wrote Arthur Judson, manager of the Philadelphia Orchestra, Leopold Stokowski, conductor, stating that I would like to engage the Orchestra with Stokowski for the Rivoli City Concerts. "Yes," said he but "I would have to guarantee the Orchestra for a week — six concerts, $30,000.00" — a goodly sum. But, hurrah, I could have the illustrous Symphony, all I had to do was meet the conditions! With only one concert in Toledo, six brave men underwrote $5,000.00 each — one was John N. Willys, another Thomas DeVilbiss. I then resold Chicago, Pittsburg, Dayton, managed Toledo and Detroit myself, and Everett Jones, whom I came to know when he was associated with "The Miracle" production, took charge of the Cleveland concert for me. The dates were booked one year in advance for the week of February 25, 1926. I would have sold the Detroit concert to the reigning manager there, Jimmie DeVoe, but as he said, "the orchestra doesn't exist for which he would guarantee $5,000.00," so I engaged the date in the new Masonic Auditorium, one year before the building was completed, having faith that it would be finished in time — and it was. This brought me into focus as the manager of the gala Auditorium Opening, mentioned previously. This event netted me $2,000.00, but the entire amount was lost on the Philadelphia Orchestra concert in Cleveland.

For the Philadelphia Orchestra concerts Stokowski brought an unexpected feature — the Hammond piano — a two-keyboard instrument, with pianist Lester Donahue, a luminary of Los Angeles, as soloist.

As Stokowski made it his personal responsibility to check all details in relation to the stage for his concerts — space, lighting, orchestra seating, — he came to Detroit in advance of the orchestra, his train arriving at 6:00 A.M. This was an early hour to route out members of the stage crew and myself, but it was done. After the session Stokowski calmly sat at a table on stage and worked at designing jewelry for his new wife — formerly Evangeline Johnson.

Other events that year on the Rivoli Series were Fritz Kreisler, Beniamino Gigli, Sigrid Onegin, Toti dal Monte, a stellar list.

Years later in the Toledo *Blade*, Dorothy Stafford wrote a series of articles entitled "Yesterday's Concerts." A headline for one was: "No Other Fiddler Charms Dorothy as Kreisler Did." She wrote, in part, "It was at the Rivoli Theatre on January 22, 1926, at a Grace Denton concert, that I heard Kreisler for the first time and after hearing him play the 'Kreutzer' Sonata, I decided that he was the greatest violinist in the world . . . I recall that I was fascinated by Kreisler's personality. Suave, genial, sure of himself, elegant, with a monocle cord around his neck — the Viennese was everything one could expect of a great artist. Looking back down the years, it seems to me that Fritz Kreisler more than any other musician had a popular appeal. Even the most unlettered had his record of 'Humoresque' on the Victrola and by his records he did more to acquaint the public with good music than any other artist I can remember. His playing had a human note. Coming out of the Rivoli, my companion said, 'You act as if you were in a trance.' 'I am', I said, 'and don't wake me up. I never want to hear another violinist. No one can ever come up to him.' "

The Kreisler concert brought an edict from the Stage Hands Union. To accommodate the ticket buyers, it became necessary to put 100 chairs on the stage. I could have placed the folding wood chairs myself, but was required to have four stage hands at seven dollars each.

The Zonta Course continued with some attractions to crow about. This was the year that Will Rogers went on a concert tour with a male Quartet — The DeReszke Singers — a program like none other. When the show was over Will Rogers and I sat on stools at the Secor Hotel lunch counter for refreshments. I liked his writing on the photo he gave me — "Champion Manager."

What a gem of an attraction, the Barrere Little Symphony led by Georges Barrere, the inimitable flautist, with the Scotch baritone, Cameron McLean, as soloist, an artist also beyond compare as was his accompanist, Mabelle Howe Mable.

Last of the three events was Ninon Romaine, Toledo pianist, who had a face like chiseled marble and played divinely. Later on a tour in India, she contracted the deadly black smallpox and was buried secretly in the middle of the night.

Two extra concerts brought widely different stars, each a peer in his own realm — Ignace Paderewski, Polish pianist-patriot in his last Toledo concert, and John Philip Sousa, Band Master, he of "Stars and Stripes Forever," and the majestic marches heard in all parades.

Either as conductor or pianist, Ossip Galbrilowitsch was essentially a poet. He developed the Detroit Symphony to new levels of excellence, and as a solo performer on the piano, or in duo-recital with Harold Bauer, he built a huge and loyal public.

The stately Masonic Temple in Detroit houses two theatres, the large Concert Hall seating 4600. The opening performance by the Detroit Symphony Orchestra, Ossip Gabrilowitsch conducting, Luella Melius, soprano, the soloist, was managed by Grace Denton. Thereafter she presented the Chicago Civic Opera for three seasons, also great theatre, dance attractions and concerts in the beautiful edifice.

E. Goldensky Photo

Leopold Stokowski built the Philadelphia Orchestra into the greatest organization in the world. The silky strings, the precision and control plus the nuances which he could command from a hundred men, gave him a unique place among all conductors.

Keystone Photo Service Photo

Always concerned with the new in music, Leopold Stokowski introduced the Hammond double keyboard piano in his 1926 tour of six cities with the Philadelphia Orchestra, managed by Grace Denton. To Lester Donahue, a young artist from Los Angeles, fell the opportunity of playing this instrument with the Orchestra, which he did with brilliant effect.

Stokowski at the controls during a recording session.

Ignace Paderewski played his final Toledo concert under the management of Grace Denton. Obviously, his years as a statesman, particularly as the Premier of Poland, gave new depth and emotional coloring to his last performances.

The mellifluous and robust tenor of Beniamino Gigli was remindful of Caruso. He was considered by many to be the greatest dramatic tenor of his day in roles at the Metropolitan.

Fritz Kreisler was certainly one of the immortals among the great violinists of history. His tone was extraordinary, and his technique so facile that it hid technique. He overwhelmed in the classics and charmed in the playing of his own compositions.

Will Rogers on the concert stage complete with rope and bandanna. There was a deluxe quartet also, the DeReszke Quartet. This was an evening to delight. Rogers wrote on a photo "To Grace Denton, Champion manager," and underscored Champion!

FROM THE WILD WEST via the

— Ziegfeld Follies —

WILL ROGERS

WITH COMPLETE PARAPHERNALIA
LARIAT, CHAPS, BANDANNA and ALL

In Toledo, Friday Eve., October 23

with DeReszke Male Quartet

SEATS—
MONDAY, OCTOBER 19th

	AMPLIFIERS
PRICES $2.75, $2.20, $1.65, $1.10	will be used making every seat satisfactory.
NICHOLAS BUILDING LOBBY	

THE ZONTA COURSE · Direction: Grace E. Denton

The Bettmann Archive, Inc. Photo

John Philip Sousa's Band received plaudits the length and breadth of the United States in annual tours. His march, "Stars and Stripes Forever," holds an undying place in the sinews of this country. His marches are played by all bands and by Symphony Orchestras on occasion.

Ninon Romaine, pianist, evoked a very distinct style, particularly in the classic repertoire.

Cameron McLean was a Scottish baritone par excellence. What character, lilt and warmth a Scotsman can bring to his songs. His admirers were legion and his excellent accompanist, Mabelle Howe Mable, shared in his honors.

1926~1927

GRAND OPERA held the spotlight in Madame Impresario's fourth season. The Chicago Civic Opera, then in its zenith under the aegis of Samuel Insull, was seen in four performances at the Masonic Auditorium. The guarantee of $70,000.00 was underwritten by prominent Detroiters. The dates were in March 1927, one year after the opening of the Auditorium. The glamorous repertoire included "Tosca" with Claudia Muzio, "The Jewels of the Madonna" and "Aida" with Rosa Raisa, and "Resurrection" with Mary Garden. This was opera in the grand manner. With the entourage of an opera company of this stature, carloads of scenery, the costumes, large orchestra, ballet, chorus, stage crew; the air was charged with commotion and excitment. Top-ranking in the publicity field, Ben Atwell was the company publicist, quite an assignment with so many prima donnas. I recall he said, "I aim to suit myself, then I know someone is pleased." The prima donnas brought great glory to the performances.

Opening with "La Tosca," Claudio Muzio with her special gifts, vocal and histrionic, brought to the role of La Tosca a quality that transcends. As she came on stage in a trailing sequined gown, turquoise in color, carrying an armful of real, yard-long-stemmed American Beauty Roses, it was an enthralling sight.

Also on both the Detroit and Toledo subscription series, none other than Feodor Chaliapin, the incomparable Russian basso, starred in a traveling production of "The Barber of Seville," a Hurok enterprise.

95

Not often did I have trouble with artists failing to keep their dates, but the Prima Ballerina of the Metropolitan Opera Ballet, Rosina Galli (she was the wife of the Met manager, Gatti-Cazzasa) became ill and cancelled. In her place the Adolph Bolm Company brought delight to the audience.

Adolph Bolm, who, with Nijinski, came to America with the Diaghileff Ballet Russe, remained in this country and founded his own ballet ensemble — the Bolm Ballet Intime, with the delightful Ruth Page. Bolm, of course, was a former member of the Russian Imperial Ballet. He was adept as a choreographer and producer. He appeared with remarkable success in the Hollywood Bowl. His "Spirit of the Factory" remains the gauge by which other ballets are judged in the Hollywood Bowl. A native of Russia he was of Scandinavian descent.

Dance in America also has been graced by the creativity of the petite and gifted dynamo in relation to dance, from Indianapolis, Ruth Page, who danced with Pavlowa at age 15. To name a few of her multiple accomplishments in addition to being prima ballerina with the Bolm Ballet in tours throughout this country and London, she performed the leading role in John Alden Carpenter's "The Birthday of the Infanta;" was prima danseuse with the Municipal Opera Company in Buenos Aires; was guest artist at the enthronement ceremonies of Emperor Hirohita, Tokyo, Japan; guest soloist, Ballet Russe de Monte Carlo; Co-director with Bently Stone, Les Ballets d'Americaine at Theatre des Champs-Elysses, Paris; Director of Chicago Opera Ballet. The list of ballets choreographed by Ruth Page is imposing. Isaac Van Grove was the musical arranger for many of them.

The list of events presented that season in Detroit included a repeat of the Philadelphia Orchestra with Stokowski conducting. There was a recital by scintillating Mary Garden. I met her as her train arrived. In the taxi, enroute to the hotel, she discoursed on many topics including current politics. Her mind was chisel-sharp. At a press interview she would answer the questions instantly upon the asking. The press was goggle-eyed, likewise the audience who heard her concert.

Dusolina Gianini, a soprano newcomer, who looked stunning in her medieval costume, appeared in joint recital with Mischa Levitzki, pianist. A novelty on both the Detroit and Toledo series was the Tipica Orchestra of Mexico. Soprano opera singer, Lucrezia Bori, was soloist. Ruth St. Denis, Ted Shawn and their company returned to Toledo.

A second series in Toledo, sponsored by The Orchestra Society of Toledo, offered the Detroit Symphony Orchestra, Ossip Gabrilowitsch, conductor; the Cincinnati Orchestra, Fritz Reiner, conductor; the Cleveland Orchestra, Nicolai Sokoloff, conductor, at the Keith Theatre. I was proud of the distinguished Board of Directors who supported this effort.

Edith Rhetts Tilton, who achieved brilliantly for the Detroit Symphony Youth Concerts, gave a Preview lecture. Charles Isaacson spoke on Opera prior to the Chicago Opera season in Detroit. A Morning Musicale took place at the Toledo Commodore Perry Ballroom with Canadian soprano, Eva Gautier, delighting her listeners.

Eva Gautier was an exotic. Physically, she was a rather petite brunette, and her face and figure on the platform had her audience charmed before she sang a note. Her specialties were the uncommon songs ranging from German lieder to Reynaldo Hahn, and she was the first to sing the songs of George Gershwin in a so-called serious program. She was particularly fond of the music of Maurice Ravel.

And so ended another stimulating season.

The Claudia Muzio Club

Regal Claudia Muzio as Tosca. The roses were real American beauties. The sequined dress turquoise in color, and her voice liquid gold, thrilling to hear.

Edith Mason enacted many lyric soprano roles with the Chicago Civic Opera. In the Detroit season, she was cast as "Madame Butterfly" and as Marguerite in "Faust." She was the wife of the Opera Conductor, Giorgio Polacco.

fernand de Gueldre Pho

Claudia Muzio's tomb. A group of her devoted young followers issued this photo and tribute:
"In loving memory of our beloved Claudia Muzio, on the fourth anniversary of her death, May 24th, (1936-1940). She brought joy and beauty to us in life — We shall think of her always with love in our hearts."

fernand de Gueldre Photo

Feodor Chaliapin was a colossus of the
operatic stage. His performance of
"Boris Godounov" has never been
equalled. In concert, his magnificent
voice and his histrionic ability were
unique in the whole recital field.

Sol Hurok persuaded Chaliapin to go on
tour singing Don Basilio in "The Barber
of Seville," not a large part, but as done
by Chaliapin, unforgettable.

Mira Photo

"Sol Hurok Presents." Under this
banner a plethora of fine music and
ballet has taken place in practically
every city from Coast to Coast.

The name of Adolph Bolm looms large in the annals of Ballet in America, although his initial activity was with the Diaghilev forces. Bolm toured his Bolm Ballet Intime, choreographed for motion pictures and in later years had a teaching studio in Hollywood. His influence will be felt for years to come.

Adolph Bolm

Morse-Pix Photo

In her exotic dances of the Orient, Vera Mirova added a rich luster of motion and costuming to the Bolm Ballet Intime programs.

Maurice Goldberg Photo

The versatility of Ruth Page is remarkable. She could choreograph new dances in the modern mode, or revert to the classic roles with the greatest distinction. Here she is dancing to a Chopin etude, as Prima Ballerina with the Bolm Ballet Intime.

Ruth Page was not only a very versatile dancer, mistress of many styles, but a choreographer of great imagination. Here she is shown in her own version of Peter Pan.

Ruth Page, pictured here as Susanna, the maid, in her choreographed Ballet of "The Barber of Seville." Among her multiple activities on behalf of Ballet, she choreographed several ballets using Grand Opera librettos. Dynamic Ruth, her accomplishments for Ballet are manifold, her versatility enormous.

A dance in lighter vein choreographed and danced by Ruth Page that captured plaudits was her fanciful "The Flapper and the Quarterback," with Paul DuPont the Quarterback. It personified John Held Jr.'s Flapper, an individual of the 1920s.

Nicholas Muray Photo

Rosa Raisa starred in the dramatic repertory at the Chicago Civic Opera with pronounced success. Her stage presence and rich vocal attainments brought her great prestige.

Rosa Raisa as Norma, a role in which she excelled through her abundant gifts as an artist.

For her concerts, the Italian beauty, Dusolina Gianini, soprano, wore medieval costumes of rich fabrics and hues. She made a picture as she sang in velvet tones.

Because of her individual interest in composers not often listed on programs, Eva Gautier, songstress from Canada, had a large and ardent following. This drawing by John Singer Sargent, exemplifies her charm.

Lucrezia Bori brought an authentic atmosphere of Spain as soloist with the Tipica Orchestra of Mexico, in Detroit. She was a great favorite in Opera, especially at the Ravinia summer season of Opera, where this picture was taken.

Sculpture of Ossip Gabrilowitsch.

For the Detroit Symphony concert in the Toledo Symphony Series, Ossip Gabrilowitsch served both as conductor and piano soloist, providing an enriching evening of music. This photo was given by his wife, Clara Clemens Gabrilowitsch, to Dr. Maurice Bernstein, who was Orson Welles' guardian when Orson was a boy.

Fritz Reiner conducted the Cincinnati Symphony in Toledo, also when the Cincinnati Symphony appeared in Detroit on the Masonic Auditorium Series. Reiner later became the regular conductor of the Chicago Symphony. His approach to orchestral music was intellectual yet he had a sympathetic warmth in his interpretations of composers.

GREATNESS IN MUSIC, DRAMA, DANCE ~ 1927~1928~1929

It was a Roman candle of stars until 1929 when drastic changes came. For its second season in Detroit, the Chicago Civic Opera's repertoire included "La Gioconda" starring Rosa Raisa, "Madame Butterfly" with Edith Mason as Butterfly, Mary Garden in her superb delineation of "Carmen," "Il Trovatore" with Claudia Muzio.

The third and final season of four operas listed an enthralling performance by Mary Garden in "Thais," Rosa Raisa in "Norma," beauteous Marion Claire as Elsa in "Lohengrin," Edith Mason in "Faust."

This once great Chicago Civic Opera was a victim of the 1929 stock market "crash" when Samuel Insull, its benefactor, and other supporters lost their fortunes.

There was American Opera, too — a touring company of the opera which had been produced at the Metropolitan — "The King's Henchman," by Deems Taylor, text by Edna St. Vincent Millay. Presented both in Detroit and Toledo, it was sung in English. With orchestra and chorus there were 105 in the touring company. Frances Peralta, Rafaelo Diaz and Henri Scott enacted the leading roles. Though it had mildly enjoyable features, it went into oblivion as have quite a few operas composed by Americans. Richard Hale, later to win acclaim in classic roles in motion pictures, was in the cast. In years to come we became friends when he taught diction in the Music Academy of the West, which I founded in Santa Barbara, California.

Theatre appeared on the scene in Detroit with flair, first in the New York Theatre Guild Repertory Company in a series of four plays — each performed for three nights and matinee in Detroit, one night in Ann Arbor, two nights and matinee in Toledo — the regular eight performances per week. I migrated from place to place on the street-car for the four weeks. When did I sleep, I wonder, for there were concert events, too, to look after.

The Theatre Guild announcement read: "The Theatre Guild Repertory Company with George Gaul and Florence Eldridge." In the roster of actors listed below was the husband of Eldridge — one Frederic March, then just on the threshold of his renowned future. The four plays were: "Arms and the Man," George Bernard Shaw; "The Silver Cord," Sidney Howard; "Mr. Pim Passes By," A.A. Milne; "The Guardsman," Molnar.

Also there was a week's engagement in Detroit and one performance in Toledo of "Porgy," the play that preceded Gershwin's mighty "Porgy and Bess." Alexander Woollcott wrote of "Porgy" in the New York World: "An evening of new experience, extraordinary interest, and high, startling beauty . . . In a dozen years of first nights I have not seen in the American Theatre an example of more resourceful and enkindling direction . . . in the ballet of the mourners' shadows upon the wall, 'Porgy' reaches one of the most exciting climaxes I had ever seen in the theatre . . . the Guild has begun its tenth season magnificently."

For the second season of the Theatre Guild Reportory plays, Elizabeth Risdon and Robert Keith carried the leading roles. The schedule included: "The Doctor's Dilemma," George Bernard Shaw; "The Second Man," S.N. Behrman; "Ned McCobb's Daughter," Sidney Howard; and "John Ferguson," St. John Ervine, which had launched the Theatre Guild on its history-making career. Each play was given as before in Detroit, Ann Arbor and Toledo.

The following year, 1929, my last in Toledo and Detroit, Clara Nobel, a theatre buff, and I rented the Palace Theatre in Toledo for a series of plays. There was a subscription series of five Theatre Guild plays, each having a week's run. These included "Strange Interlude," by Eugene O'Neill, which was accepted with consternation. It began in the afternoon, there was an intermission for dinner, it then continued with an evening session. Pauline Lord and Ralph Morgan had the starring roles. Lynn Fontanne and Alfred Lunt appeared in their charm-oozing delineation of "The Guardsman." In the season there was the musical comedy, "Blackbirds," which brought out the perennial "I Can't Give You Anything But Love."

"Strange Interlude" also was given at the Wilson Theatre in Detroit.

In Detroit that year a stage event of majestic stature which I presented for a week in the 4,600 capacity of the Masonic Auditorium was the stupendous Gordon Craig "Macbeth," produced by George Tyler, who specialized in the production of master classics of the theatre. The noted Craig, son of Ellen Terry, executed the scenery all in a neutral shade, the startlingly beautiful effects done with inspired lighting. This was his first and only production in the United States. The sets were massive — a bridge in the rear weighed a ton. There was a long flight of stairs at stage right front, down which Florence Reed as Lady Macbeth descended slowly, trailing her clinging robe of white as she spoke the famous lines "Out damned spot." Never could this sequence be more gripping. Lyn Harding was the Macbeth, William Farnum was Banquo, Basil Gill, the Macduff. One performance was given at the Rivoli in Toledo.

The New York reviews were raves. "Epoch-making, eye filling and ear filling . . . it was just such an entertainment as most of us hope for but seldom get," William Trapp, New York *Evening World*. "By all odds the most beautifully staged 'Macbeth' that has yet been seen," New York *Times*. "Great is our elation, therefore, when Mr. Tyler, noblest of showmen, provides us with one of the best endeavors as 'Macbeth' . . . I felt that all of Avon's obligations to me had been paid in full," Percy Hammond, New York *Herald-Tribune*.

Another "Macbeth" made well-deserved history, though at another end of the spectrum as far as diversity is concerned. This was the all-Negro cast "Macbeth" directed by young Orson Welles, his first opus with the WPA Unit — that of Harlem, New York. Orson, just out of his teens, already had infused the theatre with more creative originality than dedicated thespians find possible in a lifetime. How come? Well, this was genius in full bloom. Many artists in various fields are gifted in one category. Orson, like the heroic Da Vinci, was many-sided.

Since this Chronicle is a tale of *Madame Impresario*, I mention only artists and productions that I personally presented. An exception is the Welles "Macbeth." This I did not have the privilege of managing, however, I saw it repeatedly during the Broadway run of ten months. It made no less than a prodigious impression! Also there was a tour of major cities continuing for many months.

I came to know Orson during my Chicago years — the '30s. I first saw him as an actor in the role of Svengali in "Trilby" which he staged and directed at the Todd School where he was a student, his only formal schooling. As I was a manager, Orson's guardian (Orson's parents were deceased), Dr. Maurice Bernstein, who was deeply interested in his ward's future, would talk with me about ways and means of developing opportunities for Orson.

Actually, from his beginnings Orson was wont to make his own opportunities, such as his going on a bicycle sketching tour through Ireland at age 16, during which he attended a performance at Dublin's Gate Theatre. He then proceeded to introduce himself to the Company as an actor from the New York Theatre Guild, whereupon soon he was on stage playing parts far beyond his years. It was the sonorous, rich quality of Orson's voice that first attracted the attention of John Houseman with whom Orson teamed in the development of the Mercury Theatre, a great page in theatrical history. Orson was 19 then and appearing as Tybalt in the Katherine Cornell Company of "Romeo and Juliet," when Houseman found him.

I was fortunate in attending a performance of "The Cradle Will Rock," by Marc Blitzstein, which was the final opus of Welles and Houseman, under WPA, yet when it was shown it was done so privately by the intrepid producers.

Some technicality in connection with the performance being given on the stage precluded either actors or scenery being on stage. There was an old upright piano on center stage and a single stage light. Outside of this the stage was bare to the back wall. The actors rose from the front row of seats and the loges in the theatre and spoke their lines. Incredibly this did not deter complete dramatic intensity.

About this time I met Orson under the clock at the Astor Hotel — a place to meet in those days. He sipped lemon juice, being concerned with weight. I tried to interest Harry MacGuire in putting money in the Mercury. I believe he did invest moderately. We went to Harry's apartment. His collection of Hogarths was something to behold.

It has been stimulating to watch the skyrocketing achievements of Orson Welles, a chapter in greatness.

I was privileged to present another drama group that held Detroit audiences spellbound — The Irish Players from Dublin seen in "The Whiteheaded Boy," by Lennox Robinson; "Juno and the Paycock," and "The Plough and the Stars," by Sean O'Casey. Sara Allgood and Barry

Fitzgerald, peerless as the leads, later became famous in motion pictures in Hollywood.

Morris Gest was responsible for the traveling company — The Moscow Lyric Art Theatre — for which I managed the Detroit appearance. I had taken a trip to Boston with Gest for the opening there. The two productions given were "Lysistrata" and "Carmencita and the Soldier," the artistry of which belies words. For "Carmencita," a version of the familiar "Carmen," there was a curving staircase at the rear of the stage. A senorita, dressed in red, stood on each stair looking out on the stage. Each held a large black fan, eyes looking over the top of it. They could flutter the fans in rhythm with the action on stage, intensely or placidly, a very dramatic effect.

Even back in 1927, Sol Hurok had an interest in Russian Ballet. He arranged an appearance of famed Fokine and Fokina and a company of 70 with the New York Philharmonic at the Lewisohn Stadium which was witnessed by some 40,000 people in three programs. This Company with a symphony orchestra came to the Masonic Auditorium in November for two performances; one on the subscription series, the other on Armistice Day, a benefit for the Lincoln Memorial University in the Appalachian Mountains.

The Fokines formerly were leaders in the Imperial Russian Ballet. They exerted strong influence in revision of ballet movement. Fokine's choreography of "The Dying Swan," with music by Saint-Saens, was performed by Pavlowa and by dancers ad infinitum around the world.

Another company of dancers which attracted enconiums at this time was the Jooss Ballet. Their "The Green Table," particularly memorable, had an all-male cast — diplomats discussing affairs of State. This engagement took place in Toledo.

The Concert Series for 1927-1928 in Detroit was varied in scope. There was the unsurpassed Boston Symphony Orchestra, Serge Koussevitzky conducting. What a feast of sound! There was Fokine and Fokina and Ballet Company; George Gershwin and Marguerite D'Alvarez, Peruvian mezzo soprano; the opera, "The King's Henchman;" The Barrere Little Symphony, conducted by Georges Barrere the first flutist of the New York Symphony and considered the world's greatest virtuoso on this instrument, with as soloist Emile de Gogorza, the suave Spanish baritone, the husband of Emma Eames. There was to have been a Grand Opera Trio — Jeanne Gordon, contralto of the Metropolitan, who came from Detroit; Edward Johnson, tenor of the

Metropolitan; and George Baklanoff, Russian baritone. Several days before the concert, the phone rang and I was advised by Jeanne Gordon's manager that she would be unable to sing on the scheduled date. What to do had to be decided right then and there. Since Gordon had a large Detroit following that would be disappointed not to hear her, I accepted a postponed date, always complicated with notifying subscribers, etc. So far, so good, but on the original date, Edward Johnson arrived ready to sing. He had not been told by his manager of the change of date! He was on his way to New York for the Christmas vacation with his family and refused to return, so the concert took place sans tenor and this was awkward for me — some tickets had to be refunded.

Artists on the Rivoli Series in Toledo that year included Jascha Heifetz, Rosa Ponselle, the Russian Symphonic Choir, the Detroit Symphony with Ossip Gabrilowitsch appearing both as conductor and pianist (he played the Rachmaninoff Second Concerto in C Minor, Op. 18), and there was the much admired tenor, then in his zenith, Tito Schipa.

The 1928-1929 Concert Series in Toledo brought the titan composer-pianist, Serge Rachmaninoff; the famous Negro lyric tenor, Roland Hayes; The English Singers who sang a cappella madrigals and early song forms, sitting around a table as was the custom in the sixteenth century; soprano Dusolina Giannini and the Cleveland Orchestra, Nicolai Sokoloff conducting.

Extra events claimed attention — a recital by Marion Talley, whose youth attracted attention but whose career was short lived. I managed a lecture by Clarence Darrow — his subject, "Is Life Worth While?" The audience was large. He began by saying that "he was surprised to see that so many had come to hear that Life was NOT worth while." Not all of his listeners shared his opinion.

These were the years when there evolved a little black box, which when one put on ear phones, voices could be heard from distant areas — the advent of radio!

For my final year in Detroit, 1928-1929, the Concert Series was sparked by glamorous Maria Jeritza who had made headlines through her performances in "Tosca" at the Metropolitan when she sang "Vissi d'arte" lying on her stomach. Heifetz gave one of his exalted recitals. There was Roland Hayes, and the Cincinnati Symphony, Fritz Reiner conducting.

110

Also there was the first appearance in Detroit of Andreas Segovia, whose artistry on the guitar ushered in a whole new concept for this instrument. I had to contact Segovia about some business detail and went to the Statler Hotel to see him, whereupon he regaled my assistant Anita Bates, who was with me, and me with a private recital in his room. What a delight this was!

There were social teas at the College Club which had its own attractive building. Lawrence Langner of the Theatre Guild spoke concerning the first Theatre Guild Repertory Season. Walter Pritchard Eaton, the noted dramatic authority and critic, gave a talk on the second Theatre Guild season. There was a tea for Jeritza who exuded her special brand of charm.

Jeritza came into my life many times thereafter. In Chicago, after the Civic Opera had vanished, I produced with Isaac Van Grove "Tosca" starring Jeritza, but this is a later story. In Santa Barbara, California, she sang in a County Music and Drama Festival which I developed. She was then Mrs. Winfield Sheehan, wife of the motion picture producer, and had lavish homes in Beverly Hills and Hidden Valley to which I was invited at various times.

Bookings for the big, 4,600 seats, Masonic Auditorium in Detroit became increasingly difficult as I was number two on the Detroit management totem pole. Because of his many years' priority, Jim DeVoe was number one and had first claim on the top drawing cards among artists.

I had succeeded better than I might have expected with three seasons of Chicago Civic Opera, "The Barber of Seville," with Chaliapin, "The Kings Henchman," in the Opera category. In Symphony there were The Philadelphia Orchestra (two engagements), Boston, Cincinnati, Detroit. The Ballets of Fokine and Fokina, and Adolph Bolm, plus a goodly array of famed artists. The dramatic offerings included the Gordon Craig "Macbeth," The New York Theatre Guild "Porgy", and two seasons of the Guild Repertory Company; also "Strange Interlude." The Irish Players (these in the smaller Scottish Rite Theatre in the Masonic Temple), and the Moscow Lyric Art Theatre.

It had been a creditable array for a somewhat novice of an "Impresario," in her thirties. Ticket sales in my two towns, Toledo and Detroit, totaled into the hundreds of thousands, yet costs kept pace with incoming amounts. I never was good in driving a hard bargain in signing contracts, and as I operated on the so-called "shoestring" basis, it was a wonder that I stayed on top, and I didn't always. In the midst of all this I was offered the position of Assistant Manager of the Detroit Symphony at a sizable salary, but I did not accept being too involved in my own machinations.

The Rivoli in Toledo also had become too expensive to continue, plainly indicating it was "time for a change." The Keith vaudeville theatre in Toledo (1,600 seats) came up for lease. I obtained underwriting for guaranteeing the lease (quite a procedure) but I did not get the lease — a motion picture concern in Buffalo (Shea's) outbid me. This was a disconcerting blow. The muse had carried me far in my six years as Madame Impresario, but now I had reached a stalemate. I was depleted physically and economically but somehow I did not feel defeated. It was 1929. The stock market was whizzing downward. Just how do I pick up the pieces? Motivation — it couldn't be money for this I didn't make, and I had no interest in something called "fame." It must be that I still had music in my system, though now for a couple of years I digressed to include other events.

In Detroit a project evolved called "Town Hall." In fact, there were two of them, each having a capable woman in charge, in competition with each other but both succeeding in reaping handsome profit. The "Town Halls" presented famous lecturers and took place in the largest movie houses at 11:00 A.M. and were followed by luncheons.

In Toledo a newspaper friend's job on the Toledo *Blade* came to an end. She needed to work so I said to her, "Why don't you do a Town Hall?" She liked the idea so I helped her. I gave her my mailing list, my office equipment, went to New York and booked attractions for her. She was successful and continued for many years in bringing both music and lectures to Toledo — Flora Ward Hineline.

One of the lecturers I engaged for her was the eminent psychologist, David Seabury. He said to me he thought I would do well with a "Town Hall" in Chicago. Well, why not? Blithely I bought a train ticket for Chicago. Life began again to be full of promise!

But heartfelt memories remain of Toledo and the wonderful cooperation I had from so many. Samagama, an organization, the members of which are all club presidents, made me an honorary member, and still send me their bulletins. The Toledo *Blade,* where Mitch Woodbury wrote on the theatre and had a column on general topics which, after some fifty years, is still a *Blade* feature. Clippings of his writings about me arrive at intervals. In a "Thanks for the Memories" column in 1946 he wrote: "Let's discuss Grace Denton who brought many a concert and theatrical world winner to Toledo during the years she functioned hereabouts as a feminine entrepreneur. In the Fall of 1923, she brought the Irish tenor, John McCormack and in 1927, Jascha Heifetz, who was then a mere youth. After the concert backstage, I saw the artist tenderly wiping his beloved instrument (a Guarnerius valued at $50,000.00) with a soft handkerchief. On a Sunday afternoon in 1926, the master of them all, Ignace Paderewski, Premier of Poland as well as unparalleled pianist, played to a well-filled house in the Coliseum. He added to his program six extra numbers. For his last number he played his own 'Minuet,' the best known of his compositions. And still the audience would not let him go. It was six o'clock and semi-darkness was upon the house. As I remember many were standing but the stillness of the house was such that a whisper could have been heard — mute testimony to the genius of the artist."

My thanks to Mitch Woodbury for recalling my Toledo days in print.

Kubey Rembrandt Studios Photo

Serge Rachmaninoff could not decide whether his greatest merit was as composer or pianist. He was a master at both, however his compositions bid fair to remain in the repertory of pianists for years to come. Rachmaninoff forsook his native Russia and lived largely in the United States. He succumbed in California.

Jascha Heifetz burst upon the musical scene in 1918 like a meteor. He had a facility and brilliance that placed him among the select few master violinists of all time.

The lustrous tone of Rosa Ponselle's soprano voice, her acting ability and dark Italian beauty made her a star in dramatic roles at the Metropolitan. She was sought for concerts in which her brilliant performance won enormous favor.

Tito Schipa had a lyric bel canto tenor voice that placed him in the forefront of tenors at the Metropolitan in this country and European opera companies. In concert, listeners responded to his singing and his charm with bravos.

Maria Jeritza, a blond beauty, came to the Metropolitan from Austria. She had attained stardom and her individual approach to her roles was widely publicized. She had verve and was an opera personality.

Roland Hayes had a significant career, which was due to his sincerity as an artist and his musicianship. He plumbed the depths of the classics in several languages.

Andres Segovia with his expert virtuosity in performing classical music on the guitar caused a resurgence of classical guitar playing all over the world. He has attracted huge audiences world-wide for more than fifty years.

George Baklanoff like many men of Russian origin had a deep and sonorous baritone, which he used well in both opera and concert. He was tall and made a handsome appearance.

Edward Johnson came from Canada and became an integral part of the music scene in the United States as a tenor soloist, and later Manager of the Metropolitan Opera.

George Barrere, perhaps the most distinguished flautist who ever lived, organized and conducted the Barrere Little Symphony. His treatment of music was very special and everything he did confirmed his great style.

Drawing from life by Carl Bohn

Clarence Darrow

Muray Photo

The Boston Symphony, one of the foremost in this country and the world, has had a succession of significant conductors. Serge Koussevitzky's reign with the Boston can only be termed as marvelous.

THE
THEATRE
GUILD
REPERTORY
COMPANY

with
GEORGE GAUL
and
FLORENCE ELDRIDGE

THE GUARDSMAN
By FRANZ MOLNAR

is the best light comedy of the new season. Often lightness in the theatre is achieved by the simple device of putting very little into the container, but this time we have true deftness of touch and a dancing mood with an ample wealth of incident."
—Heywood Broun—N. Y. World.

"One of the gayest things in town . . . "
—Percy Hammond—N. Y. Herald-Tribune

"The most iridescent trick the season of comedies has yet turned. Excruciatingly funny scenes." *—Gilbert Gabriel—N. Y. Telegram.*

"No comedy of the Guild list has been more cleverly or intelligently directed." *—Burns Mantle—N. Y. News*

Ran A Solid Year in New York at The Garrick and Booth Theatres

THE
Guardsman

SHAW'S
ARMS
AND
THE
MAN

ARMS AND THE MAN
By BERNARD SHAW

"Best of the Guild revivals . . . a brilliant and entertaining comedy. Playgoers who know their way about will see ARMS AND THE MAN. The others ought to." *—John Anderson—Post.*

"The play emerges as one of the stellar achievements of the new theatrical season. The Theatre Guild merits sincere congratulations on this perfect revival of Shaw's 'tut tut' at the childishness of the human race." *—Gordon—Wall Street Journal.*

"One of the brightest of comedy satires." *—Burns Mantle—News.*

"More timely, more trenchant and more delectable than ever . . . One of the most satisfying revivals of many seasons."
—H. Z. Torres—Commercial.

The Guild's Production of This Play Ran for Nine Months on Broadway

Theatre Guild productions managed by Grace Denton
in Detroit, Ann Arbor and Toledo:

John Ferguson	St. John Ervine
Arms and the Man	Bernard Shaw
The Silver Cord	Sidney Howard
Mr. Pim Passes By	A.A. Milne
The Second Man	S.N. Behrman
The Doctor's Dilemma	Bernard Shaw
Ned McCobb's Daughter	Sidney Howard
Strange Interlude	Eugene O'Neill
Porgy	Dubose and Dorothy Heyward
The Guardsman	Franz Molnar

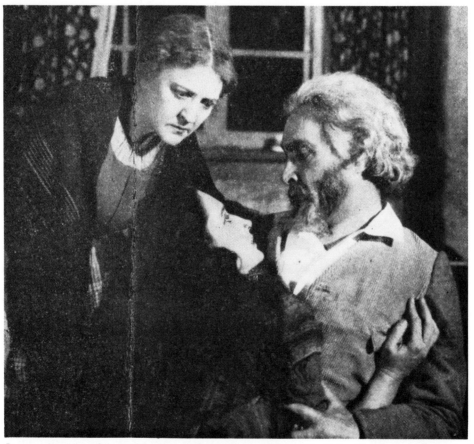

It was the powerful production of "John Ferguson" by St. John Ervine, that launched the New York Theatre Guild on its momentous career. Since that time the list of fine plays the Theatre Guild has produced and toured is formidable.

Complementing each other
to the nth degree in their joint
performances the Lunts, Alfred
and Lynn, graced the
American theatre scene with
such scintillating charm and
verve that attending their
dramatic appearances became a
fine art in theatre-going.

Does she or doesn't she know
that her husband and the
Guardsman are one and the
same? Alfred Lunt who
appeared as the fictitious
Guardsman, here seems to be
pondering this question, as
Lynn Fontanne, his wife on
stage and in life, smiles at
him seductively.

PORGY

A FOLK PLAY

BY DUBOSE & DOROTHY HEYWARD

Dubose and Dorothy Heyward's Folk Play, "Porgy," became the libretto for George Gershwin's remarkable opera "Porgy and Bess," a slice of life which as play or opera, was dramatically stirring.

"STRANGE INTERLUDE"
By EUGENE O'NEILL

THE THEATRE GUILD OF NEW YORK extends to subscribers and patrons of the Theatre Guild Repertory Company the opportunity of reserving seats preceding any mail order or public sale for

EUGENE O'NEILL'S
EXTRAORDINARY NINE-ACT PLAY

"STRANGE INTERLUDE"
At the new WILSON THEATRE
Two weeks beginning December 31st.

This application will be alloted first choice of seats if mailed with check prior to December 17, when regular mail orders are filled, and the public sale opens.

There will be *no matinees* of this play due to the length of the production. *The curtain will rise promptly at 5:30, with an intermission of about an hour and a half for dinner at 7:30.*

The cast includes such distinguished artists as PAULINE LORD, RALPH MORGAN, DONALD MacDONALD and HARRY C. BANNISTER.

Fill out and mail with check to

GRACE DENTON
GRINNELL BROTHERS
1515 WOODWARD AVE.,
DETROIT, MICHIGAN.

The luxurious costuming for "Macbeth" was in keeping with the matchless staging of Gordon Craig. Here is shown Florence Reed as Lady Macbeth and Lyn Harding as Macbeth.

Drawing by Gordon Craig of stage set for "Sleep-walking scene" in "Macbeth."

Gordon Craig, son of the late Dame Ellen Terry, is recognized as the Master of modern theatrical design. An aloof genius, he has nevertheless given to the theatre the inspiration which has been followed by Reinhardt in Germany, Stanislavski in Russia, Gessner, Genier and Coupeaux in France, Lindbergh in Sweden, Schanke in Norway, Johannes Paulsen in Denmark.

The cast for the Craig "Macbeth" was chosen from leading stars of the English-speaking stage: Florence Reed, Lady Macbeth; Lyn Harding, Macbeth; William Farnum, Banquo; Basil Gill, Macduff. George Tyler was the producer. Florence Reed, clad in a trailing white robe, seemed to flow as she descended the long stairway at stage front right, while speaking the fateful lines of Shakespeare.

The New York *Times* wrote: "By all odds the most beautiful 'Macbeth' that has been seen."

Orson Welles' "Macbeth" with all-Negro cast, produced by him under war-time W.P.A. received tremendous acclaim. Here Orson, a young thespian, exhibits a plaque awarded to him by Drama Study Club in 1938. His accumulated honors now would fill a museum wing.

Orson Welles as the mature actor, writer, director. A titan he is in all phases of theater fare.

Barry Fitzgerald was a star in the Irish Players tour of the United States. He became famous also in motion pictures produced in Hollywood.

The Irish Players from Dublin—what glory they brought to the art of the stage in "Juno and the Paycock," "The Plough and the Stars" by Sean O'Casey, and "The Whiteheaded Boy," by Lennox Robinson, and other dramatic plays. The star, Sara Allgood, later had a fine career in motion pictures.

Barry Fitzgerald and Eileen Crowe in the Irish Players production of "Juno and the Paycock."

Edna St. Vincent Millay

Deems Taylor, the eminent composer and music critic composed the opera, "The King's Henchmen," with poet Edna St. Vincent Millay providing the libretto. It was produced at the Metropolitan and had a brief tour, but did not achieve lasting success.

The King's Henchman

By

Deems Taylor *and* Edna St. Vincent Millay

The Fokines, Michael and Vera, were luminaries in the history of Ballet. The ballets choreographed by Fokine such as "Les Sylphides" to the music of Chopin are standard works in classical ballet regimes the world over. Fokine's "The Swan" has remained one of the most popular of ballets.

the chicago years

1931-1932

"Chicago, Chicago, that wonderful town," as the song goes, and so for me it was. Here was the cross-roads of the nation, a railroad center, then the second city in size in the United States. It had supported one of the world's great opera companies and top-ranking Symphony Orchestra. Life, cultural and economic, burgeoned in Chicago.

A former Toledo friend who lived in Chicago took me in and so did the Palmer House, which accepted having a "Town Hall" Series to be given in its Empire Room, a fine locale. I was given desk space. The first objective — to obtain the elite of the city as Patrons. The key to this was to have the support of the reigning arbiters of society — Mrs. Edith Rockefeller McCormick, and Mrs. Waller Borden who later married composer, John Alden Carpenter.

This was 1931 and somehow in those days I was not lacking in confidence. I managed to obtain Mrs. McCormick's telephone number, and unbelievably got her personally on the phone, when I asked her to be a "Town Hall" Patron. She said, "Yes." Now I was on my way! Other illustrious Patrons followed, among them Mrs. J. Ogden Armour, Mrs. Wilhelm Ludwig Baum, Mrs. Joseph M. Cudahy, Mrs. Robert M. Hutchins, Mrs. George Taylor Langhorne, Mrs. Howard Linn, Mrs. Philo A. Otis, Mrs. Stuyvesant Peabody, Mrs. Walter Dill Scott, Mrs. Silas H. Strawn, Mrs. James Ward Thorne, Mrs. Patrick A. Valentine, the British Consul General Godfrey Haggard and Mrs. Haggard, the

127

Hungarian Consul L. L. Medgyesy and Mrs. Medgyesy and a few dozen others. Mrs. Charles S. Clark, President of the "Council of Club Presidents" was a staunch supporter of my endeavors. The announcement folder had for its heading: Public Affairs — Literature — Discovery — History — Philosophy — Education — Art — Drama. The list of speakers might well draw attention even in the depth of depression. Here it is: The Right Honorable Winston S. Churchill (Subject, "The Destiny of the English-Speaking Peoples"); Mary Garden (in a Debussy Recital); Countess Margit Bethlen, wife of the Hungarian Prime Minister ("Sketches of Famous Personages"); William Lyon Phelps of Yale University ("Some Contemporary Books)"; Rafael Sabatini, novelist ("Fiction in History and History in Fiction"); Baroness Helene Nostitz von Hindenburg, niece of Paul von Hindenburg ("The Old and the New Germany"); Cosmo Hamilton, English author ("What is This Thing Called Life?"); Evangeline Adams, Astrologer ("Your Stars and How to Know them"); Lennox Robinson, Irish dramatist ("The Building of a Play"); Princess Der Ling, Chinese Princess ("At the Manchu Court"); Jehan Warliker, authority on India ("India and Her Millions"); H. V. Kaltenborn, writer on international events ("We Look at theWorld") — all for twenty five dollars admission. The Series went well even though it was in the midst of the "depression."

Winston Churchill's appearance needed a larger seating capacity so took place at Orchestra Hall, scheduled for Sunday afternoon. The final advertising had been run in the newspapers, the seats were practically all sold, when there came the widespread news that Churchill, being used to English traffic, had stepped in front of a car on Fifth Avenue in New York and been knocked down. He was not seriously hurt but his Chicago lecture had to be postponed. This required the extra costs of mailing and newspaper advertising — all of which came to some $400.00. I felt the manager should share this with me — he thought differently, and for the only time in my life I was sued; however, in the end we had an out-of-court settlement and the manager did share half the extra cost with me, but what a nuisance. The appearance of Churchill came off with his usual oratorical magic, heard by a packed house. Samuel Insull introduced him.

1932-1933

As I look over old programs for 1932-1933, I am surprised at myself. How could so much have happened during my second year in Chicago? There was the Town Hall series of twelve lecturers, which moved to the

Drake Hotel ballroom. Music again caught up with me. The "depression" had curtailed the concert calendar in Chicago, and I couldn't resist plunging. I organized a series — "The Monday Night Concerts" — at Orchestra Hall, with recitals by Lucrezia Bori, Tito Schipa, Jascha Heifetz, Sigrid Onegin, Swedish contralto; and the one and only Feodor Chaliapin. When he walked on stage his reception was tumultuous, taking several minutes to subside.

One had to seek special means of selling tickets. For this series, the boxes and main floor seats benefited the Girl Scouts.

There was no Opera in Chicago. Whatever prompted me to enter this precarious field on a "shoe-string" with Isaac Van Grove, whose career in Chicago had been long and laudable. We produced "Tosca" with Maria Jeritza as Tosca; John Charles Thomas as Scarpio. Van Grove was the able conductor. Harry Beatty, for years a technical pillar with the Chicago Civic Opera, was Technical Director. The Opera took place in the Auditorium Theatre, once the revered home of the Chicago Opera. It was presented as the Fiftieth Anniversary benefit for the Women's Board of the Presbyterian Hospital. Pictorially it was a strange performance. Jeritza sallied back and forth across the stage, her red, floor-length velvet cape billowing after her. She did her routine singing of "Vissi d'arte" while lying on her stomach on a divan. John Charles was not at his best in Grand Opera. In this one with his white wig, he looked more like George Washington than Scarpio and there was little that could be called romantic about his acting, but the voice was super! However, it was Opera and this brought cheer to the opera-prone gala audience.

Spurred by this success Van Grove and I took on the producing of "Emperor Jones" with Lawrence Tibbett, whose portrayal of the Emperor brought chills to the spine — so superb it was. The Negro cast was recruited in Chicago. The double bill included "Pagliacci" in which Tibbett also starred as Tonio. What a night — to hear this consummate artist in two roles, in one performance, something he had not done before. Mario Chamlee was Canio, Marion Claire, Nedda. Van Grove conducted both operas. Given twice — the post season dates were May 2 and May 5, 1933. The beneficiary was "The Hungry School Children's Fund of the Chicago Public Schools" — I cannot recall how that came about.

I began to receive generous and favorable publicity. Edward Moore in the *Chicago Tribune* wrote: "Ordinarily the music department of a newspaper is but little concerned with managements . . . but the manager of the coming operas is more than commonly connected with the operatic situation in Chicago. This manager is Miss Grace Denton, who has been the means of bringing some of the most notable artists of the world to Chicago. A lecture series of similar order brought other interesting personalities. She presented Maria Jeritza in "Tosca" a few weeks ago and Lily Pons in concert a few nights ago. Now she is taking up these opera projects — "Emperor Jones" with Lawrence Tibbett and "Aida" to welcome the Balbo Flyers.

"In other words she has been stepping out and doing things in a time when many others have been 'hemming and hawing' and finally deciding that times were not propitious. Of course the times have been about as unpropitious as any in history. It would seem to have been mainly a question of intelligent courage. It is certainly true that lacking Miss Denton's efforts the season would have been much duller. This department therefore desires to extend her its congratulations and best wishes in her operatic projects. It believes them to be well worth support and encouragement."

The Town Hall Series was proudful including as it did: Dr. Robert Andrews Millikan, who opened the Series (Science — "New Results in the Field of Cosmic Ray"); Stuart Chase (Economics — "The End of an Epoch"); Dr. John Grier Hibben (Philosophy — "The Quest for a Practical Philosophy of Life"), Sir Frederick Whyte (Asia — "Asia in the Twentieth Century"); Vicki Baum (Life — "Looking at Life"); Clemence Dane (Drama — "Drama in Life and on the Stage"); Max Eastman (America — "America's Changing Ideals"); Victoria Sackfield-West and Harold Nicolson (Marriage — "What I think of Marriage"); Richard Boleslavski (Theatre — "The Universal Theatre"); Baroness Keikichi Ishimoto (Japan — "The Women of Japan"), Thomas Wilfred (Invention — "Light as a Fine Art"); and Irvin S. Cobb, the famous Journalist.

Vicki Baum's lecture took place on her birthday so we celebrated with a luncheon. How little I dreamed then that years later I would be conferring with her husband, Dr. Richard Lert, during several months concerning plans for the Music Academy of the West in Santa Barbara which I founded and for which he served as the first Musical Director. Vicki was generous with helpful advice. She had been a professional harpist before her writing claimed her. The Lerts were in Germany and knew the after World War I hardships, when Vicki sold her book, "Grand Hotel," for a pittance. She reaped none of the rewards from this best seller except world-wide fame.

1933-1934

Life really took on new dimensions in 1933-1934. The Monday Night Concerts moved to the Auditorium Theatre — capacity 3600. They could well generate enthusiasm and did. There was Lawrence Tibbett, Lily Pons, the youthful Yehudi Menuhin, a joint recital by Elizabeth Rethberg and Tito Schipa, and for the first time in Chicago the leading dancer and ballet-master of the Paris Opera—Serge Lifar and his "Russian Ballets Russes Company." Lifar was wined and dined by Chicago elite, and to appear at his best he decided to use an orchestra of Chicago Symphony players, which he paid for himself. Will one ever again see "L'Apres-Midi d'un Faune" danced as this handsome Lifar did it, and his program also included "Le Spectre de la Rose." Some said he even rivaled Nijinsky in this role.

Since Lifar was responsible for the orchestra, I came out rather well — my net totaling a couple thousand dollars — but the glorious remembrance of that great evening of ballet is worth even more.

For this the third and final year I offered the Town Hall Series of lectures, the listings were: William Lyon Phelps ("Contemporary Books Worth Reading"); Lloyd C. Douglas ("The Flight to Freedom"); Clyde Fisher, Curator of Astronomy, American Museum of Natural History ("Earth and Neighbor Worlds"), E. de Gramont, representative of the two oldest Ducal families in France ("Chateaux and Chateau Life in France"); R. D. Blumenfeld, Editor of the London *Daily Express:* Elliot O'Donnell ("Personal Adventures in Ghost Hunting"); Sisley Huddleston, representative from Europe of the *Christian Science Monitor;* Julian Duguid, author of *Green Hell,* ("The Romance and Fascination of the South American Jungle" — illustrated); Bruce Lockhart, author of *British Agent.* Admiral Richard E. Byrd gave a thrilling lecture on "Little America" with remarkable motion pictures.

This was the year that Sol Hurok introduced the Ballet Russe de Monte Carlo to the United States. I went to New York to see performances at the St. James Theatre and there and then decided that while the Ballet's success in New York had been limited, it was my destiny to present the Ballet Russe de Monte Carlo in Chicago. Some other Chicagoans had the same idea, but although I was still operating without capital, Hurok signed a contract with me for nine performances, for which the first guarantee to him was $20,000.00. To this must be added $12,000.00 for operating expense: rent, advertising, orchestra, stage-hands, etc. etc. Then a 50-50 percentage.

I returned to Chicago and rolled up my sleeves. I hired Hazel Moore, wife of Edward Moore, Chicago *Tribune* music editor, to make talks on Ballet at clubs, schools, organizations; and Elsie Johns, publicist and wife

131

of Otto Frankfurter, brother of Felix Frankfurter, late Chief Justice, to book dates for her. The news media were wonderful. We serviced with foreign language and suburban press some 400 newspapers and covered a mailing list of twenty thousand. My expense was nearly fourteen thousand instead of twelve. Chicago went wild over the Ballet Russe de Monte Carlo, and why not—with Alexandra Danilova, Tatiana Riabouchinska, Tamara Toumanova, Irina Baronova, David Lichine and the great Leonide Massine, a dozen other stars, and unsurpassed Corps de Ballet.

Reviews ran like this;

"The ultimate in Ballet as far as this generation might venture to hope." — Edward Moore, *Tribune.*

"The week of revels by the Monte Carlo Ballet Russe was the most stimulating event of the theatrical year. Chicago has seen nothing like it in years." — Charles Collins, *Tribune.*

" 'Presages' is one of the greatest triumphs I have ever witnessed in the theatre." — Herman DeVries, *American.*

" 'Tapestry Alive' as Russian Dancers do their acting. Opera House throbs like an old violin." — Ashton Stevens, *American.*

"It represents in the most important way one of the most important movements in present day art." — Eugene Stinson, *News.*

"There were shouts of approval and cheers." — Glenn Dillard Gunn, *Herald.*

"Strange sights at the Auditorium. Male patrons increase nightly in number and enthusiasm. The lobby looked like the between-halves period of a football game. The dancers are shod with fire — a mass explosion of spirit." — Lloyd Lewis, *News.*

Tower Town Topics, a monthly magazine, used pages of glamorous ballet photos, and in a story about me wrote: "If you think business men have their troubles, how's this for a business girl's problems? Suppose you went to bed some night with the little worry on your mind that you had 39,935 seats to sell, $35,000.00 to raise, and had on your conscience the fact that you were bringing 64 dancers, 27 orchestra men and 18 stage hands from New York to Chicago — that the seats in the Auditorium Theatre had to be sold, the money raised and the deal put over in about three weeks. Would you have a headache? We ask you."

132

Despite the success of the first engagement, I had to talk even harder to get the Auditorium Theatre to rent for a repeat in April but twelve performances came off with the gross going from $37,746.85 for the first engagement to $53,381.86 for the second.

I again had the Ballet for thirteen performances the following December 26 to January 2, 1935 (gross $46,003.41) and again for five performances the following March 1935 (gross $20,510.18) — the total gross $159,642.39. Now Ballet was a going concern in Chicago. I received an eight-column banner headline in the Chicago *American:* GRACE DENTON DARES TO PROVE THAT CHICAGO IS A DANCE-LOVING CITY. Hurok had not lost by having faith in me.

But after all this, Hurok now said he would have to have underwriting for the guarantee. George Woodruff, a banker and ballet enthusiast, agreed to back me with $10,000.00 against loss. Hurok said this was not enough. By now the Ballet could be managed by himself to advantage, so I was ushered out of the Ballet business. My success somehow brought defeat more than once as life unrolled. Hurok reaped the harvest from my work!

In his autobiography, Hurok stated: "Wonderful Chicago! Long before New York became a ballet town, Chicago was running London a close second in its devotion to ballet." Just how did this come about? Madame Impresario's efforts started the ball rolling. In a listing of Ballet receipts sent out by Hurok, the nearest one to Chicago was Los Angeles which was $31,201.76, while Chicago was $73,604.70. My work brought results.

It was the summer following my first two engagements of the Ballet Russe when I was requested to manage "A Century of Progress" World's Fair concerts by the Chicago Symphony Orchestra. This I have mentioned previously in connection with my association with George Gershwin. The series included Wagner-Strauss Program, Claire Dux, soprano, the soloist, Frederick Stock, conductor; Tschaikowsky program, Rudolph Ganz, soloist, Frederick Stock, conductor; Ballet Night — with Ruth Page, Novikoff and Corps de Ballet, Isaac Van Grove, conductor; American Night with George Gershwin, pianist, the soloist and also the conductor.

1934-1935

The Monday Night Concerts offered brilliance. There was Feodor Chaliapin, so highly revered by Chicagoans. When I met him on his arrival, a newsman took a picture of Chaliapin kissing my hand which was printed on the first page of the Chicago *American*. What a great study it was of his remarkable face.

Artur Schnabel, pianist, gave a program consisting of four Beethoven Sonatas. I wondered how a Chicago audience would react to this heavy fare, but the audience listened throughout in rapt attention, a tribute to Schnabel's genius.

The Metropolitan Opera tenor, Nino Martini, sang for the first time in Chicago — the gifted young Chicago pianist, Rosalind Kaplan, sharing the program. Lotte Lehmann, the illustrious opera and lieder soprano, sang divinely, with Georges Miquelle, famed French cellist, the assisting artist. Extra excitement for me, Maurice Esser was in the audience.

The once-in-a-lifetime event on the Series was the opera "Four Saints in Three Acts," text by Gertrude Stein, composed by Virgil Thomson, and directed by John Houseman. The fascinating opera was produced in New York by Harry Moses in the Spring of 1934, with an all-Negro cast. The scenery was entirely of cellophane, including the palm trees, with striking color effects produced with lighting. It was a singular success. I was inspired to bring the entire company to Chicago and did in the Fall of 1934. Virgil Thomson conducted.

There was a clash with the stage hands' Union which insisted the lights had to be supplied by Chicago; however, the intricate lights were not available in Chicago so after many conferences, it was agreed the New York lights could be used — and were.

Such excitement for the press. Gertrude Stein had arrived in New York. It was decided that she should fly to Chicago for the opening to which she agreed, although she had never been on a plane. United Air Lines consented to compliment her with the passage, but there also was Anna B. Toklas, Stein's constant companion and likewise Carl Van Vechten, her friend, who must accompany them, so I split the travel cost paying half the total amount and United Air Lines the other half. Elsie Johns, my publicity girl, worked on the arrangements and the press of Chicago turned out in force when the plane arrived. "A rose is a rose" had a field day in the newspapers. The opera occurred on November 7, 8, 9, 10 with matinee on the 10th — a gala Gala.

Since Chicago had taken Dance to its heart, I arranged for a Dance Series which included the peerless La Argentina (her last appearance in the Windy City), a performance of the Ballet Russe de Monte Carlo with the American premiere of Igor Stravinsky's "The Fire Bird" programmed. There was Doris Humphrey and Charles Weidman and their Dance

Group in Modern Dance, and Clotilde and Alexander Sakharoff of European fame, a Hurok importation. The Series was given under the auspices of the chic group — the Bohemians of Chicago.

A week's engagement at the Studebaker Theatre of Hurok's "Continental Varieties," brought the svelt Parisian, Lucienne Boyer, who charmed Chicago with her French chansons. She introduced the entrancing songs "Speak to Me of Love" and "Hands Across the Table," always impeccably gowned in blue velvet. With her were Vincente Escudero, Nikita Balieff of "Chauve Soiree" fame; Raphael who played a pint-sized concertina accordion; Carmencita and Gypsy guitarist, Iza Volpin's Continental Quartet. Although definitely a concert production, James Petrillo, then head of the Musician's Union in Chicago, insisted that four musicians for the pit had to be paid nightly even though they never drew a bow. The stagehands union and musicians union made constant and increasing demands, contributing to the precariousness of presenting music and theatre in Chicago.

Extra events that year embellishing the season were Paul Whiteman and his Concert Orchestra, the Don Cossack Chorus, and a lecture by Drew Pearson, the columnist.

A sad mistake was my being led into managing a Spring engagement of an Opera Comique Company. It was sponsored by a blue-blood New York Committe, with the dominant name of Mrs. Paul D. Cravath, as President. Mrs. Sara Delano Roosevelt was Chairman of Life Members. The event was built up to the hilt in Chicago. Mary Garden had a box for the opening — but the Company was a complete flop — tawdry scenery and costumes — a debacle. I flew to New York and got those in charge to pay for getting the company out of town, and learned a lesson — to be certain of the quality of any attraction I assumed managing. I had always prided myself in presenting only the top echelon of artists.

1935-1936

Life took an amazing turn at this time — season 1935-1936. The new Chicago Opera House, since the Civic Opera Company was extinct, was something of a pink plush, yet white elephant. Of all things, I was approached to take over the management of this edifice with a salary and generous working fund. I accepted the offer, opened an office there and began to think of possibilities.

At the Brooklyn Academy of Music there had been a series of concerts called "The Enjoyment of Music" for which teachers were given an

135

"Alertness" credit for attending, a system of the New York Public Schools. Olin Downes, music editor of the New York *Times*, presided and gave a preamble at the opening of each concert concerning the program. The concerts had such subjects as: "Songs of Schubert, Schumann and Brahms"((Hall Johnson Choir), "Operatic Song in the Hands of European and American Composers" (Lawrence Tibbett); "The Golden Age of English Song" (The New English Singers); etc. etc.

I proceeded to copy this plan and booked ten concerts for Chicago. I made an appointment with Dr. Samuel N. Stevens, Dean of Northwestern University. At our meeting I turned on all facets of persuasion that I could command. He succumbed, accepting that the Series be presented under the Sponsorship of Northwestern University which offered a credit for attendance.

About this time Fortune Gallo, whose traveling San Carlo Opera Company appeared at the Auditorium Theatre annually, came to me, acting as an emissary from the Auditorium Theatre. He entreated me to return to the Auditorium. I told him this was impossible, that I had accepted money from the Opera House personnel including a "booking of artists" trip to New York. He vouch-safed that he would pay back these sums to the Opera House, would buy me back as it were, assuring me that I belonged at the Auditorium. Having a fond feeling for the Auditorium I accepted the offer. This was heady business, my being sought as manager by the two largest theatres in Chicago.

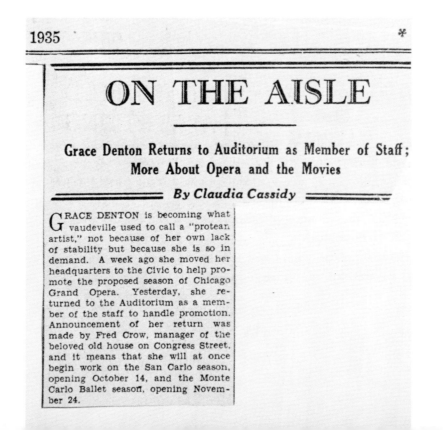

1935

ON THE AISLE

Grace Denton Returns to Auditorium as Member of Staff; More About Opera and the Movies

================= *By Claudia Cassidy* =================

GRACE DENTON is becoming what vaudeville used to call a "protean artist," not because of her own lack of stability but because she is so in demand. A week ago she moved her headquarters to the Civic to help promote the proposed season of Chicago Grand Opera. Yesterday, she *re*-turned to the Auditorium as a member of the staff to handle promotion. Announcement of her return was made by Fred Crow, manager of the beloved old house on Congress Street, and it means that she will at once begin work on the San Carlo season, opening October 14, and the Monte Carlo Ballet season, opening November 24.

The Auditorium offered me a salary and I was to have a share of the income from the "Enjoyment of Music" series, which I had gotten underway. All very agreeable. The Series was a smash hit. Over 3000 subscription tickets were sold.

Professor Felix Borowski, noted Chicago composer and lecturer, gave the commentary before each program though I arranged for Olin Downes to appear as guest speaker at the performance of the Ballet Russe de Monte Carlo. The first artist in the Series was the beauteous Metropolitan Opera soprano, Lucrezia Bori, followed by the San Carlo Opera Company in "Samson and Delilah," with Cyrena Van Gordon; also "Tannhauser" with Goeta Ljungberg. The Moscow Cathedral Choir provided an evening of Choral Music; then came a thrilling Debussy program featuring Mary Garden, the friend of Claude Debussy. Garden had the stage extended over the orchestra pit in order to be closer to the audience as she gave the commentary about the program, which the noted pianist, Rudolph Ganz, shared with her.

Gowned in a stunning black creation, completely sequined, with shoulder bouffant net sleeves, she spoke eloquently of Debussy and then sang his music accompanied by Ganz, who also was heard in Debussy's piano works. Audience eyes teared as Garden told of the Debussy cortege moving slowly through Paris streets with the ominous roar of "Big Berthas," the enormous German cannons, bombarding his beloved Paris.

The Chicago Symphony Orchestra with Frederick Stock conducting provided a symphony concert. John Charles Thomas, the eminent baritone, and Albert Spalding, noted American violinist, each gave a concert, and the final event was no less than historic, the first concert in Chicago by the incomparable contralto, Marian Anderson. She had recently returned from European successes, but the enthusiastic advance notices in no way prepared Chicago for what was to be heard, that hauntingly vibrant voice soaring to the rafters.

Fate was kind to me and this was the year when the Auditorium coffers were enriched by the presentation of the Max Reinhardt "A Midsummer Night's Dream," its glories delineated at the beginning of this book.

Under the heading "Woman Manager in Show Business," Charles Collins, drama editor of the Chicago *Tribune,* wrote: "Now comes a young woman who had never managed a theatre or staged a play in her life to give the old codgers a lesson in resourcefulness. She is Miss Grace Den-

137

ton, sponsor of concerts, operas, and ballets, a promoter of the musical arts charmingly free from the sterile cynicism of show business. She went out on a field expedition and came home with a contract for the Reinhardt 'A Midsummer Night's Dream' at the Auditorium, much to the surprise of the men who are thinking seriously of converting their dead playhouses into cabarets. It happens, however, that Miss Denton has a magic touch at the trick to which showmen devote their lives. She knows how to sell tickets. As an organizer of audiences for amusements she is probably the national champion. Whenever she has sponsored an Opera or concert, the customers have turned out in droves. She has the gift of box office salesmanship that theatrical executives seem to have lost. Grace Denton is my choice for the title of 'Joan of Arc of the Chicago drama.'"

Ashton Stevens headed his column with: "WOMAN MANAGER SOLD FULL HOUSES WHEN OLD SHOWMEN GAVE UP" with these lines following: "Grace Denton has a system quite different from the trustful trial-and-error system of the ordinary catch-as-catch-can showmen and so far her system has never failed her. What's her system? Simplest thing in the world. Grace Denton merely sights an attraction that in ordinarily good times would be likely to pack the house. Then she goes among the swell and unswell clubs and whatnots and sells them a large number of seats that they can resell to members as 'benefits.' She personally gets up subscription seasons, while we wait, incidentally making the strangely fulfilled and unfulfilled seasons of the Theatre Guild and American Theatre Society look like thirty cents. The pay-as-you-enter crowds follow the 'benefit' crowds and Grace Denton makes good her guarantees without making the acquaintance of red ink, thereby beating the best-so-called minds of Broadway at its own showman game."

The caption under a photo of Madame Impresario in *Variety*, theatrical trade news journal, read: "Grace Denton, one of Chi's big shots in legit theatre."

That Spring at the Auditorium, I managed performances by the Detroit Opera Company, ably directed by Thaddeus Wronski. "The Dybbuk" with Rosa Raisa and "Prince Igor" were splendidly given with orchestra support of musicians from the Detroit Symphony; however, it was late in the season (May) and the effort was not a financial success for the Detroit backers, which I regretted.

This season marked the end of my years at the Chicago Auditorium Theatre through an inexplicable fact. A young inexperienced chap, who seemed to have an "in" with Dr. Stevens at Northwestern University, convinced him that the "Enjoyment of Music" series could be given to financial advantage without me, so I was eliminated. The Series was a money-maker for the Auditorium as well as the University, so why pay me? Once more success had defeated me. I had failed to insist on a contract when I returned to the Auditorium, but with the University Series, the Reinhardt "Dream" and other attractions, I had provided the Auditorium with a secure position. The ingredients could continue. The "Enjoyment" series was a success for many seasons. In 1940 when I was in Santa Barbara, two years after leaving Chicago, a letter came from the manager of the Auditorium theatre there, who wrote; "I have not heard about you in a long time, but often think of you and would be glad to know how you are getting along. Our season is slow." After suggesting that I work on arranging for some attractions for the Auditorium, he added, "You should be able to handle the publicity and promotion better than any one else, and I would be most cooperative so far as the theatre is concerned." Was this a bid for me to return to the Auditorium? Well, not me.

The Chicago summer of 1936, however, proved exciting for I became one of the original signers of the incorporation for reopening Ravinia Park for concerts by the Chicago Symphony Orchestra, which were mentioned in Chapter I.

It was futile to attempt to rekindle a new regime in Chicago, although I was undaunted. I brought to Orchestra Hall Lawrence Tibbett, the Cleveland Orchestra, Arthur Rodzinski conducting. He later became conductor of the Chicago Symphony which proved a very stormy period and short-lived. Rosa Ponselle arrived for her concert but became ill and could not appear, creating many problems and this marked the end of my Chicago years — not easy years but full of great moments. My imprint remained long after, however. During the depression years I had certainly prevailed.

My final home there was at Ambassador East, where Ernest Byfield provided a plush suite for a nominal sum — depression still lingering with hotels. A friend, Winifred Ralston, now married to Georges Miquelle, the French cellist, shared it with me.

139

"In War: Resolution. In Defeat: Defiance. In Victory: Magnanimity. In Peace: Goodwill."
Words of the Right Honorable Winston S. Churchill, British Statesman and Orator.
Soldier, Traveler, Writer. He turned while just a stripling to politics. This photo by
Yousuf Karsh depicts the "bull-dog" tenacity of the man that carried him through
vicissitudes of life that would have downed a lesser stalwart.

His lecture in Chicago in November, 1931, under the management of Grace Denton,
brought the S.R.O. sign at Orchestra Hall. Samuel Insull introduced him.

William Lyon Phelps was a magnet of interest for students of literature at Yale. As a lecturer his authoritative discussion of contemporary books received national recognition. Here he is shown in his study.

H.V. Kaltenborn, graduate of Harvard, was a writer and lecturer on international affairs. He was Dean of news commentators for several decades and his books were widely read.

In the 1920s Evangeline Adams became famous as an Astrologer. She devoted years to reviving and spreading this ancient subject. She numbered among her ancestors the two Mr. Adams who signed the Declaration of Independence and who became Presidents of the United States.

DR. ROBERT A. MILLIKAN

SIR FREDERICK WHYTE

VICKI BAUM

STUART CHASE

RICHARD BOLESLAVSKI

V. SACKVILLE WEST and HAROLD NICHOLSON

THOMAS WILFRED

CLEMENCE DANE   DR. JOHN GRIER HIBBEN   BARONESS KEIKICHI ISHIMOTO   MAX EASTMAN

The Town Hall Series, Grace Denton, manager, brought an array of twelve notables for Saturday morning lectures in the Drake Hotel ballroom. The elite of Chicago attended.

142

Beauteous Lucrezia Bori sang the opening concert of the "Monday Night Concerts," Grace Denton's first effort for music in Chicago.

Drew Pearson, political analyst, the Co-Author of "Washington Merry-go-round" gave an evening lecture in Orchestra Hall, October 25, 1932. His subject was "On Washington and Politics." Pearson was a stormy petrel in his daily syndicated column.

The Bettmann Archive Inc., New York

Dr. Lloyd C. Douglas was heard by Town Hall patrons in a lecture on "The Flight to Freedom." Dr. Douglas, author of "The Robe" and "The Magnificent Obsession," was a remarkable author and man.

Maria Jeritza, the Viennese beauty, came to the Metropolitan Opera with fanfare. She was an established star in the Opera houses in Europe and repeated her success in the United States. She married Winfield Sheehan, motion picture magnate, and lived in California for many years.

John Charles Thomas, American baritone, became a Cavalier of the Crown of Italy. He officially received his decoration from Dr. Giuseppe Castruccio, Italian Consul General of Chicago at the time Thomas sang with the Chicago Opera Company. The ceremony was witnessed by Mr. Harold F. McCormick, Chicago's opera Patron, principals, orchestra and chorus members of the Opera Company.

Foto-Ad News Photo

Lawrence Tibbett brought not only his vibrant baritone to the opera stage, but he was a skilled actor as well. His roles brought him enormous acclaim with resounding "Bravos." In "Emperor Jones," his performance was masterful.

matically, Musically, a Performance of the Age!

LAWRENCE TIBBETT

BY ARRANGEMENT WITH EVANS & SALTER, INC., NEW YORK CITY

in

"Emperor Jones"

EUGENE O'NIELL • LOUIS GRUENBERG

Eight audiences jammed to capacity at the Metropolitan in New York acclaimed "Emperor Jones" with Tibbett in the leading role as the greatest event in American Operatic history. Chicago is realizing the importance of this presentation and orders already are pouring in at the box office.

•

GRAND DOUBLE BILL INCLUDES

"PAGLIACCI"

LAWRENCE TIBBETT as Tonio

with a brilliant cast . . .

MARION CLAIRE » MARIO CHAMLEE
MARIO FLORELLA » GIUSEPPE CAVADORE

•

ISAAC VAN GROVE, Conductor for Both Operas

TECHNICAL DIRECTOR, HARRY BEATTY » Management: GRACE DENTON

...mperor Jones" was given its world premiere, ...stant and sweeping success, yesterday after- ...n the Metropolitan Opera House. Mr. Tibbett ...hed in a cruelly difficult part, triumphed as ...nd singer. Up to the present time Emperor ...is his supreme achievement, and it is one ...w of the greatest singer and dramatist and the ...t traditions of the musico-dramatic stage.
New York Times, Jan. 8, 1933.

★

...s a monumental piece of work, and, when you ...ed in amazement last night to remember that ...as opera, you wondered also whether any ...singer known to this public could have done ...he role what he did.
Philadelphia Ledger, Jan. 11, 1933.

★

...ole is one of pitiless exactions, and Mr. Tibbett ...d it off with intelligent and unflagging care and ...n degree of skill, from the bombast of the self- ..."emperor" through all the variations of terror ...utter abasement of the end.
New York World-Telegram, Jan. 9, 1933.

...esday Evening, May 2 . . . and Friday Evening, May 5
at 8:15 . . . Auditorium Theatre

Marion Claire was a star in the Chicago Civic Opera singing many soprano roles. For Grace Denton she was the Elsa in "Lohengrin" in Detroit and Nedda in "Pagliacci," in Chicago.

Mario Chamlee was a valued member of the Metropolitan Opera singing tenor roles. He enacted the Canio in "Pagliacci" in Chicago for Grace Denton and Isaac Van Grove.

Maurice Seymour Photo

Isaac Van Grove was a pillar of the Chicago musical scene. His abilities took him often for engagements in New York and in other cities. When Chicago was minus opera, Van Grove joined with Grace Denton in producing "Tosca" with Jeritza and John Charles Thomas, also "Emperor Jones" with Tibbett and the same evening "Pagliacci" with Tibbett, Mario Chamlee and Marion Claire. Van Grove was the conductor for the operas. He was adept in composing and arranging, provided many scores for Ruth Page's ballets. He was accompanist for Mary Gordon and Grace Moore on their concert tours.

146

Elizabeth Rethberg had charm, beauty and a lovely soprano voice. These attributes she used effectively at the Metropolitan Opera and in concerts, delighting her audiences. Here she is shown with an armful of zinnias.

Lily Pons, the petite French prima donna soprano, graced with her lustrous coloratura the Metropolitan Opera, leading Opera houses in Europe and in concerts around the world. She divides her retirement between her homes in Palm Springs and in Dallas.

Edward Moore, music critic of the Chicago Tribune, regarded his job as more than a reviewer of concerts and opera. He played a great part in converting a somewhat lethargic audience in the Chicago area into enthusiastic and sophisticated patrons of the Chicago Opera and its great stars and unhackneyed repertoire.

Yehudi Menuhin, the boy prodigy was still a youth when he was first presented in Chicago by Grace Denton. He captured his listeners in the large audience with his tone and virtuosity executed with his young hands.

Claire Dux, the lovely blond soprano, curtailed her career in opera and concert after she became Mrs. Charles Swift and made her home in Chicago. She did consent to be the soloist with the Chicago Symphony at the opening Wagner-Strauss program, Frederick Stock conducting, of the 1933 Century of Progress World's Fair Symphony Series.

The former Italian Minister of the Air, Italo Balbo, led a history making mass flight of 100 aviators from Italy to the Century of Progress Chicago World's Fair in June 1933. The Italian Consul General, Giuseppe Castruccio and a committee planned, with Grace Denton as manager, to greet the fliers with a gala outdoor performance of "Aida" in Soldier's Field. Weather conditions interfered, a date could not be set, and the project had to be abandoned.

148

A drawing of Serge Lifar, Director of the Paris Opera Ballet, in the role of the Faun in Debussy's "The Afternoon of a Faun." It was done by a Chicago American staff artist and published in that newspaper. Lifar was another "first" for Chicago and drew an S.R.O. audience. It was a gala event!

Irina Baronova, prima ballerina with
the Ballet Russe de Monte Carlo.

Sono Osato, young and gifted Chicago
ballerina, became a member of the
Monte Carlo Ballet Russe.

150

Leonide Massine and Alexandra Danilova in
"Gaite Parisienne".

Alexandra Danilova

Tamara Toumanova was the youngest of the ballerinas, aged 16, when the Monte Carlo Ballet Russe first came to Chicago, also one of the most talented and beautiful. Fame became hers in abundance.

Blond and beautiful, Tatiana Riabouchinska was a favorite Ballet Russe ballerina.

Back stage scenes of the Ballet Russe de Monte Carlo.

As though bodily grace had not been trained to its highest powers in the ballet, lights and shadows are called upon to lend their aid in the general breath-taking beauty of the stage picture. The moon may be artificial, but the effect is prompt.

An example of dance composition, what those learned in the art call choreography, still in the old fashioned manner, but showing how bodies and costumes may be grouped so as to form a definite and powerful outline in a dance figure.

Ashton Stevens—what influence he dispersed through his coverage of music, dance and many other subjects in his newspapering, particularly with his last assignment before his demise, on the Chicago American. He had a host of friends.

Antol Dorati was an important factor in the success of the Ballet Russe de Monte Carlo inasmuch as he wielded an expert baton in conducting the orchestra for the Ballet's first appearances in the United States. Dorati now is Music Director of the National Symphony Orchestra in Washington D.C.

Sol Hurok and Leonide Massine discuss Ballet programs.

In 1951 Rear Admiral Richard Byrd revisited his old hut at the site of original Little America. He tried out some twelve-year-old tobacco and a corn cob pipe left there previously.

Rear Admiral Richard E. Byrd, officer in charge of Antarctic Exploration, on board ship with his mascot. Byrd's illustrated lecture at the Chicago Auditorium was a highlight of the season.

Feodor Chaliapin was incontestably the giant of the Opera vocally and historically. He rose from a simple peasant to sing at last in the Czars' great theatres, an unprecedented feat in itself. On this photograph dedicated to Grace Denton he wrote: "To dear and sweet Mlle. Grace Denton from all my soul."

It was the custom for artists to be met as they arrived, usually by train, sometimes by plane. Newspaper reporters often were there to get an arrival photo. When Chaliapin stepped off the train in Chicago the Chicago American reporter took his picture kissing the hand of Grace Denton. This resulted in a fine study of Chaliapin's mobile features and was given front page coverage.

To Grace Denton the great and charming impressario with love and admiration

Georges Miquelle

Recitals of German lieder by opera star Lotte Lehmann were vocal treats, so rich was her soprano and so flawless her interpretation of lieder. Georges Miquelle shared the Chicago program with her. Miquelle had soloed with most of the ranking symphony orchestras and made many concert tours, which were with Dame Nellie Melba. He was first chair cellist with the Detroit Symphony for over twenty-five years and toured the Middle East for the State Department.

Pianist Artur Schnabel was a specialist in playing Beethoven. His Chicago recital consisted of four Beethoven sonatas.

The Saints' procession in Act III.

Saint Teresa being photographed with the Holy Ghost. Act I.

Virgil Thomson,
composer.

When Virgil Thomson, composer, importuned Gertrude Stein, she of "a rose is a rose is a rose," to write an opera libretto for him, she agreed. Her favorite Saints were Teresa of Avila and Ignatius of Loyola who became the basis for the work—Spanish Saints but the fine singers portraying them were all Negroes.

John Houseman was Director; Alexander Smallens, then assistant conductor with Stokowski at the Philadelphia Orchestra conducted; Florine Stettheimer designed the stage set made of cellophane, Kate Lawson, the costumes. Ashton Stephens, principal choreographer for 17 years for Britain's Royal Ballet arranged the dance sequences. It all came together as one of the lasting delights of music and the stage—Opera.

The New York showing in 1934, was under the aegis of Harry Moses, the Chicago engagement was managed by Grace Denton, with Gertrude Stein present. One line often repeated was "Pigeons on the grass, alas". The following line was "If they were not pigeons, what were they."
Virgil Thomson conducted the Chicago performances.

159

CHICAGO AMERICAN

Possibly the most improbable confrontation was the meeting in Chicago on stage following the performance of "Four Saints in Three Acts," of the unique Gertrude Stein, who wrote the libretto for the Opera, and the great Chicago multimillionaire, Harold McCormick, long a patron of Opera. It is impossible to know which person was the more impressed! Alice B. Toklas in the background, seems to have her own emotions!

La Argentina, she of the flashing Spanish dances, became the greatest solo dancer of Iberian genre. Her fame was world wide. The December 8, 1934 appearance in Chicago became her final one. She was greatly missed.

Argentina's colorful costumes and her lithe figure were entrancing.

This caricature of Paul Whiteman typified the popular band leader. His concerts drew large audiences, who applauded him to the echo.

Lucienne Boyer, the French songstress, a picture in her blue velvet gown, captivated Chicago with her lilting songs. She introduced those favorites, "Speak to me of Love," "Hands Across the Table," and many other French chansons that go straight to the heart.

After their indoctrination at Denishawn, Doris Humphrey with Charles Weidman went on to become an important force in American Dance, touring their own Dance Group. They abandoned the theory that a dance should tell a story and created a choreography emphasizing rhythmic motion.

As solo dancer with the Denishawn tours, Doris Humphrey had enormous success with her "Dance With a Hoop."

Doris Humphrey and Charles Weidman in "Exhibition Piece". These two talented dancers interpreted symphonies with the Philharmonic, Cleveland and Philadelphia Orchestras. They emphasized the art of rhythmic motion as well as theatre expression in their dances.

Marian Anderson became something of a legend
in her own time. A Philadelphia girl, she made her
debut in this country with the Philadelphia
Orchestra. It was after her great success in Europe
that she became one of the most beloved of singers
from Coast to Coast in the United States. She
made several world tours. Grace Denton, always
interested in presenting new artists, managed her
first concert in Chicago. It was a triumph, despite
the fact she had broken her foot and had to take
her position by the piano before the curtain went up.

Negro Spirituals were given a place
on all of Marian Anderson's programs.
These she sang with understanding
fervor. A favorite was "He Has the
Whole World in His Hands." Here she
is pictured studying her own hands.

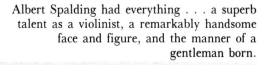

Albert Spalding had everything . . . a superb talent as a violinist, a remarkably handsome face and figure, and the manner of a gentleman born.

Dr. Felix Borowski, composer, conductor, authority in the field of musical history, held an important position in Chicago music circles. He prepared the analytical program notes for the Chicago Symphony. He lectured for the School of Music at Northwestern University for some fifteen years, and presided over "The History and Enjoyment of Music" series, inaugurated by Grace Denton and sponsored by Northwestern.

The American violinist, Albert Spalding, ranked with the foremost fiddlers who came from Europe. He chose music instead of using his abilities in connection with his family's business—the Spalding Company, sports equipment.

Olin Downes served as music critic on the Boston Post from 190 until 1924, then took up his long tenure as Music Editor of the New York Times. He was a guest commentator for the "History and Enjoyment of Music" series in Chicago, speaking briefly on "The Union of Symphony and Ballet" prior to the performance of the Monte Carlo Ballet Russe.

...dolph Ganz, conductor and pianist, was ...integral factor of music in Chicago, ...ough he toured in piano recitals and ...eared as soloist with leading Symphony ...chestras. Ganz shared a program with ...ry Garden on "Debussy—the Man and ...Music" on the "History and Enjoyment ...Music" series. He was adept in playing ...bussy—was the first pianist to play the ...rks of the French composer in this country. ...served as conductor of the St. Louis ...mphony and from 1929 to his demise, was ...rector of the Chicago Musical College.

In the words of Eugene Stinson, Chicago critic, "Lucrezia Bori was born to be a celebrity." Her first success in opera was in Italy, then in Buenos Aires from where she came to the Metropolitan. She made her debut at the Met with Caruso in "Manon." After the regime of Gatti-Casazza, Bori was made a Director of the Opera, recognition of the esteem in which she was held. She opened the "History and Enjoyment of Music Series in Chicago.

It was Theodore Thomas who brought the Chicago Symphony into being in 1891. Dr. Frederick Stock followed him as Director in 1905 and continued for 38 years until his death in 1942. During his long tenure, the Chicago Symphony became one of the great symphonies in this country. Frederick Stock was highly revered by all Chicago.

Magazine

Geoffrey Landesman Photo

Arturo Toscanini and Artur Rodzinski talk shop as they loaf on a terrace in the Italian Alps, and plan readings of the symphonic masterpieces with which the NBC Symphony Orchestra delighted millions of music lovers.

The final concert managed by Grace Denton in Chicago was the Cleveland Orchestra, Artur Rodzinski conducting. When Rodzinski first came to the United States he was Assistant to Leopold Stokowski with the Philadelphia Orchestra. After his tenure with the Cleveland Orchestra he became Conductor of the Chicago Symphony.

To my darling Hazel with much love

Fondly

Raisa

Rosa Raisa was the soprano star in the opera "The Dybbuk" presented by the Detroit Opera Company in the Auditorium Theatre, Chicago, May 1936. Thaddeus Wronski was the Director. Raisa gave a magnificent performance as was her custom.

chicago to california-
santa barbara 1938-1940

How it developed that I was employed to go to California as "advance" for a touring company of "Tonight at 8:30" by Noel Coward, I do not recall. Robert Henderson was the producer, his wife, Estelle Winwood, the star. In the cast were Helen Chandler, Bramwell Fletcher and Mary Astor. This was a new field of endeavor and intriguing. After the performances in Los Angeles, San Francisco came next, and there in the Maurice Hotel dining room, I ran into stage play producer, Arthur Beckhard. He was putting together a repertory season of plays in Santa Barbara at the Lobero Theatre, a charming theatre seating 600, a historical landmark. In the early days there were rocking chairs in the boxes. Now it is handsomely restored by architect, George Washington Smith.

Arthur assured me that Santa Barbara was the place for me and that he needed me. This was an enticing opportunity. I fell for it and landed in beautiful, wonderful Santa Barbara. Lotte Lehmann, who lives there, always said, "Santa Barbara is Paradise."

I soon found out that finances were precarious and that the plan was not going to succeed. Arthur's wife was the estimable Esther Dale of motion pictures. The County of Santa Barbara had built a beautiful outdoor Bowl with "depression" W.P.A. aid. With the stimulus of the fascinating aura of Ravinia still floating in memory, I was intrigued to the hilt with this Bowl. Sam Stanwood, the enterprising County Supervisor, listened to

167

my plea that there should be a Music Festival in this made-to-order setting. He managed to get me employed by the County, maneuvering the funds from the special San Francisco World's Fair budget. I had an office in the magnificent County Court House, and I was on my way.

Sam Stanwood was a patriarch of Santa Barbara. He saw that needed mountain roads were built, managed to have the Lobero Theatre and Art Museum, an Architect Stanford White building, owned by the County, leased to a Board of Directors for $1.00 per year, thus saving taxes. He was El Presidente of the town's celebration "Old Spanish Days" from 1927 to 1947, and he instigated the building of the picturesque County Court House.

The first County Music Festival offered the Los Angeles Philharmonic Orchestra, the glamorous opera soprano Mme. Maria Jeritza, the Adolph Bolm Ballet, Lester Donahue, pianist, and several others. It seems Santa Barbara, which is nestled between mountains and the sea, can have fog. This I knew nothing about, but I learned. It rolled in full measure the night of the first concert. The Steinway grand was dripping, so were orchestra instruments and orchestra men. The dancers skidded — luckily no bones were broken. The audience too was soaked. I recall Mrs. Alma DeBrettville Spreckles (Mrs. August), her sizeable form swathed in silver fox furs, with beads of fog dripping from every fur tip. Leopold Stokowski was present with his friend, Henry Eichheim, composer of Oriental music, who, like Stokowski, lived in Santa Barbara at that time.

One does survive calamities and the next concerts were greeted with glistening stars.

Eichheim had a valuable collection of Oriental instruments which he bequeathed to the Santa Barbara Museum where a special room is alloted for the collection.

In considering plans for the Festival at the Santa Barbara Bowl, I wrote to Leopold Stokowski concerning an "Eichheim Festival" as Henry Eichheim was greatly beloved in Santa Barbara. Also I was much interested in orchestra training for youth. Knowing that Stokowski was a great believer in youth orchestras, I broached this subject to him. His reply:

26
OCTOBER
1939

Miss Grace Denton
Lobero Theatre
33 East Canon Perdido Street
Santa Barbara, California

Dear Miss Denton

I think the idea of an "Eicheim Festival"
is excellent. As you know Heinrich Eicheim is the
greatest living authority on Oriental music.

I fear you will find it difficult to present
Oriental music to western audiences. I have not
time to go into the details of this, but I have
given much thought to it.

The second of interest of a young orchestra
training school is also excellent. The main dif-
ficulty would be to find teachers of high enough
quality in Santa Barbara, but they could easily be
found in Hollywood and I can help you to find them.

I would not be able to assist in the arrangements of this Festival because all my time is already
taken, but if I can help you with suggestions and
any knowledge I have I shall be happy to do so, just
as I have tried to do so in this letter. With every
good wish for the success of your project.

Sincerely

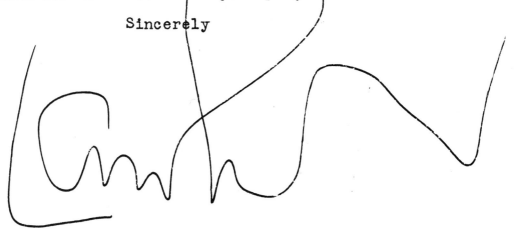

Leopold Stokowski

A youth orchestra now flourishes at the Music Academy of the West, which was my brain child, in Santa Barbara with Maurice Abravanel the conductor.

For my second year in Santa Barbara, the County continued my salary, instigating my being manager of the Lobero Theatre as well as the Summer Festival, which became "The Santa Barbara County Drama and Music Festival." The Festival had some real highlights, one being the World Premiere of "Ladies and Gentlemen" by Charles McArthur and Ben Hecht, with Helen Hayes and Herbert Marshall the stars. The demand for seats can be imagined. Every theatre-oriented person from Los Angeles wanted to attend. The theatre's capacity was more than taxed. The other plays were "Outward Bound" by Sutton Vane, and a new play, "The Great American Family," by the Los Angeles newspaper man, Lee Shippey.

The concerts were exciting, too: Albert Coates conducted the Los Angeles Philharmonic Hollywood Bowl Orchestra with the phenomenal pianist, Alec Templeton, soloist. A second event was Lawrence Tibbett with the Symphony. When he sang Wagner's "O Thou Sweet Sublime Sweet Evening Star," the actual star was there and the soul was stirred. The San Francisco Ballet, also with Symphony, was the colorful final event. Janet Reed was the prima ballerina. Her dancing met with bravos.

For the August "Old Spanish Days Fiesta" Luther Greene produced a play filled with enchantment at Lobero, "The Mistress of the Inn" by Goldoni. The star-studded cast included Misha Auer in glistening white satin breeches, a new phase for him to be so elegant.

It was a fine year at the Theatre artistically and financially. I was fortunate in being able to book an almost continuous listing of events glowing with interest such as: Cornelia Otis Skinner, Angna Enters, Paul Draper, star tap dancer, and Larry Adler, artist on the harmonica; Elsa Maxwell in one of her inimitable lectures; the superlative dance duo — Veloz and Yolanda. They had held Chicagoans enthralled for months at the Palmer House Empire Room, where I had met them.

They were considering a coast-to-coast concert tour and discussed with me my assuming the booking of dates. This was an enticing idea, sounded like some real money! Albert Fuller, who was public relations at the Palmer House when Veloz and Yolanda were having spectacular success there wrote to me these flattering words: "I am going to write Frank Veloz and tell him that I think he could make no better arrangement for his remaining years as a dancer than to tie-up exclusively with you — Grace Denton." I went to New York to start on the assignment.

Ah, but "the best laid plans" — Yolanda found she was pregnant and the tour was off.

In 1941, through John Houseman whom I came to know from "Four Saints in Three Acts," I was employed by David O. Selznick to do publicity in San Francisco for Ingrid Bergman in the stage play "Anna Christie," produced especially for her when she first came to this country and was awaiting a motion picture vehicle. What a pleasure this was! I arranged press and radio interviews, took her as honored guest to the Women's Club for a luncheon. She was shy — would only say on being introduced, "I am very glad to be here," but her beauty, peaches-and-cream complexion captured all, and in "Anna Christie" she was a spectacular, overwhelming success.

I then did promotion and publicity for the Festival celebrating the 75th Anniversary of the City of Berkeley, California. The events took place in the Greek Theatre, the handsome outdoor structure given to the University of California by Phoebe Hearst, mother of the publisher. One concert had to be moved into the gymnasium because of rain — that of "Elijah" with Claremont Choral Society — the San Francisco Symphony, Bruno Walter, conducting, John Charles Thomas, baritone soloist — a rarely beautiful occasion. John Charles' luscious tones in his singing of the aria, "It is Enough," are not to be equaled. What a voice!

Other events included: The San Francisco Opera Ballet, complete stage productions of "Orpheus in the Underworld," Offenbach; "Saint Joan," George Bernard Shaw; "Twelfth Night" by William Shakespeare.

Then came December 1941, with fateful "Pearl Harbor" on the 7th. Katherine Dunham and her Company were scheduled for their first appearance in San Francisco at the Curran Theatre between Christmas and New Years, for which I was the manager. Katherine, the M.A. in Anthropology from the University of Chicago, had assembled and trained a ranking Company of Negro dancers. San Francisco recognized its superlative quality and Katherine was to become the toast of the town.

"Blackouts" came often in those days in San Francisco. On the last night of the Dunham engagement the sirens called for a "blackout" about 7:00 P.M. I stood at the window in my tenth floor Maurice Hotel room and watched the lights on the San Francisco hills fade into darkness. "Blackouts" meant traffic stopped on the bridges right where it was. What was to happen concerning the Dunham performance? Its income was needed. Well, about 8:00 P.M. the lights came on, the audience arrived at the theatre, the curtain went up about 9:00 and the final performance was cheered.

War was upon us. I felt the urge to do some small part, so went East and began working as an inspector on B 24 planes at Willow Run near Ann Arbor, Michigan, I was assigned to the under surface wing having the wheel well. In this area the riveting was deafening! I was there a year and a half joining the hoards of thousands trooping in and out on various shifts and punching the time clock together with University of Michigan professors' wives, teachers and people from all walks of life. This was a far cry from the music business, yet an experience in another slice of life I would not have missed.

Then back to Santa Barbara for some relaxation. I received a letter from Hurok who wrote: "I still think you are one of the best promoters in the business and I am sorry that you are not actively engaged in selling talent to the public."

BILTMORE THEATRE
LOS ANGELES
TWO WEEKS ONLY, *Opening* MONDAY, *September 20*

ROBERT HENDERSON and ESTELLE WINWOOD
present
By arrangement with Mr. John C. Wilson

NOEL COWARD'S
Latest International Hit
"to-night at 8:30"

The Entire Cycle of Nine Short Plays—All Different

starring

ESTELLE
WINWOOD

HELEN
CHANDLER

BRAMWELL
FLETCHER

AND

MARY **ASTOR**, *Guest Artist*

The Direction by ROBERT HENDERSON

The Settings designed by Norman Rock

—de Meyer
ESTELLE
WINWOOD

—Hurrell
HELEN
CHANDLER

—Monroe
BRAMWELL
FLETCHER

AND

—Hurrell
MARY
ASTOR

Grace Denton went to the Pacific Coast from Chicago, in charge of publicity for the "Tonight at 8:30" Company.

QUEEN OF THE MISSIONS—Keeping silent watch over the city of Santa Barbara, California, Old Mission Santa Barbara marks its 186th anniversary this year. The church is regarded as the most splendid in the chain of 21 California missions built by the Spanish padres, and is still in daily use. Visitors can tour the mission buildings and grounds, viewing historical exhibits, quarters of the original padres and the ancient cemetery. In the city below stand original adobe buildings of the Presidio, or fort, and pueblo of Santa Barbara.

When employed by the County of Santa Barbara to develop a Festival in the County Bowl, my office was in this grandiose Court House.

Sam Stanwood, County Supervisor and patriarch of Santa Barbara. He engaged Grace Denton to manage a Summer Festival in the County Bowl and to manage the County owned Lobero Theatre. Here he is shown in Santa Barbara's "Old Spanish Days" Fiesta attire. He was El Presidente of "Old Spanish Days" for 20 years, 1927 to 1947.

An "Old Spanish Days" procession at the County Court House. There are no motorized vehicles in the Fiesta Parade, only those drawn by horses.

Karl Obert, A.P.S.A. Photo

To Miss Denton
reminding her of
Henry Eichheim
Santa Barbara
1930

Henry Eichheim, a composer in the oriental idiom,
lived in Santa Barbara. He was a close friend of
Leopold Stokowski who had a home in Santa
Barbara at one time. Henry's house was a mecca
for every musician who came his way. He had a
remarkable collection of Oriental instruments
which he gave to the Santa Barbara Museum of
Art. He was an extraordinary musician and a
delightful personage.

Albert Coates, the conductor, was part Russian
and part English, and he developed a very personal
style of conducting, which some orchestras found
difficult. In the end, his success was achieved
by his obvious sincerity, and this got through to
the orchestra musicians.

Alec Templeton at the New York World's
Fair in 1940, with Tom Bennett (left),
composer of the Ford Motor Company's
show at the Fair, "A Thousand Times
Neigh," written and directed by Edward
Mabley (right). The production cast consisted
of dancers from Lincoln Kirstein's group
that later became the famed New York City
Ballet. Grace Denton arranged for Mabley
to meet Kirstein.

Mabley has been active for many years as
both writer and director in radio, television
and theatre. His best known play is "Glad
Tidings," a comedy that enjoyed a long run
on Broadway and is still extensively
performed here and abroad. His most recent
book is "Dramatic Construction."

Alec Templeton, although blind, brought joy to
uncountable thousands with his adroit, ingenious
renditions on the piano. In addition to his
recitals given from Coast to Coast, he was soloist
with major Symphony Orchestras. He had a gift
of musical satire that brought spontaneous
laughter from his listeners.

Fred Melton Photo

Titian-haired Janet Reed, petite and beautiful, was prima ballerina with the San Francisco Ballet before she went on to a brilliant career in New York City, first with the Eugene Loring Company then with the American Ballet Theatre of Lucia Chase and Oliver Smith and with the New York City Ballet of Lincoln Kirstein and George Balanchine. Here she is seen in the New York City Ballet's "Nutcracker."

Janet Reed added to her fame as the star of the original Broadway production of "Fancy Free", composed by Leonard Bernstein. Sailors from left: Jerome Robbins, John Kriza, Harold Lang.

Janet Reed flashed across the ballet scene and left an indelible impression. In this picture she appears in another distinguished success "Bourree Fantasque" choreographed by Balanchine and danced with the New York City Ballet.

Fred Fehl Photo

The Lobero Theatre, a restored landmark in Santa Barbara. The olive trees, old and gnarled, also are early California.

Arthur Beckhard produced a Summer Season of Theatre at the Lobero Theatre in Santa Barbara. He engaged Grace Denton to do promotion and publicity. Later Miss Denton became manager of the theatre.

Ben Pinchot, New York

Cornelia Otis Skinner, highly talented daughter of the notable actor, Otis Skinner, was indeed a one-woman theatre. The dramatist, actress, producer, gave her entrancing monologues from Coast to Coast, and wrote highly entertaining books, a recent one being "Madame Sarah," the life of the great tragedienne, Bernhardt.

Elsa Maxwell played the piano, engineered international parties and gave lectures, all teeming with and motivated by the Maxwell personality. At Lobero she talked entertainingly about life in general. One bromide apropos of amassing possessions she said, "You do not own things, things own you."

History will accord Martha Graham a great place as one of the most dedicated and dynamic figures in the American scene. A distant relative of Miles Standish, she literally created an entirely new dance form. Instead of dance being programmed and stilted as in classical ballet, Martha Graham displayed the power of the body movement to project ideas most eloquently. Her contribution has been immense, and has deeply influenced the dance attitude of young Americans.

The winsome beauty of Helen Hayes and her great gifts as an actress brought her the appellation of "First Lady of the Theatre." The play "Ladies and Gentlemen" authored by her husband Charles MacArthur and Ben Hecht, had its Premiere with Helen Hayes the star at the Lobero Theatre in Santa Barbara, a feature of the 1939 County Drama and Music Festival.

Paul Draper, tap dancing to classical music, approached this type of dance as an art. His program was shared with Larry Adler, an artist who played classical music on the harmonica. It was a diverting and enjoyable evening at the Lobero Theatre.

VELOZ & YOLANDA, MOST GRACEFUL OF DANCERS, BEGIN VIENNESE WALTZ

DAY AT CONEY ISLAND WAS INSPIRATION FOR THIS MERRY-GO-ROUND DANCE

THEY SELDOM REHEARSE, SIMPLY TALK IT OVER, ABSORB MUSIC. ABOVE: A MAXIXE

Nothing greater has been seen in ballroom dancing than Veloz and Yolanda. They were supreme and were laud
in full measure. They appeared usually as ballroom entertainment but gave a full evening's recital at Lobero wi
the S.R.O. sign in eviden

Pierre Monteux was the regular conductor of the San Francisco Symphony at this time. His was a monumental career. His first assignment in this country was as a conductor for the Metropolitan Opera Company. He then had a fine tenure with the Boston Symphony. In San Francisco he held sway for 17 years—1935-36 to 1951-52— with the Symphony. His summer school for conductors in Vermont was highly successful. The list of his attainments is prodigious.

Homage was paid to Bruno Walter, master musician and conductor around the world. His interpretations of orchestral music were majestic. He conducted the San Francisco Symphony at the Festival celebrating the 75th Anniversary of the city of Berkeley.

A drawing by Lupus of Bruno Walter reflecting in his face the great compassion and understanding of life and music that was his.

Everett L. Jones (Left) Grace Denton and Leonide Massine meet at the Greek Theatre on the University of California campus in Berkeley, to discuss the possibility of performances by the Ballet Russe in this charming outdoor Theatre. Phoebe Hearst, the mother of William Randolph Hearst, was the donor of the Theatre.

Everett Jones spent a lifetime in the managerial field of artists and concerts. He was personal manager for John Charles Thomas.

The combination of her thrilling beauty and talent made Ingrid Bergman an international star of the first magnitude.

When she first came to the United States, Ingrid Bergman was cast by David Selznick in the stage play, "Anna Christie," which was presented with magnificent success in San Francisco and other California cities. Grace Denton did the publicity. Here Bergman is shown with Selznick.

Shiffer Photo

In the annals of dance, Katherine Dunham is a bright star. After obtaining her M.A. in anthropology from the University of Chicago, Katherine went to Haiti. The dances of Negroes has an innate quality, as does Negro music, that is highly effective and praise worthy. These rhythms she incorporated in her programs.

The dancing legs of Katherine Dunham might well serve as a model for sculpture. This stance was in the dance, "Finale."

Katherine Dunham's dance art resulted in international tours including the Orient. Here she is shown at the Imperial Palace in Tokyo.

Raymond Voinquel Photo

Iris Photo

Katherine Dunham has beauty of feature, grace in motion, and brought into being a touring Company ranking in the topmost bracket of creative dance in America.

As a solo dancer Katherine Dunham was no less than marvelous. She had style, beauty, class and reigned over unforgetable productions.

The beauteous Katherine Dunham evolved a highly personal concept of dance in her choreography. Based on strong rhythmic pattern, and vivid color, developed in the finest detail, her creations brought gay and joyful excitement.

AN IDEA IS BORN

Occasionally with a friend, son of stockbroker Ray Skofield, I would ride to a vantage point on a hill having a breath-taking view and a half-completed chateau Hobart's father had started to build in Santa Barbara before he lost his fortune in 1929. How could this magnificent structure be used? What a site for a special school of music but how costly to complete. I took Lotte Lehmann to see it. Her reaction, "Let me know when you get your first million."

But the school idea persisted. I started thinking and talking school, exploring the American Academy in Rome, the Sorbonne in France, etc., etc. I became immersed in the subject of a school with artist teachers and top talents in students on the West Coast. The only response I received was: "It can't be done." "Santa Barbara is not the place for this." I disagreed. Step by step I gained ground. In order to have artist teachers who have winter concert schedules, its needs must be a summer school.

Several people, mostly men, accepted coming to a meeting which developed into a Board of Directors. I spent hours discussing with Dr. Richard Lert in Los Angeles as to ways and means of a curriculum. My next move was to invite some twenty-five people for a luncheon at the Montecito Country Club. Lotte Lehmann remarked, "People are always talking about a music school — if something doesn't happen this time, this will be the last meeting I will attend." I had Merle Armitage talk on the "need" for an advanced music school on the West Coast. Enthusiasts included Mildred Couper, Santa Barbara pianist and composer; Rex and Sonya Miller, Sonya, a pianist of Beverly Hills; Isabel Morse Jones who had been music editor of the Los Angeles *Times;* and with her, Doris Kenyon Mynarski — a total of twenty-five guests.

Fate was kind. At the home of Mrs. Jessie Ford, a queen of a person, where I was residing, a man and his wife rented a cottage on the grounds. He had just returned from a war assignment in India but Jessie said that he previously had been connected with a school. She introduced me to Paul Cameron Sherbert who had been in charge of the Catalina School for Boys

185

before the war. Handsome, Harvard, musical — this was all to the good as he said he would help me.

I took him to the next Board meeting. The school subject was at low ebb. Sellar Bullard, an important citizen, read a three-page statement on the premise, "It can't be done." Tall, commanding Paul arose and made a speech to the effect that "he was not a banker or lawyer, but he did know how to run a school." This soothed the elements and he saved the day. The next subject, "Where would the school be located?" I had inspected every likely place but had not found a usable facility. After the meeting we went to Mildred Couper's handsome studio. Curtis Cate was there. The perfect location, the Cate School with Paul in charge. Glory be! It had living quarters for the faculty and for a hundred students, class rooms, fine dining and assembly rooms, all in a divine area overlooking the Pacific. The stipulation, the faculty must be completely engaged by March 15, surely late enough to start a summer school.

What to name the school? I considered many names, finally chose "Music Academy of the West." Paul Sherbert and I got busy in contacting possibilities for the faculty by long distance phone. We had no money to offer, but agreed teachers would receive all tuition that came in from their students and would be given their living arrangements. Most of the faculty we wanted were in New York. It was difficult to close contracts by phone. We had a Board meeting at which I announced the fact that to meet the deadline I would need to go to New York. Alfred Harcourt, the publisher, took out his checkbook, wrote a check for $500.00, handed it to me and said, "Go to New York." What a moment! I flew there on March 7, 1947, was back by the 15th with faculty contracts completed, without having guaranteed one cent of remuneration. What rapport there was. Richard Bonelli, in charge of the voice department, was an important asset. He aided so much in auditions and chose a brilliant array of students for scholarships. There was Roman Totenberg, now violin instructor at the Boston Conservatory; The Griller String Quartet from England; Harry Kaufman and Mildred Couper, pianists; Ernest Bloch, composer; Richard Lert, orchestra.

Dr. Richard Lert was a tower of strength. What a great musician for all generations and man. He and his wife, Vicki Baum, came to this country from Germany after the calamity of World War I when the film of Vicki's "Grand Hotel" was being premiered in New York. Lert began his career as a student in Vienna and became an orchestra musician. He played violin and viola under Nikisch, Mahler, Richard Strauss. His first post as a conductor was at Dusseldorf in 1909. Later the young conductor was called to Berlin to stage the Wagner "Ring" cycle, then to Hanover and Mannheim where he became General Music Director in 1923. In 1928 the Lerts moved again to Berlin, his wife, formerly a harpist, was gaining fame as a novelist.

It was in 1931 that the Lerts began living in Hollywood. Lert had conducted his first Hollywood Bowl concert in 1930. It was in 1936 that he took over the young Pasadena Civic Orchestra from which players found their way to positions in every important Symphony in the country. Lert held this conducting post for 36 years. At age 86, he conducted his final concert in 1972 except for guest appearances to come. Lert is far from closing out his career. He admits, "Never have I enjoyed conducting as much as teaching; working with young people, helping young conductors — that is where the real rewards are found." For several years Lert has been conducting summer Orchestra Workshops in Orkney Springs, Virginia. These will continue, and an additional Lert project is developing from the workshops some 100 video tapes to be used on college campuses. And so this man whose greatest interest was training the youth of America in the field of orchestra and conducting, gave five summers in teaching at the Music Academy of the West, setting a standard that has continued. He deserves a laurel wreath!

With the Academy location and faculty solved, the next objective was obtaining tuition scholarships and talented students. Lawrence Tibbett agreed to be Chairman of the Scholarship Committee. Others were: Edward Arnold, Ronald Colman, Doris Kenyon, Herbert Marshall, Jeanette MacDonald, Walter Pidgeon. The scholarship letter had their signatures.

Lawrence Tibbett, Chairman

Edward Arnold

Herbert Marshall

Ronald Colman

Jeanette MacDonald

Doris Kenyon

Walter Pidgeon

Committees were established in San Francisco, Salt Lake City, Los Angeles, Bakersfield, to select scholarship students. Somehow it all came together with such students as Lucine Amara who became a star at the Metropolitan Opera. Donald Gramm, basso, also has gained fame at the Met. The Music Academy's first season opened for July and August in 1947 and still continues, with a record of aiding in the development of dozens of professional artists.

That first season there was a young conducting student from Korea, Won Sik Lim. He did not know a word of English, but a beautiful Korean soprano, Florence Ahn, who had been a feature of Arthur Godfrey's radio hour, sat beside him and translated Lert's words of wisdom. That Fall Lim went on to Juilliard to try for a scholarship. By then he could write to Lert saying that he watched the contestants come in with scores under their arms, and became very apprehensive. "But," he wrote, "I went into the water closet and tried to remember everything you had taught me." He won a Juilliard scholarship and later one at Tanglewood. A voice student that first year, Charles Davis from Hawaii, has had a notable professional career.

The dining room at the Academy served as a center of musical discussion. A faculty member sat at the head of each round table seating ten. What "jam" sessions there were! Students would scramble to be seated at composer Ernest Bloch's table to enjoy his great understanding. There was chamber music playing far into the night, student concerts, faculty concerts, rehearsals, music and more music — beach parties, too — all enriching young lives. Orchestral instruments, conducting under the Master, Richard Lert, and composition were emphasized. The original compositions by the students were performed — a privilege for students to hear their own works. Composers instructing, in addition to Ernest Bloch, included Darius Milhaud and Charles Jones (for three years), Arnold Schoenberg, with guests George Antheil, Roy Harris, Virgil Thomson.

Among other faculty members were such valiants as Simon Kovar who was first bassoon in the New York Philharmonic for 27 years, a teacher of woodwinds at Juilliard School of Music (22 years), Columbia University, the New York College of Music. His teaching at the Music Academy resulted in providing top woodwind players for Symphony orchestras all over this country.

For four years I lived and breathed for the Music Academy of the West with Paul Sherbert in about the same frame of mind. It was a marvelous period, so many talented young people and inspiring musicians mingling study and performing for the cause of music.

Artists who gave concerts benefiting the Scholarship Fund included Lotte Lehmann, Rose Bampton, Stella Roman, Jarmila Novotna and Brian Sullivan, all of the Metropolitan Opera; Nan Merriman, American soprano; Lois and Guy Maier, duo-pianists; Lester Donahue, pianist. Faculty members who appeared in concerts were: Richard Bonelli, Joseph Schuster, The Griller String Quartet, Roman Totenberg, Gabor Rejto, cellist with Adolph Baller, pianist; Jascha Veissi, viola; Nikolai Grauden, cellist, and Joanna Grauden, pianist; Soulima Stravinsky, pianist; Martial Singher, Metropolitan Opera baritone. Arthur Fiedler conducted the Academy Orchestra.

For one concert Lert conducted excerpts from "Die Meistersinger" in the Santa Barbara County Bowl, a local chorus augmenting Academy students. Richard Bonelli was Hans Sachs. This was soul stirring!

As a backdrop "shell" was needed, I negotiated with Leopold Stokowski for purchasing the one he obtained personally in order to have the sound to his dimension standard when he was conductor for a season at the Hollywood Bowl. This he had stored in his Beverly Hills garage. The Academy paid him $1,000.00, however, when it was assembled, the ceiling had deteriorated and split into pieces. A new ceiling had to be installed whereupon "Stoki" graciously refunded the thousand dollars.

At a concert given by Brian Sullivan for the scholarship fund, from the stage he paid tribute to Dr. Lert, announcing that he had "acquired his musical knowledge in large measure from Lert," and expressed his deep appreciation. Lert, the complete classicist, then listened to Brian's encore, which happened to be "Danny Boy." Sitting back of me, Lert was heard to say, "What in the world is that?"

It was at this concert that Alice Corbeil, (she doubled as violinist and being available as "house mother,") acted for the students who had decided to give me a large bouquet of red roses, a token of appreciation. I was called to the stage and given the roses by Donald Gramm who made a little speech.

I wish it were possible to list the many students who were at the Academy during my four years as Executive Director, also their achievements for the world of music. What a proudful list it would be.

So many people up and down the Pacific Coast, who were contributors to the culture of the West, rallied to the support of the Music Academy of the West. One of the foremost was Artie Mason Carter, founder of the Hollywood Bowl. Later she was responsible for my Palm Springs friend, Muriel Fulton, another zealot for music, and me in having hard-to-get tickets for the Los Angeles Philharmonic concert, Zubin Mehta conducting, at the opening of the Music Center Pavilion, a memorable occasion.

Mme. Ganna Walska, the gorgeous and intrepid Opera prima donna, sent me a check for $1,000.00 to aid in the founding of the Music Academy. This was a great boost. Her telegram from New York in reply to my asking her if she wished the gift used for a particular purpose:

**"Do as you please dear Miss Denton   Do as
it is more useful for wonderful work you
are helping with so devotedly   May good
luck be with your great enterprise
Blessings   Ganna Walska"**

She maintained residence on Park Avenue, New York, at this time and had a box at the Metropolitan for the entire season, this box being the first one next to the stage. Once when I was in New York she sent her chauffeur to call for me and I was a guest in this box with her for a performance of "Lakme" with Lily Pons, the star. Walska's flair for the exquisite in her attire, her jewels, her gardens on her estate in Santa Barbara, "Lotusland," cannot be adequately expressed. That night at the Opera she was resplendent with magnificent amethysts — necklace, earrings, bracelets.

Everything in her life was on a fabulous scale. When she married she chose millionaires — two of them. No garden in the world can equal her cactus gardens in Santa Barbara which can boast of practically every known variety in the entire world. The small lake covered with lotus blossoms, her rose garden, her outdoor theatre — all bear the stamp of this beautiful and amazing woman who once owned an Opera House in Paris and sang the great roles of Opera in it.

It was a sad day for me when certain members of the Music Academy Board of Directors decided to supplant faculty members who had so valiantly worked and delivered for the Academy, with others of their choice, such as engaging John Charles Thomas. His magnificent voice I recognized, but did not feel that his metier was teaching. It was impossible for me to join in this premise, so I resigned. John Charles Thomas was at the Academy one year only. Lotte Lehmann then became a powerful influence coaching and giving Master Classes for some twenty years.

The Music Academy passed its twenty-fifth anniversary in 1971. Its significant achievements have fulfilled the early dream — and its future portends even greater glory under the musical aegis of Dr. Maurice Abravanel. My longest shadow — the founding of the Music Academy of the West.

A building at the Cate School, private school for boys, which was the home of the Music Academy of the West for its first four years. Students and faculty were housed on the grounds and all classes took place there.

The study of composition was given prominence in the Music Academy curriculum. Ernest Bloch was the first composer in residence. Here he is shown on the steps of the Santa Barbara Mission.

Darius Milhaud, world famous French composer, was resident composer at the Music Academy for two summer sessions. His charming wife, Madeleine, a talented actress, taught French.

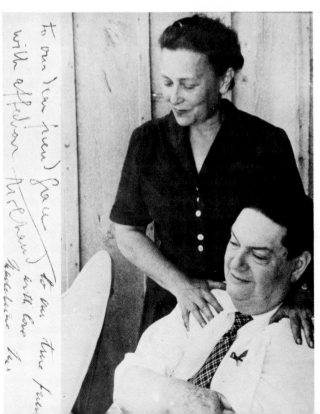

Reprinted with permission by the New York Times and the artist, Don Freeman

Milhaud discusses his Octour, given its second public performance by Music Academy students.

Darius Milhaud (seated center) and a group of his students in composition at the Music Academy. In the front row center is the young Burt Bacharach. Murray Adaskin from Canada standing left. Ruth Anderson, standing right, a talented flutist, composer, conductor.

Arnold Schoenberg
taught his theories
of composition
during one session
at the Academy.

Georges Antheil was a guest
composer at the Music
Academy teaching and giving
lectures.

Three composers
and Curtis Cate
(right) who made
the Cate School
available for the
Music Academy for
four years. Standing
is Charles Jones,
assistant to Darius
Milhaud. At the
left, the famous
musician and
composer, Virgil
Thomson, with
Milhaud in the
center.

Soulima Stravinsky, son of Igor Stravinsky, taught piano. He wrote on this photo: "To dear Grace Denton, the soul of the Music Academy of the West. Affectionately Soulima Stravinsky."

Soulima Stravinsky with his father, Igor Stravinsky, who was a guest at the Academy.

Richard Lert, a musician of limitless ability, finds his greatest satisfaction in training young musicians. Practically every leading Symphony in this country has players who have been under Lert's tutelage. He retired in 1972 at age 86 from the Pasadena Symphony, which he had conducted for 36 years, however he is continuing his work with young musicians through the American Symphony Society, conducting orchestral workshops. Lert was Music Director of the Music Academy of the West giving invaluable aid in its early years of development.

An Orchestra session at the Music Academy led by Richard Lert.

Richard Bonelli of Grand Opera fame and Alexander Schreiner, Tabernacle organist in Salt Lake City, serve as judges for the Music Academy of the West scholarship contest held in Salt Lake City for Utah talents.

The opera career of Richard Bonelli was extensive and distinguished. He sang leading baritone roles with the Metropolitan Opera for fifteen years, also with Chicago Civic Opera, the New York City and San Carlo Companies, in Berlin, Munich, Paris and other European opera centers.
As a teacher of voice, Bonelli ranks high. He held the position as principal of the vocal faculty at Curtis Institute in Philadelphia. His contribution at the founding of the Music Academy of the West was invaluable.

Richard Bonelli (right) and his wife, Mona, meet scholarship winners in contest sponsored by Salt Lake City *Tribune*. Tom Hutchins (left) from Pocatello studied piano with Harry Kaufman, Flora Lundahl Neilsen (second from left) with Bonelli at the Music Academy.

Donald Gramm, bass-baritone, a Music Academy student, has achieved stardom as a member of the Metropolitan Opera roster and with major opera companies in this and other countries.

Richard Bonelli with group of students at the Music **Academy**.

Christian Steiner Photo

A group of faculty members at the Music Academy of the West in its first years: From left standing, Gregor Piatigorsky, cello master class and lectures; Nicolai Grauden, cello; Richard Lert, orchestra; seated, Martial Singher, voice; Joanna Grauden, piano.

Music Academy faculty wives: from left, Sally Jones, Francoise Stravinsky, Harriet Okeson (formerly Veissi), Mona Bonelli, Melanie Totenberg, Mrs. Joseph Schuster.

Mildred Couper taught theory and piano at the Academy. She composed a number of works using **the quarter-tone system.**

Richard Hale, well known actor on the stage and in motion pictures, also as an opera singer, taught diction **inspiringly at the Music Academy.**

Roman Totenberg with
Richard Lert.

Totenberg with Darius Milhaud.

Totenberg with Murray Adaskin who
composed a concerto for him.

Roman Totenberg (center
without instrument) with his
class of violin students, most
of whom now are members of
Symphony Orchestras.
Marilyn Wright, the lovely
blond at far left, has been
concertmaster for New York
City Opera for many years and
still holds this position.

The woodwind class of Simon
Kovar, (fifth from left standing)
who was first chair bassoon
of the New York Philharmonic
for 27 years and held important
positions at Columbia
University, New York
University and elsewhere. In
addition to teaching individuals,
the Chamber Music classes
under his tutelage made
great music. Most of these
woodwind players hold
positions in Symphony
Orchestras.

Roy Harris (left) has gained the laudable position of being one of America's most important composers. His works are programmed by all leading Symphony Orchestras. His wife, Joanna, is a gifted pianist. She gave a benefit concert for the Music Academy Scholarship Fund. Roy held classes in composition.

Gabor Rejto, cellist, and Adolph Baller, pianist, such wonderful musicians they are and wonderful as persons! They played a concert at the Music Academy. Since then "Gaby" who is on the faculty of the University of Southern California, became a faculty member at the Music Academy, a position he has held for over twenty years.

The Maiers, Guy and Lois, were accomplished pianists. Guy teamed with Lee Pattison in playing two-piano concerts. They were a favorite attraction on their many tours. Later Guy and his wife used this form of music. They both also had fine reputations as teachers. Their concert benefiting the Music Academy Scholarship Fund proved enjoyable.

Mme. Lotte Lehmann at her home in Santa Barbara enjoying life and her dogs.

When the Music Academy of the West opened in 1947, Mme. Lotte Lehmann gave the first benefit concert for the Academy. When she retired from her operatic and concert career, she taught Master Classes at the Academy for many years. Grace Bumbry, now a star at the Metropolitan Opera was among the large number of singers who journeyed from all over the country to be in her class and to be coached in German Lieder in which Lehmann is a peerless exponent.

Artists who appeared in concerts benefiting the Music Academy
Scholarship Fund in 1949: (top row from left) Rose Bampton, Brian
Sullivan, Jarmila Novotna, (second row) Jascha Veissi, Martial Singher,
Soulima Stravinsky, (bottom row) Nikolai and Joanna Graudan, Roman
Totenberg, Stella Roman.

The brilliance of Madame Ganna Walska streaked across continents like a comet. An international beauty, the alabaster quality of her skin, her raven tresses and violet eyes, her supreme taste in attire, made her the cynosure of all eyes as she sat in her season box at the Metropolitan Opera. Her position as an Opera singer had been enviable. Ganna Walska was a star in the realm of music for decades.

Since her retirement on her estate, "Lotusland," in Santa Barbara, California, Mme. Ganna Walska has continued to lend her influence and support for important objectives in music, such as the Music Academy of the West, the important center for specially talented students bound for professional careers. The magnificent gardens at "Lotusland" have been the scene of events of signal importance in aid of music.

ur Fiedler conducted the Music Academy Orchestra in an August concert
fiting the Scholarship Fund. It was a splendid evening of music.

Following his tenure of four years as business manager for the Music Academy of the West, Paul Sherbert
went to Madras, India, for the State Department. During his six years there he frequently was in contact
with Nehru and Indira Gandi. Here he is shown with these great people.

Since 1950, the Music Academy of the West has had its own permanent home on an eighteen acre estate within a block of the Pacific Ocean, the gift of Helen Marso. It recently acquired a new building for rehearsals and concerts—Abravanel Hall.

The Music Academy Orchestra in 1972, directed by Dr. Maurice Abravanel, in performances of major Symphonic works.

here and there for music

As it occurred that Walter Paepcke, founder of the Aspen Institute for Humanistic Study, sought to engage me in relation to organizing the Music School of the Institute, I accepted and went to Aspen, Colorado. Several of the Music Academy faculty joined me there. Darius Milhaud became composer in residence, remaining in this capacity for twenty-five years, his assistant, Charles Jones. Roman Totenberg became head of the violin department, Martial Singher, the vocal. Now in 1973 Roman teaches at the Boston Conservatory and Martial is back at the Music Academy.

When I went to Aspen, Paul Sherbert left the Academy for several years' service for the U.S. Government in Madras, India.

Somehow my theories for a performing arts music school did not coincide with those of Mr. Paepcke. At that time he was strongly against giving tuition scholarships which I considered essential in order to enroll students of exceptional talent. I soon realized this was not the place for me.

After my Aspen sojourn, John Rosenfield, Music Editor of the Dallas *News* and arbiter of matters musical for a large area in that vicinity, decided that I should be associated with the Dallas Symphony. I became assistant to that prince of managers, Morgan Knott, for three years. Walter Hendl was the able conductor. Soloists of the stature of Kirsten Flagstadt, Vladimir Horowitz, and Jose Iturbi, as piano soloist and conductor, embellished the concerts. Miklos Rozsa, the composer, came for the premiere of the Concerto he wrote for Jascha Heifetz, played with all brilliance by Heifetz.

A Santa Barbara friend had steered me to the Jack Westsmiths in Dallas. I became a member of this family, a plus arrangement for me. Jill Westsmith ran a great household. The five children were beautiful and special — Gay, John, Dick, Nancy, Sally.

Roman Totenberg of Music Academy and Aspen days, then teaching at the Mannes School of Music in New York, appeared as a Dallas Symphony soloist. He suggested that I aid in setting up a campaign for funds in relation to the Mannes Music School becoming the Mannes College of Music which it now is. With my deep admiration for David Mannes, this met with a ready response. Quite a few years had elapsed since I had been involved with the New York scene. The pace had changed since my salad days. After several months I was glad to journey back to California.

A former Music Academy student, Bess Eller, invited me to her Palm Desert home, in California. The desert won me. I managed a series of Ensemble groups in concerts, held at the handsome Jewish Community Center, under the auspices of the Palm Springs Civic Chorus, Harry Tomlinson, director. These included Gabor Rejto, cellist, and Adolph Baller, pianist; the Schoenfeld Trio; Mitchell Lurie Woodwind and Piano Quintet; Vertchamp Piano Quartet; Trojan String Quartet from the University of Southern California; Yaltah Menuhin, piano, and Eudice Shapiro, violin; Martin Ruderman, long the flautist of Disney Studios, and Laurindo Almeida, guitarist; Jascha Veissi of the Music Academy, viola artist.

Dan Eller, the son of my Palm Springs friend, who also was a Music Academy student, embarked on a great career of teaching piano and composition. A student of Soulima Stravinsky, he taught at Cornell, Claremont and now at the Boston Conservatory.

In Palm Springs somehow I became involved with the idea of presenting Fred Waring and His Pennsylvanians on the spacious grounds of the Desert Inn, then owned by Marian Davies. The thrill of music under the stars still held sway. Muriel Fulton, a staunch music and art devotee, joined me in this venture. I assured Music Corporation of America, Waring's manager, that it never rained in the Fall in Palm Springs. I couldn't have been more wrong. It rained often during the whole month of October. While it stopped on November 14, the night of the concert, it was cold and damp. The daintily clad lovely girls shivered as did the capacity audience which braved the weather to revel in Fred Waring's music. A spot-light was turned on Marian Davies, who sat in a place of honor.

In the Spring of that year I was enlisted to aid for three weeks a fund drive for the Orange County Symphony. I was persuaded to continue for three years as manager of the Orchestra, and lived in Corona del Mar on the shores of the Pacific. When I resigned a member of the Symphony Board of Directors, Adrian Pelletier, who was Board Chairman of Purex Corporation Ltd. importuned me to work for him at Purex. This was far removed from the music business. The salary was good but I certainly did not feel equipped, also as I told Mr. P. I was seventy years old. This he waved aside. He gave me a secretary to take his correspondence and Board meeting minutes. I could not ever take shorthand. I managed his office for a year and a half and then gave up and went back to music aiding in the organizing of a Council of Arts in Newport Beach. The University of California provided a "Living Arts Series" as a benefit for the Council. The Berkeley campus theatre group was seen in "Don Juan" by Moliere. From the UCLA campus there was a "Salute to the New UC Irvine" by its 80 piece Symphonic Band; programs from the Dance Department and the Motion Picture Division (documentary, dramatic, animation films and "Image of the Sea," the film that represented the United States at the Cannes Festival that year); and "A Rendezvous with Opera" from the Opera Workshop.

The desert beckoned. I contacted the Desert Southwest Art Gallery in Palm Desert and was engaged as assistant to the manager. This was a new world. I enjoyed learning more about art and artists.

One exhibit I arranged met with particular enthusiasm, attracting hundreds of viewers. It was called "Collector's Choice." Thirty noted collectors in the area loaned paintings. Mrs. Dalzell Hatfield from Los Angeles sent Aubusson tapestries. There was a "Grandma Moses" from Bob Hope. The Howard Ahmansons loaned a Millard Sheets. The Dan Thorntons (he was Governor of Colorado at the time) loaned paintings by Dwight Eisenhower. Others represented in this exhibit included the Justin Darts, Leigh Battsons, Leonard Firestones, Donald Gilmores, Sol Lessers, Harpo Marx (a Thomas Hart Benton), Floyd Odlums, Irene Rich (a terra cotta sculpture of Diego Rivera by Frances Rich) and many others. The exhibit was a benefit for the local public library, the results generous.

The following Fall, 1964, Paula Garrison Penney, wife of artist Frederick D. Penney, opened THE GALLERY in Palm Springs. It was my good fortune to be a member of her staff for four years until I became

Mrs. Maurice Esser, November 22, 1968. Paula had knowledge and verve. What a parade of great exhibitions she brought to Palm Springs. French Impressionists, German Expressionists, the best of American art — early and contempory, Western art, Desert art, particularly James Guilford Swinnerton — great man and great artist. Paula honored him in The Gallery on his ninetieth birthday.

Each season there was a special showing in collaboration with the Dalzell Hatfield Galleries of Los Angeles with paintings by Utrillo, Claude Monet, Matisse, Raul Dufy, Valtat, Mary Cassatt, Pisaro, Picasso, Vlaminck, Roualt, Gabriel Munter, Kandinsky, Pechstein, Jawlinsky. Paula grossed $150,000.00 her first season, a goodly sum.

I had come full circle — music, theatre, dance, the graphic arts.

When I walked down the aisle with artist Sterling Moak and was married by Judge Donald Redwine at the Bel Air Hotel in West Los Angeles, among the guests who toasted us with champagne in the beautiful gardens were Frederick W. Sleight, Director of the Palm Springs Desert Museum, and Mrs. Sleight. Through the expertise of Fred Sleight the Desert Museum has become outstanding. It offers not only natural exhibits of desert flora and fauna, Indian culture and other subjects pertaining to the desert, but also significant exhibits of Art, Sunday afternoon concerts, lectures on a plethora of subjects and each year presents a benefit concert of such stature as Artur Rubinstein, Isaac Stern, the Los Angeles Philharmonic, Zubin Mehta, conductor.

I was asked in 1968 to be the publicist for the Museum. That year the benefit concert was the Los Angeles Philharmonic, Eugene Ormandy, guest conductor, Mischa Dichter, the piano soloist. Mrs. Walter Annenberg was Chairman of the event. She later became President of the Board of Directors. The Museum is building a new facility to house its riches. It also maintains a "Living Desert Reserve" of 350 acres where an active program in relation to the desert is offered.

A memorable event that took place at the Museum in 1969 was the Retrospective Exhibition of the sculpture of Frances Rich. So many distinguished American artists merit a whole book instead of the few paragraphs I can do about them in this Chronicle. One of these is Frances Rich, the beauty and power of whose sculpture is remarkable. A proudful name is hers in the annals of Art in America.

After early study in Switzerland, graduating from Smith College and service in the Waves that brought her the rank of Lieutenant Commander, sculpture took the lead in her life activity. She studied with Carl Milles at Cranbrook and enjoyed his friendship until his death. She fulfilled a request of his in executing a St. Francis, which was placed at his graveside in the sculpture garden at Lidingo, Sweden.

There was the time when Frances made a bronze head of Diego Rivera as he was making a fresco portrait of her. Frances Rich, the daughter of Irene Rich, the beloved actress, worked with many noted artists. At Cranbrook, in addition to Milles there was Eliel and Eero Saarinen. At Scripps College in Claremont, California, Albert Stuart and Millard Sheets, and in New York, Malvena Hoffman.

To list a few Frances Rich sculptures which have gained distinction there is: "Army and Navy Nurse" (10 feet) Pink Tennessee Marble, in Arlington National Cemetery; "Our Lady of Combermere" (10 feet) bronze, at the Madonna House, Combermere, Ontario, Canada; "The Laughing Pelican", 10 foot wing spread, bronze, the Pelican Magazine Building, University of California, Berkeley, California; "St. Francis of Assisi" (1) 7 foot, Bronze, St. Margaret's Episcopal Church, Palm Desert, California (gift of Mr. and Mrs. Leonard Firestone); (2) four foot, bronze, Millesgarden, Lidingo, Sweden; (3) 7 foot bronze, Pierce College, Mt. Hymetus, Athens, Greece. Some of her portraits include Margaret Sanger, Lawrence Langner, Katherine Hepburn as Cleopatra, Diego Rivera, Virgil Thomson, Lotte Lehmann.

Frances now may well gain inspiration from her Pinyon Crest mountain-top studio in California.

It also was in 1969 when Fred Sleight turned over to me the responsibility of the arrangements for honoring James Guilford Swinnerton on his 94th birthday. There was a special exhibit of his paintings, and how beautiful Swinnerton paintings are! At the exhibit opening reception, Jimmie blew out the 94 candles on the cake, with friends attending from all over California to cheer him.

Jimmie's first fame was in drawing cartoons. He began at age 17 on the staff of the Hearst San Francisco *American*. He remained on the William Randolph Hearst papers for nearly fifty years. His first cartoon for Hearst was a little bear, which daily told of the weather. His was the first syndicated comic strip cartoon, "The Little Bears and the Little Tykes," which led the way for this whole field of cartoons such as "Little Orphan Annie," "The Katzenjammer Kids," "Dick Tracy," and others. In 1905 Swinnerton moved to New York and launched "Little Jimmie" about a whimsical little boy who seemed always to be in trouble. This strip ran for 40 years across the country. The "Canyon Kids" ran for 42 years in *Good Housekeeping* magazine.

When he contracted tuberculosis, Hearst sent Jimmie to Palm Springs to recover. He began painting the desert, the first artist who really grasped the beauty of its ever-changing light and color. His malady vanished and his fame soared as a revered artist. Soon he was painting canvases of the entire Southwest. His admirers are legion, not only for his great ability as an artist, but also as a man.

Although he laid aside his brushes at age 90, he is still with us, bless him, at age 97.

In my gypsying across our country, in and out of theatres, there are so many delightful people I would like to include in this Chronicle. A salute to the fine secretaries who lent their skill to the events that went on behind the footlights. In Toledo there was Mary Curran and the Day sisters, Ruth and Edna. Ruth was a pillar of strength in Detroit. In Chicago my first secretary was Mrs. Myron Adams, whose husband instigated the Century of Progress Fair in 1933. Next was Charlotte Baylie, who later became secretary for Gertrude Lawrence in New York. Helen Bolsum aided much in Chicago, and at the Music Academy there was Beatrice Du Pree, Frances Flock and Jennie Alice Fatherree. Mrs. Frances MacArthur in Newport Beach wrote a birthday poem for me:

> To a "boss" who's a friend
> On a job without end -
> Who knows the whole "score"
> In music and more -
> Who goes like a jet,
> Or a missle in flight -
> Even dreams up new schemes
> In the dead of the night;
> Who tries to save money
> For the Society's goal,
> And always comes up
> With an ace in the hole -
> Who combines all this drive
> And talent and charm,
> And, more than all these,
> A heart that is warm.
>
> To a "boss" who's a friend
> What more could I say -
> But I'll just close with a wish
> For a most happy day.

And now this Chronicle takes me to my home in "Snow Creek," eleven miles from Palm Springs with 10,800 foot Mt. San Jacinto, glistening with snow most of the year, in my back yard. I can really look at the mountain "from whence cometh my strength." My Maurice named our house "Casa Novita." With quail, rabbits, raccoons, coyotes for neighbors, in addition to the fine human neighbors who dote on "Snow Creek," it is indeed a new life, but not the life it would have been if Fate had not taken him with his great heart giving up eight months after our marriage.

Even though I could never be termed a writer, it is my wish that the photographs in this Chronicle will tell a story of a wonderful, never-to-return era in the arts. I would like to feel that besides bringing joy to myself, the performances presented under my banner brought a lasting joy to those who sat in the seats and that these pages may echo some of this joy to those who turn them.

The
Amphitheatre
at Aspen,
Colorado,
designed by
Eero Saarinen.

Concert audience
in Aspen tent
Amphitheatre.

Walter Hendl, conductor of the Dallas Symphony, when Grace Denton was on the staff in early 1950s.

Kirsten Flagstad as Bruennhilde in "Die Walkuere", an aria she sang among others with the Dallas Symphony. As a Wagnerian soprano she was unsurpassed.

As soloist with the Dallas Symphony, Vladimir Horowitz played the Tschaikowsky Piano Concerto, No. 1, Op. 23 in B-flat minor. His interpretation and brilliant execution transcended all other renditions. When he performed this concerto with Toscanini and the NBC Symphony in Carnegie Hall on April 25, 1943, eleven million dollars in War Bonds were raised.

The hands of Vladimir Horowitz.

Jose Iturbi won fame both as pianist and conductor. It was a gala occasion when he appeared in both capacities with the Dallas Symphony.

Fred Waring is an active participant in music for Palm Springs. He heads a group working for a new Concert Hall to be built at the College of the Desert. The Fred Waring concert managed by Grace Denton occurred on her birthday, so he wrote "Happy Birthday" on the photo he gave her.

Grace Denton at the entrance of the
Desert Southwest Art Gallery, where she
enters a new phase in her career, at age 73,
working with paintings, sculpture, and
other aspects of the graphic arts.

Palm Desert Post Photo

Grace Denton at her desk at "The
Gallery" in Palm Springs.

Committee for "Collector's Choice" exhibit showing paintings loaned
by thirty outstanding art collectors. Held at the Desert Southwest
Gallery, it benefited the Palm Desert Public Library, and was managed
by Grace Denton. From left, Charles Shelton, owner of the Gallery;
Thirza Williams, President of the Palm Desert Women's Club, William
Daugherty, manager Eldorado Country Club; Kal Kapp, Public Library
officer.

Robert E. Johnson Photo

216

Attendants when Grace Denton became Mrs. Maurice Esser. Judge Ronald Redwine who officiated (left), Harry Esser, Maurice Esser, Grace Denton, Muriel Fulton, Sterling Moak, Bonita Wilson.

Paul Pospesil Photo

Mrs. Maurice Esser

Muriel Fulton, President of the Palm Springs Desert Museum Women's Committee, greets Artur Rubinstein following his concert presented by the Women's Committee of which Grace Denton was a member and director of publicity.

Congratulations were extended to Eugene Ormandy (second from left) following a concert by the Los Angeles Symphony, which he guest conducted in Palm Springs, a benefit for the Palm Springs Desert Museum. Left: Frederick H. Sleight, Director of the Museum; Ormandy, Mrs. Walter Annenberg, Chairman of the event; Mrs. Red Skelton and Skelton. Grace Denton was director of publicity.

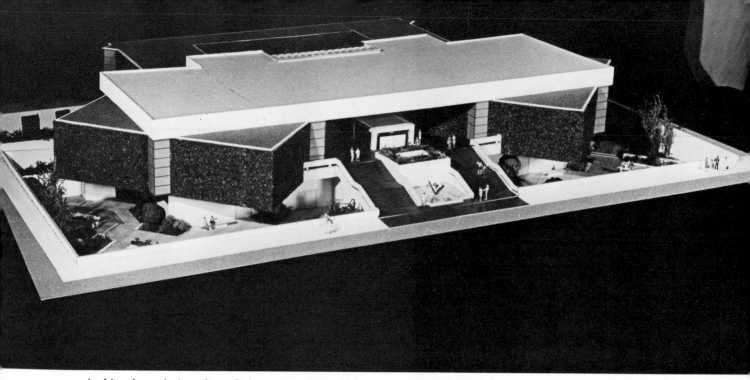

Architect's rendering of new Palm Springs Desert Museum to open in 1975, which will provide a Cultural Center for Natural History, Art, Music. Events in the Museum Auditorium will include important film series, speakers, seminars, also ten Sunday afternoon concerts under the aegis of Mimi Rudolph. Gala concerts featuring such artists as Artur Rubinstein, Isaac Stern, the Los Angeles Philharmonic Orchestra also are sponsored by the Desert Museum. Exhibits in Art cover a wide and significant range.

Important visitors frequent the Palm Springs Desert Museum. Here are (from left) Mamie Eisenhower, the late Walt Disney, Yousuf Karsh.

Mrs. Walter Annenberg (her husband is Ambassador to the Court of St. James) is President of the Palm Springs Desert Museum Board of Directors. Here she is pictured at the museum with a model of "Family" by Robert Russin, which enlarged to life size is the sculpture for the fountain at entrance of the City of Hope hospital in Duarte.

Gilbert Kahn, a member of the Palm Springs Desert Museum Board of Directors, has a wide interest in cultural developments. It was his father, Otto Kahn, who was a pillar of support for the Metropolitan Opera and innumerable cultural projects during the first decades of the Twentieth Century.

Earl Wild, pianist, who ranks with the greatest of keyboard performers, gives an annual concert in the Desert Museum Auditorium, to the delight of his host of admirers.

Alice Sleight (Mrs. Frederick W.) lends her multiple talents in various activities at the Desert Museum. A gifted pianist, she is heard in concerts, acts as a charming hostess on the many occasions honoring visiting celebrities and here she is shown giving information about the Great American Desert to a group of youngsters. The record of young people attending classes at the Museum numbers into the thousands.

The Great American Desert

"Auntie Pearl" McManus (Mrs. Austin G.) was the "First Lady" of Palm Springs for decades. Her father, Judge John G. McCallum, was the first white settler in this desert area. He purchased large tracts of land, including where Palm Canyon Drive now is for $2.50 an acre. Before her death at age 87, his daughter, Pearl, created the McCallum Desert Foundation, which contributed a million dollars to the new Palm Springs Desert Museum.

Dr. Frederick Lowe (Fritz to his friends), composer of the perennial favorites, "My Fair Lady," "Gigi," "Camelot," and more, who has a home in Palm Springs, greets Van Cliburn following the young pianist's recital sponsored by the Desert Museum. Mrs. Thomas Mancine, likewise a concert pianist, also congratulates Van Cliburn.

An extensive exhibit from Ted Weiner's famous collection of sculpture attracts many viewers at the Desert Museum. The genial gentleman in the front row is Don Wilson, formerly associated with the television hour of Jack Benny. He now is a television executive in Palm Springs.

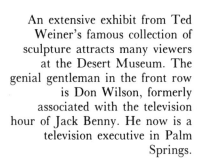

Portrait of Diego Rivera (clay in process) by sculptor Frances Rich.

223

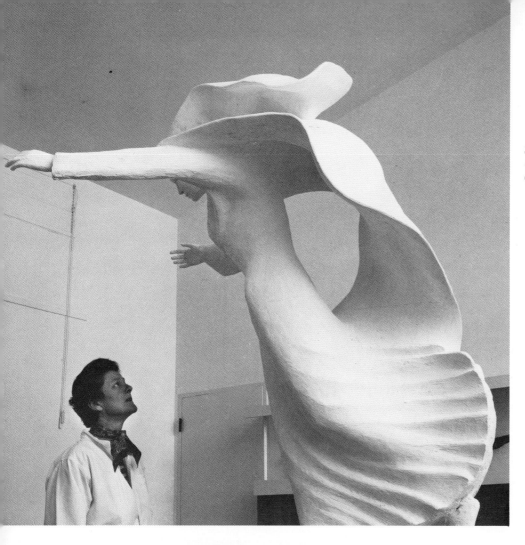

Sculptor Frances Rich with plaster (before bronze) of "Our Lady of Combermere".

Frances Rich is one of the few women who have made a great place in the art of America. Her sculpture is in many public and private buildings and estates across the country. Her St. Francis is in the sculpture garden of the great Carl Milles in Sweden by his request, as she worked for some time with this master. The St. Francis shown here is on her mountain top estate near Palm Springs, California.

Army Navy Nurse Monument, Arlington Cemetery, Washington D.C., of Tennessee marble, ten feet high. Sculptor, Frances Rich.

Lewis P. Woltz Photo

"Nunc Dimitiss" bas relief. Plastocene clay phase for bronze panel in St. Peters Episcopal Church, Redwood City, California. Sculptor, Frances Rich.

James Guilford Swinnerton paints the Grand Canyon.

A younger Swinnerton draws a cartoon.

Swinnerton (left) with fellow cartoonist, George McManus, creator of "Bringing Up Father," and Walt Disney.

Will Rogers and James Swinnerton exchange jokes.

Paul Pospesil Photo

Albino Desert trees painted by James Swinnerton.

James Swinnerton doesn't count his birthdays, but his friends remember him specially on these days. Paula Penney, (Mrs. Frederick W.) honored him on his 90th birthday with a reception at "The Gallery" which she owned. At left: Mrs. Swinnerton, Jimmy, Paula. Jimmy Swinnerton immortalized the desert smoke tree in his paintings. Here he is backed by one of these paintings with a small real smoke tree at its right.

Palm Springs Life Photo

The "Canyon Kiddies."

James Swinnerton with his 90th birthday cake, surrounded by the staff of "The Gallery." From left, Paula Penney, Georgia MacLean, Jimmy, Fred Penney, Margaret Moak, Grace Denton, Beatrice Cooper.

Grace Denton Esser in her Snow Creek home
with memories on the wall.

Jean Woodbury Photo

Grace Denton takes over the box office for
a charity event in Palm Springs.

Grace's 80th
birthday was
celebrated with a
party, Georgia
MacLean, the
hostess.
A few of the
guests: standing
from left,
Frederick Sleight,
Mrs. Sleight,
Gladys Sanborn,
Mrs. Norman
Massey, Mrs.
Sylvain Robert,
Dr. Alan Fallows,
Georgia
MacLean, Mrs.
Fallows, Merle
Armitage,
Sylvain Robert,
Sterling Moak.
Seated, Grace
Denton Esser.

Grace Denton Esser at "Casa Novita" with snow covered Mt. San Jacinto in the background, 10,800 feet in height. She can indeed "look to the hills from whence cometh strength." The tree is a graceful desert willow.

230

DESIGNED BY
MERLE ARMITAGE
AND PRINTED BY
FRANKLIN PRESS

ESSENTIAL GUIDE TO
cake decorating

Alex Barker

Bath · New York · Singapore · Hong Kong · Cologne · Delhi · Melbourne

Contents

Introduction

In the 21st Century, teatime often still means 'cake' and even though we rarely make time for tea in the old-fashioned way, most of us will not turn down the occasional offer of a slice of cake. However, turning an everyday cake into a glamorous gâteau or a crazily decorated party piece requires a little more than just baking.

Cake decorating can be a craft, a hobby or even a business. The skills used at the highest level of sugarcraft require training, practice and expertise. Most of us simply want to enjoy being creative, and taking pride in making something really special or unusual. Making a beautifully decorated cake for someone, or for a family occasion, is a real gift of love and time.

Today's cakes are as simple and stylish, or as colorful and daring as you want them to be. Finding the right design or idea is the first most important stage – frills, ribbons and roses suit some occasions; a brightly colored design with edible caricatures another; or fresh or frosted flowers or fruits may be appropriate. You may well be surprised how easy it is to make a creative cake if you take the time to select and plan a design. Look around at the tools available to turn an idea into reality.

The *Essential Guide to Cake Decorating* describes all you need to know about simple stylish cake decorating, from the basic cake recipes to a range of stunning designs. The first half of the book covers the recipes, techniques and skills that will equip you to make any of the cakes with confidence. Whether you want a Victoria sponge cake, a dark fruit cake or other favorites, like rich chocolate cake or carrot cake, they are all here. Professional tips, guides to quantities for making larger cakes, and information on choosing the right equipment are all included. Learn how to use classic methods for marzipan and royal icing, or soft sugar paste for exciting effects.

The second half of the book leads you carefully, step-by-step, through the stages in making 24 beautiful cakes. It doesn't matter how inexperienced you are, the techniques and guidance in the early pages will show you all you need to know. Discover elegant designs based on surprisingly simple piping; model charming little penguins; or succulent-looking raspberries and bramble berries. Alternatively, try your hand at pretty delicate butterfly run-outs, or stunning bronze cut-out doves. Why not simply have fun with the family, making fabulous cup cakes?

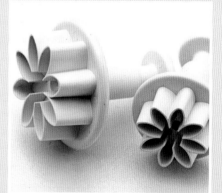

Planning Perfect Cakes

There is such an array of recipes, designs, equipment, pans, gadgets, ingredients and colors that making the right choice is the first important step. If possible, start with a design outline, then collect everything needed to make and complete the cake. If you have a specialist cake decorating supplier on your doorstep you are lucky; if not, allow plenty of time for mail order delivery of any special cutters, colors or cake boards required.

As well as a reliable recipe, turning out a great basic cake demands a good pan, prepared properly, and an oven that cooks evenly and steadily at the right temperature. Generally, there's no need to buy a new pan if you already have one of the correct size and shape – simply take care to line it properly. Pans of unusual shape or size are available to hire from catering shops or specialist cake suppliers. Make a point of keeping all your cake-decorating tools stored safely together, for example in a toolbox. Many items are tiny, easily lost and costly to replace.

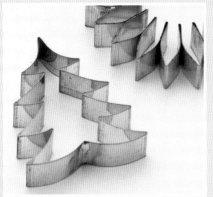

Baking Equipment

Most cooks already have a selection of baking equipment, often handed down through generations, and few have to buy everything from new. However, using the right item for the job does make all the difference, especially when it comes to baking pans and mixers.

- **Boards:** If possible use separate boards for general cooking and making sugar decorations. Small white (or colored) smooth plastic boards are available from specialist cake decorating shops.
- **Brushes:** Use a variety of sizes for greasing pans, brushing on apricot glaze, moistening surfaces with water or lemon juice, and painting fine designs.
- **Cake boards:** Available in many sizes and shapes, thin or thick, in both gold and silver,
- **Cake pans:** Available in all sizes and shapes. Choose good-quality non-stick pans with loose bases. Keep your pans really clean and dry. Hire unusual shapes or large sizes for special occasions.
- **Cooling racks:** Cool cakes and bakes on wire racks.
- **Knives:** Palette knives, both large and small, are important for spreading, smoothing and flattening. You will also need a selection of good, sharp cook's knives for cutting and trimming cakes.
- **Mixers:** If you frequently make cakes you will find a good mixer indispensable. An electric hand-held mixer is the most economical and useful for creaming light mixtures, whisking eggs, or whipping cream. A large free-standing food mixer with beater and whisk is ideal for frostings, royal icing, and fruit cakes. Food processors are not ideal for cakes, or frostings unless they have a whisk blade and a slow speed setting for gentle mixing.
- **Papers and wraps:** You will need wax paper and non-stick baking parchment to line pans, draw designs or make piping bags. Plastic wrap keeps frosting and marzipan soft and airtight. Foil is a good base on which to set chocolate and caramel designs. Paper towel can be used to support shapes and dry items.
- **Sieves:** For sifting flour and sugar; also for finely dredging cakes with confectioners' sugar or cocoa powder (unsweetened).
- **String:** To tie paper around cake pans when baking rich fruit cakes, to protect them from over cooking on the outside; also useful for measuring pans or cakes of awkward shapes.

Pictures left, from top:

- *Use brushes to keep surfaces clean, grease pans or paint decorations. Tweezers and craft knives allow pin-point precision on fine cakes.*
- *Keep cutting knives sharp. Have a good selection of palette knives to move even the smallest item with care.*
- *Good-quality pans cook evenly and clean easily; cakes will also come out easily.*
- *Cake boards can be used in many ways and can be covered with sugar paste or pretty paper to suit your design.*

A good mixer will save a lot of hard work.

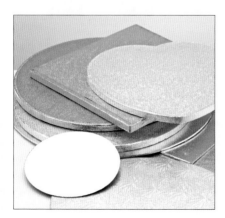

Lining Cake Pans

Preparing a Round Pan for a Fruit Cake

1 Cut two circles of wax paper for the base and a strip twice the depth and just larger than the circumference of the pan. Fold in half lengthwise and make a 1in fold along one edge of this strip. Make angled cuts into the folded edge.

2 Place one circle in the base of the pan, then line the inside with the strip, cut edge down. Overlap the cut edge to to curve it neatly.

3 Place the second circle of paper in the pan to cover the overlapping cuts around the edge. Lightly grease the base and sides.

4 Tie a band of double-thick brown paper around the outside of the pan. Place the pan on folded newspaper or brown paper on a baking tray.

Lining a Jelly Roll Pan

1 Cut a rectangle of wax paper 2in bigger than the pan on all sides. Place the pan on the paper and cut into the corners so the paper overlaps neatly in the corners.

2 Grease the pan lightly so the paper sticks. Place the paper in the pan, grease lightly and sprinkle with flour. Shake off the excess flour before filling with sponge cake mixture.

Decorating Equipment

The tools needed for decorating can be extensive, especially if you are clever and creative, and enjoy producing elaborate and artistic cakes. There are always new tools and shapes of cutters on the market, available through specialist websites, so you don't even have to go out to update your toolbox!

- **Colorings:** Edible food colors are available in several forms. Liquids are best for pastel shades; pastes for stronger, deeper shades; dusting powders can be brushed on to give subtle effects; and colored pens can be used for small areas of writing or drawing instead of using a paintbrush.
- **Crimpers:** These resemble wide tweezers with shaped ends that imprint different shapes (such as hearts, leaves or scrolls) instantly onto the top or bottom edge of a cake or in rolled-out sugar paste.
- **Cutters:** There are dozens of shapes available: novelty animals, festive shapes, numbers and letters, specific types of flowers and petals – so you can stamp out almost any design.
- **Edible glue:** Ideal for assembling flowers or attaching designs to sugar paste.
- **Embossers:** These look like small pencils and are used to press simple patterns onto sugar paste. Similar effects can be achieved with small graters, or zesters, and patterns can be pressed on using pieces of textured materials and mesh.

- **Floristry wire:** This is perfect for attaching leaves to flowers or making a bouquet, and ideal for giving ribbons some shape or fixing festive party decorations.
- **Flower Finishes:** You can buy tiny stamens and various types of coated wires for stamens. Veining tools give a realistic effect to cut-out sugar paste leaves.
- **Flower Nail:** A base on which to pipe tiny simple royal icing flowers.
- **Modeling tools:** A dog bone tool and ball tool help give the perfect shape to sugar paste designs. Available in various shapes and sizes.
- **Piping bags:** Small nylon washable bags are available in several sizes, but if you are using several different colors of icing for fine piping, or small quantities, then paper bags are much easier to use. Buy a batch in bulk or make your own (page 35).
- **Piping nozzles:** There are hundreds of small nozzle shapes for fine royal icing piping, from fine writing to buttercream shells. Buy a small selection of the basic types first, and then gradually add shapes as you become more adventurous.

Pictures left, from top:
- *Edible colors are available in paste, powder, liquid or as pens. Edible gold or silver, glue and varnish are also useful.*
- *Buy tools as you need them – there will be one for every shape and technique.*
- *Tiny shapes that you can then paint or dust over are easily imprinted with embosser pens, which are available in many different designs.*
- *Piping nozzles can produce delicate lines, and a sugar paste gun makes rope designs in seconds. String is used to tie brown paper around a prepared fruit cake pan and is useful for measuring cake sizes when rolling out marzipan or sugar paste.*

• **Ribbons:** Add a simple touch of color with a ribbon sweeping around the cake or dressing the edge of the board. Ribbons can be dramatic, in both color and style, for that final touch.

• **Rolling pins:** Marzipan and sugar paste require a standard-size rolling pin, completely smooth for the best result, but for small shapes and flowers a very small marble, plastic or steel rolling pin is useful. There are also patterned rolling pins to emboss paste as it is rolled out.

• **Ruler and scrapers:** Straight-edged metal rulers are used to flat ice the top of a cake and give a perfect, smooth surface. Some rulers have comb-ridged edges to apply a quick finish to the top or sides. Scrapers are short and wide, usually about 4in long, for smoothing excess frosting off the sides of a cake or board.

• **Craft knife:** For cutting paper designs or fine edges, or carefully inserting or removing items in a design.

• **Scissors:** You may need both tiny and large scissors for different tasks.

• **Shapers and smoothers:** For a professional finish you can buy a smoothing tool but for tight corners and short cake sides the simplest, effective way to smooth sugar paste is to use a chunk of spare paste wrapped in small polythene bag or plastic wrap.

• **Sponges:** Raised items in run-out icing or sugar paste often need supporting until set and a tiny corner of sponge is perfect for this task. Remember to

remove the sponge when the item is dry.

• **Toothpicks:** Toothpicks or small wooden skewers can be useful for shaping, supporting, or frilling edges.

• **Sugar paste and frostings:** Sugar paste, flower paste, modeling paste, pastillage, royal icing, run-out icing, and many more types are available mixed or in a ready-to-mix powder form from sugarcraft specialists. To make some items you may need specialist ingredients such as glycerine, glucose, gum tragacanth or gelatin.

• **Sugar paste gun:** A gun or pump with discs to extrude various shapes of sugar paste or marzipan.

• **Turntable:** The ideal equipment to raise and turn a cake for easy decorating. Some can be tilted.

• **Tweezers:** Invaluable if you have to remove the tiniest crumb from the top of a cake, or to place a very delicate decoration precisely.

The Finishing Touches

The right finishing touches are necessary to create a fabulous cake. Choosing the right board – shape or color – is just part of setting the final scene. Trimming with ribbons, scattering flower petals, adding table décor such a stars, or dragees, wrapping or sitting a cake in tissue, are all examples of ways to add to the total effect. The choice of trimmings in the shops is endless, so have fun staging your cake as well as making it!

Pictures right, from top:

• *Cutters come in many different shapes, some in sets of various sizes. For more adventurous designs try the larger flower sets for shapes such as sunflowers or lilies. Once cut, you can shape the paste to give a very realistic result.*

• *Ready mixed paste or powders give exactly the right frosting consistency. Most are white, but some are available in different colors.*

• *Decorations for finishing a fabulous cake include colors, candles, crackers, dragees, papers, party poppers, ribbons, sparklers, streamers – the list is endless.*

• *A turntable is a very good investment for cake decorating.*

Recipes for Success

Using the very best ingredients is the base of any good cake. For example, sponge cake especially, benefits from the use of fresh free-range eggs for their rich golden color and light-as-air texture. Fruit cakes benefit from good dried fruit that is full of moist richness. Use good quality vanilla extract – not synthetic flavoring – particularly for delicate sponge cakes in which its distinct warm flavor sings through.

Use equipment wisely: a food mixer can save time and effort but be aware of the potential for over mixing. A light sponge cake needs a light touch for a well-risen springy result. The initial creaming of fat and sugar to a pale fluffy texture helps the ingredients for a fruit cake to mix well. Beating royal icing to a thick glossy cloud can be very tough on your wrists.

Discover the right techniques that result in the perfect finish. Whether you prefer working with classic royal icing or the more immediate, hands-on sugar paste, the following pages have lots of advice and tips to share.

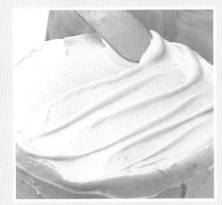

Sponge cake tips

- To test if a sponge cake is cooked, press gently on the top with your finger tips. If the imprint quickly disappears, the cake is cooked.
- Listen to your sponge cake and if it is still crackling furiously it is not fully cooked!
- For a really light Genoese sponge cake, sift the flour three times to incorporate plenty of air and whisk the eggs over a pan of hot water.
- To freeze a sponge cake, cool thoroughly. Double wrap in plastic wrap and then in foil. Allow 1 hour to thaw, but if cutting into layers do this while still part-frozen.
- Using a food processor to make a sponge cake takes a matter of minutes and the only difference is that it will not be quite as light and fluffy as the hand-mixed version. Simply mix everything together in the machine on its slowest speed for as short a time as necessary. When well mixed, spoon into the pans.

Variations
quantities for a 3-egg mixture
- **Lemon or/orange:** Add 2tsp orange flower water, or the finely grated zest of 1/2 lemon or orange with the egg yolks.
- **Chocolate:** Replace 1tbsp flour with sifted unsweetened cocoa powder and add 1-2tsp extra sugar.
- **Nuts:** Replace 1/4 cup flour with 1/4 cup of finely ground almonds or hazelnuts.
- **Coffee:** Dissolve 2tsp instant coffee in 1tsp boiling water and blend in with the eggs.

Simple Sponge Cakes

Making a good plain sponge cake does not require impossible skill, simply the right recipe and a little time. This cake can then form the base for a wide variety of other cakes, from cup cakes to fruit gâteau, novelty shapes, and elaborately decorated celebration cakes. Cake trimmings can be used in wonderful weekend desserts. A sponge cake is the most versatile cake to have in your repertoire.

Victoria Sponge Cake

The basic proportions of this cake are well worth remembering so you can whip up this popular family treat at a moment's notice. One hour from start to finish is really all it takes – even less if you use a food processor.

Serves 4-6

3/4 cup butter or margarine, softened
3/4 cup superfine sugar
3 eggs, lightly beaten with 1-2tsp vanilla extract
1 1/2 cup self-rising flour, sifted

1 Preheat the oven to 180ºC/350ºF/gas mark 4. Lightly grease the base and sides of one 7in cake pan, or two sandwich pans. Line the base with paper and grease this.

2 Cream the soft butter and sugar in a mixing bowl until pale and fluffy. Gently beat in the eggs and vanilla, gradually adding the flour.

3 When the ingredients are smoothly combined, without too much beating, place the mixture in the pan or divide it evenly between the two pans. Flatten the top or tops with a wetted knife and place in the middle of the oven, on the same shelf if possible, when baking two cakes.

4 Bake for about 20 minutes.The cooked cakes should be light golden, well risen but flat on the top and springy to the touch. Leave to part cool in the pan on a damp cloth for speed and then turn out onto a cooling rack and leave until cold.

Victoria Sponge Cake Proportions for Pan Sizes (one deep pan or two sandwich pans)

6in round pan: 1/2 cup fat, 1/2 cup superfine sugar and 1 cup self-rising flour to 2 eggs
7in round pan: 3/4 cup fat, 3/4 cup superfine sugar and 1 1/2 cup self-rising flour to 3 eggs
8in round pan: 1 cup fat, 1 1/4 cup superfine sugar and 2 cups self-rising flour to 4 eggs

Note
Remember that cooking times may vary depending on the oven used. Cake mixture in one deep pan will take longer to cook than when divided into two pans. Use cooking times as a guide.

Genoese Sponge Cake

The Genoese sponge cake (*Genoise* in French) is a whisked sponge cake with a very light open texture. Whisked sponge cakes can be fatless, but a little melted butter is added to a Genoese for a richer result and improved keeping qualities. This type of cake is used for Jelly rolls, ladyfingers, flans and layered gâteau. It is very quick to cook and impressive to serve.

1 Preheat the oven to 180ºC/350ºF/gas mark 4. Grease and line one 9in x 14in Jelly roll pan, or two 7in round sponge cake pans.

2 Sift the flour and salt together two or three times for a really light result.

3 Place the eggs and sugar in a large mixing bowl and whisk, with an electric beater, for about 10 minutes or until the mixture is really thick, creamy, and pale. A trail should be left in the mixture when you lift out the beaters.

4 Use a large spatula to fold in the sifted flour and melted butter, carefully and gently folding until smoothly mixed. It is vital to fold in all the flour evenly but try not to overmix as this will reduce the lightness of the cake.

5 Pour into the prepared sponge cake pans and bake for 10-12 minutes, until pale golden, just firm to the touch but very springy. Leave in the pan to cool for 3-5 minutes then transfer to a wire rack.

Makes one jelly roll or two 7in sponge cakes

1 cup all-purpose flour, sieved
pinch of salt
3 eggs
1/2 cup superfine sugar
1tbsp melted butter

Rolling Jelly Roll

1 While the cake is cooking, place a clean dish towel on a flat surface. Cover with wax paper and add a good sprinkling of superfine sugar. Invert the freshly-baked cake carefully onto this. Gently remove the baking paper.

2 Trim any crisp or uneven edges. Make a shallow cut 1in in from the narrow edge of the cake for easy rolling.

3 Cover with a clean sheet of wax paper. Use the dish towel to help roll up the cake, folding the paper inside. Leave until really cool.

4 To use, gently unroll and spread with filling (don't add too much). Gently re-roll the cake, using paper or a dish towel as support. Place join-side underneath – on a board or serving plate and decorate as required.

A Simple Decoration for Sponge Cake

Sifting confectioners' sugar over a template makes a very quick, simple and stunning decoration. The easiest option is to sift the sugar over a paper doily, preferably one with a wide and open design. Alternatively, you can make a template by drawing a pattern on clean card or wax paper and cutting it out neatly. Be generous with the sugar to give a strong design or color the sugar with edible powder colors.

There's no need to reserve this star design for Christmas as it is ideal at any time. Find the template on page 96 and use only the center part for smaller cakes.

1 Dredge the top of the cake with confectioners' sugar. Place the central star and outer circle templates in position, laying them gently over the sugar. Dredge with unsweetened cocoa.

2 Use tweezers and a palette knife to remove the central star, taking care not to spill cocoa on the sugar.

3 Remove the outer circle template and transfer the cake to a plate.

Madeira Cake

The British Madeira cake evolved from the American pound cake, originally made with a pound in weight of each ingredient. It has become popular (known by various names) all around the world. It is a longer-keeping, firmer cake than a whisked or Victoria sponge cake. It is ideal for those who do not like rich fruit wedding cake, is perfect for making gâteau with several layers, and it freezes very well. Often baked in a loaf pan, it is a delicious, simple teatime cake, especially if you add a warm sugar and lemon crusted topping.

Madeira Tip
• To test if a Madeira or any deep Victoria sponge cake or light or rich fruit cake is cooked, push a metal skewer into the middle. If it comes out free of sticky mixture, the cake is ready.

Variations
quantities for a 7in round or 6in square cake
• **Lemon or orange:** Add the grated zest of 1 orange or lemon, or 1tbsp orange flower water.
• **Nuts:** Replace a quarter of the flour with finely ground nuts of your choice.
• **Seeds:** Add 2tbsp poppy, caraway or mixed seeds.
• **Cornmeal or Polenta:** Replace up to half the flour with ready-to-use cornmeal or polenta.

Makes one 7in round, 6in square or 2lb loaf cake

1 cup butter or margarine, softened
1 cup superfine sugar
3 large eggs
2 cups all-purpose flour, sifted
1 1/2 tsp baking powder
salt
1 1/2 tsp vanilla extract (optional)

1 Grease and line a 7in round cake pan, or 6in square pan, or 2lb loaf pan. Preheat the oven to 180°C/350°F/gas mark 4. Beat the butter or margarine and sugar together until light and creamy. Gradually beat in the eggs until evenly blended.

2 Mix the sifted flour, baking powder and salt, and fold in gently using a large metal spoon. Add vanilla if required. Spoon the mixture into the prepared pan, level the top and bake for 1¼ hours, until a skewer pushed into the middle of the cake comes out clean and free of sticky mixture.

3 Remove the cake from the oven and leave to partly cool in the pan for 15–20 minutes. Then turn out onto a wire rack and leave to cool completely.

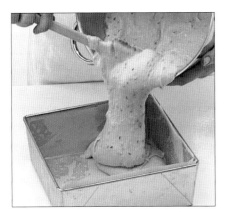

Lemon Sugar Topping

Use this variation to make a simple weekend cake that may well be eaten before it has time to cool! Spooning the topping over takes seconds and it does not need a rich filling. Bake the cake in a loaf pan so it is easy to slice.

4tbsp lemon juice
1tbsp corn syrup
2tbsp granulated or crystal sugar

While the cake is still warm and in the pan, pierce it with a skewer, several times right the way through. Warm the lemon juice and syrup together. Add the sugar and immediately spoon the mixture over the cake, so the flavored syrup soaks through leaving some of the sugar crystals on the top.

Slicing a Madeira or Sponge Cake

To slice a Madeira or sponge cake into several layers, allow it to cool completely. Chill a sponge cake briefly or Madeira for several hours if you need a fine, crumb-free cut. Place on a flat base – on a turntable if you have one – and place a sheet of wax paper on top so you do not leave finger indents. Use a large, sharp knife. Cut partly through, then give the cake a quarter-turn, keeping the knife in place, and continue cutting. Turn again and continue cutting until the cake is sliced through. The knife remains in the same position to produce even layers.

Madeira Tip

• Madeira cake freezes well so make double quantities. Bake one quantity in a rectangular or square pan, and freeze it in slabs or sections. Use it for Iced Fancies (page 56) or for quick family desserts.

• Plain cake trimmings are great crumbled into a fruit crumble dessert topping.

Madeira Proportions for Pan Sizes

Pan	Fat	Superfine Sugar	Eggs	Baking Powder	All-purpose Flour
7in round or 6in square	1 cup	1 cup	3	1½ tsp	2 cups
8in round or 7in square	1¼ cups	1¼ cups	4	2tsp	3 cups
9in round or 8in square	1¾ cups	1¾ cups	6	2½tsp	4 cups
10in round or 9in square	2 cups	2 cups	7	3tsp	4¾ cups
12in round or 11in square	2⅓ cups	2⅓ cups	10	4tsp	6 cups

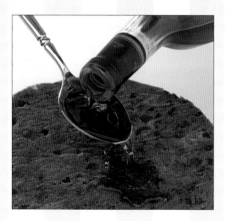

Feeding a fruit cake with brandy

• To feed your cake with brandy, rum or whisky during storage, unwrap and prick the top several times with a fine skewer. Spoon over 2-3tbsp spirit, leave to soak in well before re-wrapping and storing. Repeat 2-3 times at weekly intervals.

Fruit Cakes

A good homemade fruit cake is a rare treat these days, and festive occasions are incomplete without one. Why not make a small or individual fruit cake for a thank you or birthday gift for a special friend? It is better than any gift you might buy!

Dark Rich Fruit Cake

This dark and rich cake is made with dark ingredients – brown sugar, molasses, dark fruits – and traditionalists used to add gravy browning to ensure it was really dark! It is usually 'fed' with brandy before icing and can be kept for months, even years, thoroughly wrapped and stored in a cool dry place.

Makes one 8in square cake or 9in round cake

2lb mixed dried fruit
3/4 cup chopped mixed peel
1/2 cup candied cherries, chopped
1/2 cup pitted prunes, chopped
2-3tbsp sherry, brandy or rum
grated zest of 1 orange
grated zest of 1 lemon
3 cups all-purpose flour, sifted
1tsp ground cinnamon
1tsp ground mixed spice
1tsp salt
5 eggs
1 3/4 cups butter or margarine, softened
1 3/4 cups soft dark brown sugar
1tbsp molasses or corn syrup
Extra brandy to moisten the cooked cake

1 Prepare an 8in square or 9in round pan (page 11). Preheat the oven to 160°C/325°F/gas mark 3. In a large bowl, mix the dried fruit, peel, cherries, and prunes with the sherry, and orange and lemon zest. Leave to soak for 1–2 hours if possible to let the fruit soften and absorb the sherry.

2 Sift the flour, cinnamon, spice, and salt together. Lightly beat the eggs.

3 Cream the butter or margarine, sugar, and molasses together until paler and creamy. Gradually beat in the eggs, alternately adding the sifted flour in batches until it is well mixed.

4 Stir in the soaked fruits with any liquid from the bowl until evenly mixed. Spoon into the prepared pan and bake for 1 1/2 hours in the center of the oven.

5 Reduce the heat to 150°C/300°F/gas mark 2 and cook for a further 2 hours. If the cake begins to darken too quickly after the first hour, reduce the heat earlier.

6 Push a metal skewer into the middle of the cake to check that it is cooked. Leave to cool in the pan.

7 When cold, turn the cake out carefully. Overwrap thoroughly in double wax paper. Then wrap in foil and store in a cool place.

8 Remove the wax paper and pierce the cake with a fine metal skewer all over. Spoon a little brandy over the cake, allowing it to soak into the pierced holes.

Golden Fruit Cake

This light golden fruit cake can be decorated within weeks of baking. Using the lighter fruits, such as pineapple, apricot, ginger and golden raisins, and soaking them well with fruit juice and rum, makes a cake that is wonderfully rich and moist but in a lighter and fruitier way compared to a traditional dark fruit cake. It's a matter of taste really!

Makes one 8in round or 7in square cake

1¹/₂ cups mixed candied cherries, pineapple, ready-to-eat dried apricots, candied peel and/or crystallised ginger
1¹/₄ cups golden raisins
1¹/₄ cups raisins
finely grated zest and juice of 1 small orange
finely grated zest of 1 small lemon
2-3tbsp sherry, brandy or rum
1¹/₄ cups butter or margarine, softened
1¹/₄ cups superfine sugar
4 eggs
2³/₄ cups all-purpose flour, sifted
2tsp ground mixed spice
1¹/₂ tsp baking powder

1 In a large bowl mix together all the fruit, zest, juice, and sherry, brandy or rum. Cover and set aside in a cold place for several hours or overnight.

2 Prepare an 8in round or 7in square pan (page 11). Preheat the oven to 160°C/325°F/gas mark 3. Cream the butter or margarine and sugar together in a large bowl until light and fluffy.

3 Beat the eggs together, then gradually stir them into the creamed mixture, adding the flour, mixed spice, and baking powder in batches alternately with egg.

4 Gently stir in the soaked fruit and any juices to make a fairly soft mixture. Spoon into the prepared pan.

5 Smooth the top of the mixture and bake for 1¹/₂ hours, then reduce the heat to 150°C/300°F/gas mark 2 and bake for a further 1 hour. Check that the cake is cooked through. Cool in the pan.

6 Remove from the pan when cold and wrap in double-thick wax paper, then foil. Store in an airtight container until ready to decorate.

To Test if Fruit Cake is Cooked

• The cake should look slightly shrunk away from the sides of the pan. Press the top to check if it is firm.
• Push a clean metal skewer into the center of the cake, if it comes out with sticky mixture on it, return the cake to the oven.
• A fruit cake that is not fully cooked will definitely make a noise – a slight humming.

Fruit and nut topping

For a quick fruit cake decoration, simply arrange glacé fruits and whole nuts neatly on top of the matured cake and brush with corn syrup or honey.

Guide to Proportions for Pan Sizes (fruit cakes)

Ingredients	6in round 5in square	8in round 7in square	10in round 9in square	12in round 11in square
Dark Rich Fruit Cake				
Mixed dried fruit	1lb	1lb 14oz	3 1/2lb	5lb
Candied cherries	1/3 cup	1/2 cup	3/4 cup	1/2 cups
Flaked almonds or chopped nuts	1/2 cup	3/4 cup	1 1/4 cups	2 cups
Grated zest	1/2 lemon and 1/2 orange	1 lemon and 1 orange	1 lemon and 1 1/2 small oranges	1 1/2 lemons and 1 1/2 oranges
Orange juice	2tbsp	3tbsp	4tbsp	6tbsp
Sherry, brandy or rum	2tbsp	3tbsp	4tbsp	6tbsp
All-purpose flour	1 1/4 cups	2 1/4cups	4 cups	6 cups
Ground cinnamon	1/2tsp	1tsp	1 1/2tsp	2tsp
Ground mixed spice	1tsp	1 1/2 tsp	2tsp	2 1/2tsp
Salt	1/2tsp	1tsp	1 1/2tsp	2tsp
Eggs	3	4	6	9
Butter or margarine	1/2 cup plus 2tbsp	3/4 cup plus 2tbsp	1 3/4 cup	2 3/4 cup
Soft dark brown sugar	generous 1/2 cup	generous 3/4 cup	1 3/4 cup	2 3/4 cup
Molasses or corn syrup	1/2 tbsp	1tbsp	1 1/2 tbsp	2tbsp
Baking time	**1 1/2–2 hours**	**3–3 1/4 hours**	**4 hours**	**5–5 1/4 hours**
Golden Fruit Cake				
Mixed candied fruits: pineapple, cherries, apricots, mango, ginger, peel	1/4lb	generouse 1/2lb	1lb	1lb 5oz
Mixed golden raisins and raisins	1 1/2 cups	2 1/2 cups	2 1/4lb	3 1/4lb
Grated zest and juice of	1/2 orange	1 orange	1 1/2 orange	2 oranges
Sherry, brandy or liqueur	2tbsp	3tbsp	5tbsp	7-8tbsp
Butter or margarine	1 1/2 cups plus 3tbsp	1 cup	1 1/4lb	1lb 12oz
Soft light brown sugar	heaped 1/2 cup	1 cup	1 1/4lb	1lb 12oz
Eggs	2	4	6	10
All-purpose flour	1 1/2 cups	2 3/4 cups	5 cups	8 cups
Salt	1/2tsp	1tsp	1 1/2tsp	2tsp
Ground mixed spice	1tsp	2tsp	4tsp	6tsp
Baking powder	1tsp	2tsp	3 1/2tsp	5tsp
Baking time	**2 hours**	**2 1/2–3hours**	**3 3/4–4hours**	**5 hours**

Frostings

Frostings and fillings can transform a plain cake into a quick and simple teatime treat or a glamorous creation that keeps moist and delicious for longer. If you are making an impressive gâteau for a special occasion it can be prepared well in advance, as some of these mixtures will keep well for 3-4 days, or more.

Buttercream

This popular frosting gives a creamy rich finish. It can be flavored and colored in numerous ways. It is very easy to make and work with as its rich and creamy texture quickly covers any surface and fills any gap. Turn a simple sponge cake into an elegant gâteau in minutes by swirling buttercream delicately around the sides and piping it stylishly over the top.

1 Place the butter in a mixing bowl and beat until pale and fluffy. Gradually beat in the confectioners' sugar and lemon juice or vanilla. Beat in 1tbsp hot (boiled but not boiling) water, beating all the time to give a soft-peak consistency.

2 Add any chosen flavorings, with extra confectioners' sugar as necessary to retain the right consistency. Use immediately, or cover and chill until required. Bring the frosting back to room temperature before use.

Sufficient to fill and top two 8in sponge cakes

1/2 cup dairy butter, softened
2 1/4 cups confectioners' sugar, sifted
2tsp lemon juice or a few drops of vanilla extract

Variations

• Add 1tbsp unsweetened cocoa powder blended with 1tbsp hot water.
• Add 2tsp instant coffee blended with 1tsp boiling water.
• Add 2tsp finely grated zest of lemon, orange or lime.

Simple Finishes for Buttercream

The buttercream should be firm enough to give a good shape, but soft enough to spread easily. Simply swirling it over the top or around the sides of a cake always looks good. You can create many effects by using a fork, serrated comb, ruler or a palette knife.

1 Completely cover the cake with frosting. Use a flat ruler to flatten and smooth the top, or use the serrated edge to give a neat lined effect before adding the final decorations.

2 If you are not decorating the top and need a more stylish finish, pull a wide fork through the frosting in two different directions to make a pronounced square or angular pattern.

3 The side can be marked quickly with a small- to medium-sized palette knife. Place the clean and dry blade flat upright against the frosting. Press gently to smooth the frosting and create a luscious effect. Slide the knife upward and remove gently. Do not pull it away too sharply.

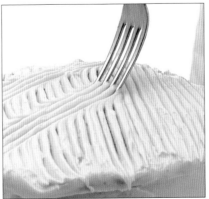

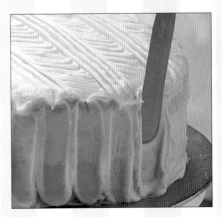

Meringue Buttercream

This richer and glossier version of buttercream is perfect for special occasion cakes and gâteau. It has a finer, lighter flavor than standard buttercream. It keeps really well in a container in the refrigerator and also on the cake.

Sufficient to coat two 8in sponge cakes
(topping and coating)

¹/₃ cup sugar
4¹/₂ tbsp water
3 egg whites
³/₄ cup dairy butter, softened
few drops of vanilla extract

Variations

• For a rich chocolate buttercream, melt and slightly cool 3 squares bitter chocolate. Work it into the meringue buttercream after the butter. This becomes quite stiff on cooling, so spread or pipe before it cools too much.
• Flavorings for buttercream (previous page) can be used in meringue buttercream.

1 Dissolve the sugar in the water in a small clean saucepan and then bring to the boil. Boil the sugar syrup to a temperature of 115°C/239°F.

2 Whisk the egg whites in a large heatproof bowl until they stand in soft peaks. Place over a pan of gently simmering water and whisk in the syrup. Continue whisking until the mixture is thick and glossy.

3 Cream the butter until it is soft. Using an electric whisk, gradually incorporate the butter into the meringue until the frosting is firm and glossy. Flavor with a little vanilla. Cover with plastic wrap and leave to cool before spreading or piping.

Glacé Icing

There is nothing simpler and quicker to make and use than a glacé icing. It can be colored and flavored, spread, drizzled and feathered, but not piped into sophisticated designs. Youngsters can make this frosting easily by themselves. Getting the consistency right is important or the frosting can run all over the place.

Sufficient to coat 12 cup cakes

1 cup confectioners' sugar
1-2tbsp water

1 Sift the sugar into a small bowl and add 1tbsp water. Mix until the water is worked in. Then add more water by ¹/₄ teaspoon at a time. When blended but thick, beat hard to remove any lumps. Then work in drops of water for the consistency you need.

2 Add flavoring and coloring to taste and use immediately. If not using the frosting immediately, cover closely with plastic wrap as the surface will very quickly crust over and the frosting with then go lumpy when stirred.

Icing cup cakes

Place the cakes on a wire rack. Place the rack on a board or over wax paper to catch any drips. Using a teaspoon, spoon frosting into the center of each cake, leave it to settle for a few seconds, then tap the edge of the cake rack very gently to help the frosting flow to its own smooth level.

Feather design

Make up a small quantity of a contrasting color of frosting. Alternatively, use melted chocolate or jelly (sieved). Spoon a little into a small paper piping bag without a nozzle. Snip off the end to make a small hole and pipe lines or circles on the wet white frosting. Use a skewer or toothpick to pull lines through the two colors to give the feathered effect.

American Frosting

Used for many traditional cakes, such as carrot cake or angel cake, this frosting peaks wonderfully and has a mallowy texture, with a slight crust when cold. It takes only 8–10 minutes to make but is best whisked until cool before using. On an uncut cake it keeps well for several days.

Sufficient to cover top and sides of a 9in cake

²/₃ cup superfine sugar
1 tbsp water
1 tbsp corn syrup
1 large egg white

1 Mix all the ingredients together in a large clean heatproof bowl. Place over a saucepan of simmering water. Whisk lightly until the sugar has dissolved.

2 Whisk hard for several minutes, until the mixture forms stiff peaks. Remove from the heat and continue whisking until the frosting cools.

3 Spread the frosting generously over the top and sides of the cake.

4 Make peaks or attractive swirls, and leave until cold, by which time the frosting will have acquired a slightly crisp surface.

Italian Meringue

Italian meringue is a very stable mixture and it is often used as a frosting. The egg whites are whisked with syrup instead of sugar. Like American Frosting, it also forms a slight crust when cold but it remains gooey underneath.

Sufficient to cover the top and sides of a 9in cake

³/₄ cup superfine sugar
6 tbsp water
2 egg whites

1 Dissolve the sugar in the water in a medium saucepan and bring to the boil. Boil until clear and syrupy.

2 Whisk the egg whites in a large heatproof bowl over a saucepan of simmering water until they are stiff.

3 Gradually pour in the hot syrup in a slow trickle, whisking hard all the time. Continue whisking until the meringue is very stiff and glossy. Remove from the heat and keep whisking until the frosting is cool.

4 Use immediately or cover with plastic wrap and keep in a cool place (not the refrigerator) for 2–3 days.

Marzipan

Also known as almond paste, marzipan is a pliable mixture of ground almonds, confectioners' sugar, egg and lemon juice. It is used as a base coat for a madeira or rich fruit cake to prevent the oils from the cake seeping out into the white frosting. Marzipan provides a smooth surface for coating and decorating, and it improves the keeping qualities of a cake. You do not have to use marzipan – or you could simply apply a very thin layer.

Bought marzipan is available natural, uncolored and known as white marzipan, or as egg yellow marzipan. Homemade is always much paler than bought. Marzipan can be colored with food colors and molded into different shapes for decoration. Both shapes and the covered cake need 10-12 hours to dry out and firm up.

Marzipan Tips

• Keep marzipan cool and do not knead too much as it can become oily.

• When rolling out, use a little sifted confectioners' sugar to prevent sticking. Do not add other flours, such as cornstarch, as they ferment during storage.

• Homemade marzipan will keep in the refrigerator for 2-3 months, or it can be frozen for up to a year.

• Leftover marzipan can be grated and added to crumble toppings or used to flavor cakes and desserts.

• A Simnel cake has a layer of marzipan placed in the middle of the mixture before baking.

• For good keeping qualities, a fruit cake must be well fitted on the board, and the marzipan should create a complete airtight seal before you begin icing.

Health Concerns

If you make cakes for gifts, or for public occasions, or are worried about the use of raw egg in marzipan or royal icing, buy dried egg products instead. These ingredients have been heat treated to ensure they are safe. Alternatively, buy marzipan or frosting. To ensure it keeps well, boil apricot glaze before use.

Marzipan

Makes about 1lb
Sufficient to cover top and sides of one 8in round or 7in square cake

2 cups ground almonds
$\frac{1}{2}$ cup superfine sugar
1 cup confectioners' sugar, sifted
1 egg, lightly beaten
1tbsp lemon juice

1 Mix the almonds, superfine and confectioners' sugars in a bowl. Work in the egg and lemon juice until the mixture is fairly stiff.

2 Turn out onto a lightly sugared work surface and knead gently for a few minutes, until really smooth.

3 Wrap tightly in plastic wrap or place in a polythene bag until required.

Apricot Glaze

Apricot glaze is used to keep the marzipan in place. Warm 5-6tbsp apricot jelly with 2tbsp water in a small saucepan. Bring to the boil, stirring, and then sieve the jelly to remove lumps of fruit. Cool slightly.

Covering a Cake with Marzipan

There are two ways to marzipan a cake. Either the all-in-one method, which is ideal for round cakes and as a base for sugar paste, or by covering the top and sides separately. The latter gives a cake with squarer edges and is used as a base for royal icing.

If necessary, trim off any slight dome of mixture to flatten the top of the cake. Brush with a little apricot glaze and invert the cake onto a board. This provides a flat surface to work on. Fill any large holes, or gaps around the base of the cake with pieces or strips of marzipan, smoothing them in place. Brush the cake all over with apricot glaze.

All-in-one Method

1 Measure the diameter of the cake. Add double the depth of the side and at least 1in extra. Roll out the marzipan on a surface lightly dusted with sifted confectioners' sugar to a circle or square the size you have calculated.

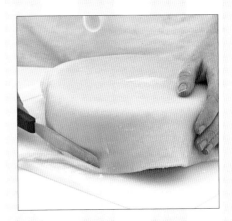

2 To lift the marzipan, roll it loosely over the rolling pin, then lift it over the cake, and unroll it in place.

3 Gently ease the marzipan down the sides pressing lightly so it sticks. Smooth out the curves and around the corners of a square cake. With a sharp knife cut away the excess and neaten the base edges with a palette knife.

Two-stage Method

1 Roll out half the marzipan and cut a circle, or square, to fit the top of the cake. Gently place this on top, easing it exactly to the edges and smooth over.

2 Roll out the rest of the marzipan and cut four side pieces measured to the height and length of the cake sides. Attach each piece individually, carefully trimming off the excess at the corners. Gently smooth over the joins. Brush each section of cake with apricot glaze when necessary, rather than glazing the entire cake, so you can hold the uncoated sides while you work.

3 For a round cake, cut a strip of paste to fit the height of the cake (including the top covering of marzipan) and long enough to fit the circumference. Carefully roll this up from the short side.

4 Place the marzipan roll against the side of the cake and unroll it carefully while turning the board. Press it gently into position as you turn. Then trim and seal the joins neatly.

Royal Icing

Royal icing is the traditional British choice for very special formal cakes. It gives an elegant bright-white covering and it can be used in very simple or very complex ways. Antique Victorian and Edwardian designs show the ultimate use of piped decoration, but even simple, minimal, icing can give a very elegant, modern result.

Make royal icing using raw ingredients or you can buy commercially prepared powder mixes. These mixes include precise proportions of albumen (egg white), glucose or glycerine necessary for making icing for different tasks. For example, glycerine is added to give a coating icing that stays soft for cutting, while run-out icing needs sufficient albumen for it to become dry and hard, but contains no glycerine.

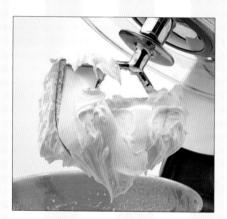

Royal Icing

Makes sufficient to coat top and sides of an 8in round or 7in square cake

2 egg whites or 1¹/₂ oz albumen powder
1tbsp lemon juice
2tsp glycerine (use only for coating icing)
1lb confectioners' sugar, sifted twice

1 Lightly whisk the egg whites, lemon juice and glycerine (if using) in a large bowl. If using albumen powder, make it up according to the packet instructions. Gradually work in the sifted confectioners' sugar.

2 Continue beating until the icing is stiff, smooth and glossy. For flat coating, the icing should stand in soft peaks, so when you lift the spoon out of the bowl the icing stands in a peak with a gentle curve.

3 Cover the bowl of icing with a clean damp dish towel or plastic wrap and leave for about 1 hour before using to allow any air bubbles to disperse.

Flat Icing a Round Cake

When flat icing a cake, you will achieve the best results by giving the top and sides 2-3 coats, allowing each coat to dry well before adding the next. Coat the top and side in separate stages, allowing them to dry between coats. Speed things up by storing the cake in an airy, dry place under a lamp if possible. Before you move on to the next stage, gently scrape off any lumps or snags with a craft knife and fill any holes with soft icing.

1 To coat the top, place 2-3 tablespoons of icing in the middle and gently spread it over with a palette knife. Do this using a flat paddling movement. The top of the cake should be even covered.

 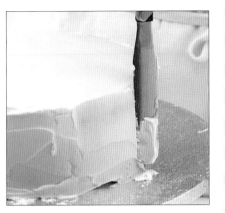

2 Draw a straight edge or clean icing ruler firmly and smoothly across the top of the cake. Hold the ruler at an angle of about 45 degrees. Do this in one movement – if you stop you will have a ridge. If necessary, repeat the whole process, but remember that the next two layers will cover up any problems. Set aside until firm.

3 To coat the side, spread the icing roughly around the cake with a palette knife, making sure all the marzipan is evenly covered.

4 Use a plain-edged cake scraper, and start at the opposite side of the cake, furthest away from you. Hold the turntable with the left hand, and the scraper in the right hand. The scraper should be vertical, and at an angle of about 45 degrees. Turn the cake steadily in one continuous movement while scraping the icing firmly. When both hands meet, carefully slide the left hand out of the way, and pull the scraper toward you. This can be repeated, but unless the coat is really uneven it will be improved when the next coating is applied. Set aside until firm.

5 When the icing has dried, smooth any rough edges carefully. Gently scrape off any rough ridges, and then coat top and sides again.

6 Once you are happy with the flat icing, cover the board in a similar way to the sides. Spread a thin coat first with a palette knife, then gently drag the scraper over the board, pulling it toward you at the end to avoid creating a ridge.

Royal Icing Tips

• Royal icing can be made in a food mixer but not a food processor.

• Royal icing benefits from being left to rest for at least 1 hour so any air bubbles can disperse.

• Keep the icing well covered with plastic wrap or a damp cloth at all times to prevent it from drying out before you have finished using it.

• Use a turntable to lift the cake to a comfortable working height and to turn it easily while you work.

• Always let one coating become totally dry before repairing it or applying another coat.

Flat Icing a Square Cake

1 Coat the top in exactly the same way as for a round cake.

2 For the sides, coat lightly all over as for a round cake. Then smooth one side at a time with the same angled and firm action. Finish at the corner by bringing the scraper off the cake toward you. Start the next side by joining up with the previous edge and continue this way around all four sides. Set aside until firm. Apply second and third coats in similar stages.

Sugar Paste Tips

• Always keep sugar paste covered when you are not working with it. It quickly forms a crust that can cause lumps. If it does dry out, cut off any hard edges, then knead it again gently inside a plastic bag.

• Keep a clean pastry brush handy to brush away any cake or dry paste crumbs that might ruin your sugar paste.

• Don't let sugar paste get too warm when handling it or it becomes difficult to roll out and handle.

• Always use sifted confectioners' sugar to dust the surface and rolling pin as any small lumps will spoil the sugar paste. Use cornflour for very fine designs in flower paste or pastillage.

• The finished coat of sugar paste can be gently polished with a special smooth plastic smoother, or with a small lump of leftover paste wrapped in a polythene bag. Dust with a little confectioners' sugar.

Sugar Paste

Sugar paste is also known as ready-to-roll icing, or it may sometimes be called rolled fondant. It is easy to use, very forgiving and great fun for everyone to use. Sugar paste gives a professional finish with little effort. A sugar paste covering will keep a cake fresher for longer than, for example, buttercream. Most larger stores sell sugar paste and specialist cake decorating suppliers have a selection of pastes.

Cakes can be wonderfully colorful and theme cakes are great fun to prepare. For the more complex designs, plaques, and lace or filigree work, there are other sugar pastes that can be made at home. These are easy to prepare if you have a mixer, but you can also buy prepared powders or pastes from specialist shops. The harder pastes used for modeling and making flowers are not intended to be eaten – they do not contain inedible ingredients but they set to a hard, unpalatable finish. Decorations made from these pastes will keep indefinitely if stored in an airtight container in a cool dry place.

Modeling paste: This is stronger than standard sugar paste, yet very pliable for making models, animals and larger shapes. It contains gum tragacanth, an ingredient that helps to give the paste strength.

Flower paste: Also known as petal or gum paste, this also contains gum tragacanth, as well as a little white vegetable fat. This can be rolled and molded thinly to make delicate decorations, flowers and foliage.

Pastillage: This dries rock hard. It is ideal for intricate, tall or arched designs.

Sugar Paste

1 egg white or 3/4oz albumen powder
2tbsp liquid glucose, warmed
1lb confectioners' sugar, sifted

Sufficient to cover top and sides of an 8in round or 7in square cake

1 Place the egg white in a mixing bowl. Alternatively, make up the albumen as directed on the packet. Lightly beat in the liquid glucose. Gradually work in the confectioners' sugar with a wooden spoon until it begins to form a paste.

2 Knead the paste gently into a ball with your fingertips. Turn onto a clean dry surface and knead well until smooth. Dust the surface with sifted confectioners' sugar if the paste sticks, and work in extra confectioners' sugar if it is too sticky.

3 If you are not using it immediately, wrap the paste tightly in plastic wrap and store in a cool place or in the refrigerator.

Covering a Round Cake with Sugar Paste

A sponge cake or fruit cake can be covered directly, without a marzipan layer, as long as the surface is flat and free from loose crumbs. Lumps will show through the sugar paste.

1 Cover a sponge cake with a light coating of apricot glaze (page 26) or buttercream. Brush a fruit cake with boiled water, or clear alcohol, such as gin or vodka.

2 Measure from the base of one side of the cake, over the top, and down to the base on the other side. Knead the paste briefly to warm and soften it, then roll out on a sugar-dusted surface, into a circle 1-2in larger than the total top and sides measurement.

3 Roll the paste loosely over the rolling pin, and lift it carefully over the cake. Gently unroll it, and smooth the paste down the sides. Trim the excess from the bottom edge.

4 For a polished result, smooth the surface with a plastic smoother, or use a small lump of extra paste wrapped in a small plastic bag.

5 To cover the board, roll out a band of paste the same width and circumference as the exposed board. Roll this up loosely. Brush the board with a little boiled water or alcohol, then carefully unwrap the paste on to it. Trim and seal the paste at the join, and then trim the edge around the board.

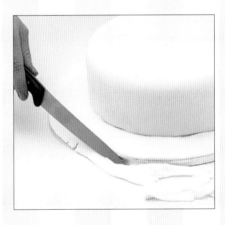

Covering a Square Cake with Sugar Paste

1 Measure from the base of one side of the cake, over the top, and down to the base on the other side. Roll out the paste large enough to cut out a square of paste 2.5-5cm (1-2in) larger than this measurement. Carefully roll the paste loosely on the pin, and then lift it over the prepared cake, and unroll in position.

2 Smooth the paste from the center out to the corners. Lift the excess paste at the corners as you smooth it on the cake and down the sides.

3 Smooth the paste well. Trim the excess paste from the edges and then cover the board, as above, if you wish.

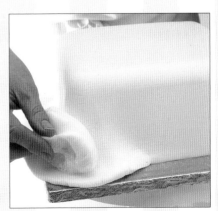

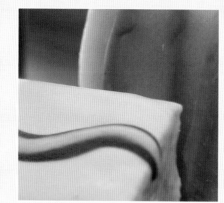

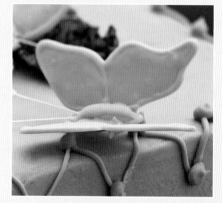

Decorating with Style

The fun part of making a cake is the decorating and finishing. Seeing your idea or design come to fruition, and hearing the appreciation of family and friends, is what it's all about. Whether you have spent a couple of hours or a couple of days creating the cake, the end result is what matters.

Map the design fully before you start so that you can assemble colors, tools, trimmings and any specialist items. If you haven't used a technique before, take time to try it out before working on the cake. Allow for breakages by making extra decorations. Plan your work in stages, working backward from the day the cake is required to the baking day.

Drying time is among the most important stages – for marzipan to harden, frosting to set, and sugar paste to firm up. Any delicate decorations, flowers and cut-outs will need at least 1-2 days to dry before they can be assembled on the final cake. Do not forget to plan for setting and drying or you may run out of time.

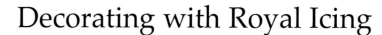

Royal Icing Tips

- Be well organised and have everything you will need at hand before you start working with royal icing.
- Make up sufficient icing in the first place, to be able to use it to firm up a small quantity of thinned icing that has become too soft.
- Remember not to add glycerine or liquid glucose for piping or run-outs – the decorations must set hard.
- Keep all bowls or bags of colored mixture covered with plastic wrap or a damp cloth at all times.
- Use a damp, fine paintbrush to correct (rub out or gently brush off) any minor piping errors, or pull out the points or corners of flowers.
- Mix the required color, then check the consistency and add a little of the original batch of royal icing to firm up the icing, or single drops of water to loosen or thin the icing slightly.

Royal icing was created for royal occasions, and often used for very intricate designs far too complex and time consuming for the majority of today's requirements. However, a traditional occasion, for example a wedding, calls for something really special by way of a decorated cake, and many people like the royal icing finish. Royal icing more versatile than it first appears to be. It can be used for delicate, simple designs that are modern and do not require great skill or too much practice. Getting the consistency right for piping royal icing is vital, particularly if you are decorating several cakes or tiers – as your wrists will ache if the icing is too stiff.

Soft Peak

This is the basic consistency for flat icing a marzipan-covered cake. The icing should hold a peak that just falls over slightly at the tip.

Full or Firm Peak

Suitable for most piping tasks. The icing peaks stay firm and sharp. Don't make it too firm or it will be difficult to pipe.

Very Firm Peak

This is the ideal consistency for a Christmas snow scene. Keep working in more confectioners' sugar until it stands up in stiff, short sharp peaks.

Run-out Icing

For outlining a template the icing needs to be almost as stiff as soft peak – maybe a touch softer.

Flooding Consistency

To 'flood' a shape, the icing needs to be much looser. To test, spoon a little into a bowl and the lines and edges of any peaks should fade within 8 seconds.

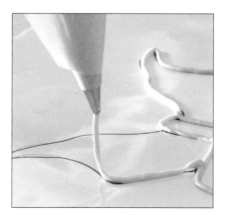

To Make and Fill a Piping Bag

You can never have too many small piping bags. Even though you may buy ready made bags, there will be occasions when you need to make one.

1 Start with a square of waxed paper, approximately 10in square. Fold in half into two triangles. Crease from the middle of the long side to the point.

2 Holding the points opposite the long side with one hand, roll the left corner over to line up with them. Do the same with the other corner so it wraps around, making a cone with all the points neatly together.

3 Shuffle the points until they meet neatly. Ensure the cone has a good shape, with a firm point at the bottom.

4 Fold over and secure the points you are holding with tape or a staple clip. If you are using a nozzle, snip a little off the tip of the bag and insert the nozzle.

5 Only half fill with icing. Then fold over the top to enclose the icing.

6 Fold the corners firmly in toward the middle, and fold the top over again. Gently squeeze the icing down into the nozzle. If you are not using a nozzle, cut off a tiny point from the tip of the piping bag equivalent to the size of the nozzle you need.

Nozzles

• For fine lines use a small plain nozzle, no. 1 or 2.

• For small rosettes, stars or shells use a no. 5, 7, 9, or 11.

• For ropes use a 42, 43, or 44.

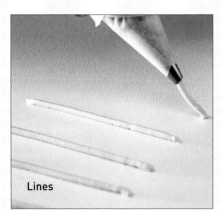

Lines

Piping

Hold the bag in one hand, between thumb and fingers, so that the thumb can be used to push the icing down the bag. Use the other hand as a support. Firmly, but with even pressure, push the icing down the bag, trying not to squeeze the whole lot with your hand.

To pipe lines: Touch the surface with the nozzle to attach the icing first. Start to squeeze as you lift up and slowly pull backward. Let the icing hang without pulling so that you can position the line or shape. Stop applying pressure when you see the end of the line. Lower the nozzle down to touch the surface and seal the line in place. Lift off the nozzle.

To pipe a snail trail: This is a delicate line with small regular dots. It looks pretty and more modern than many other designs. Start by piping a very small ball, release pressure, and drag a short, piped line. Then apply pressure to pipe another small ball. Continue for the required length.

To work cornelli or filigree piping: This looks very effective and can cover large areas quickly. You have to be very consistent with the pressure and size of line for this to look good. The design consists of m's and w's run on together without stopping. These two letters create a soft-flowing design to fill any area. Practice first.

To pipe balls: Touch the surface and pipe without moving until the icing forms the size of ball you require. Then release the pressure before lifting up the nozzle to avoid leaving a long peak. The size of the ball is dictated by the length of time you pipe on the spot.

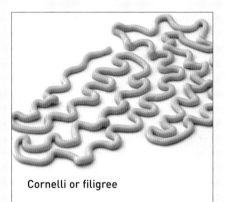

Snail trail

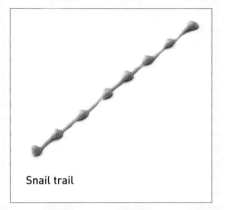

Cornelli or filigree

Stars

Rosettes

Balls

Shells

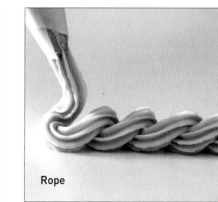

Rope

To pipe stars: Using a star nozzle, hold the bag vertical and steady on the surface. Apply pressure without moving the bag. Pull up sharply to make a small or large point. Use a larger nozzle and more pressure for a large star.

To pipe a rosette: Using a star nozzle, hold the bag vertical, touch the surface and squeeze out the beginning of a shell shape. At the same time, rotate the bag in a very small circle and raise it. Pull up and release pressure to leave a pointed tip.

To pipe shells: Touch the nozzle down on the surface, squeeze at an angle of 45° until sufficient icing comes out. Release the pressure and point the nozzle down to cut off the icing, at the same time, pull back to make a very slight tail. Start the next shell immediately on this tail to link the shells.

To pipe a rope: Begin by piping a rosette but do not finish off. Continue rotating the bag, at the same time as moving it along in a line.

To pipe a small flower: Use a flat petal tube (no. 57). Use a little icing to attach a small piece of wax paper to a flower nail. Hold the tube flat with its wide end in the center and squeeze out a petal shape, at the same time twisting the flower nail in a full circle. Pipe another petal partly over the first in the same way. Repeat. Finally pipe one petal in the opposite direction to fill the gap. Pipe yellow dots in the center and leave to set.

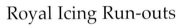

Royal Icing Run-outs

A run-out is a hard icing shape. The outline is piped and the center filled in or 'flooded' with softened royal icing. Run-outs have to set hard, so glycerine must not be used. If different colors are used, it is important to ensure that one area has set and formed a dry skin before piping adjoining areas.

Trace the design on wax paper. Cover with silicone paper, securing it in place with a little icing. Using run-out consistency icing, pipe over the design outline and any inner lines. Leave to dry – place under a warm lamp to speed up the drying time. Fill the outline with softer, flooding-consistency icing. Leave for up to 24 hours to dry completely. Use a palette knife to lift the run-out off the paper. Attach to the cake with a little icing.

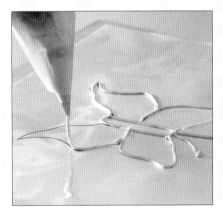

To create run-outs with a three-dimensional effect, pipe and fill separate sections. Assemble the sections at different angles or levels directly on the surface of the cake, supporting each piece with soft paper or a corner of sponge until firm.

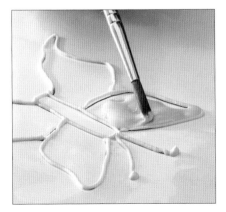

Decorating with Sugar Paste

Sugar paste is a versatile and forgiving medium to work with, especially for fun designs and theme cakes. Be as adventurous or creative as you dare because you can re-model a shape – whether it's a teddy bear or a fine rose – until you get it right. Effects like frills and folds, pleats and patterns, ribbons and bows are easily made using cutters, crimpers, and specialty modeling tools available. Colors can be used to shade and marble the paste, or to dust, paint, and sponge on. Once finished, sugar paste does not take long to dry, so the cake can be assembled in a day or two.

Cut-out Shapes

All sorts of flat shapes can be cut out of sugar paste. Letters, numbers, flowers, or animals – there are endless cutters, or for a specific design, draw a template and cut it out in cardboard or firm paper. Once the shapes are cut, leave them on a board to dry out for 1-2 hours. Cut-outs can be given a three-dimensional effect by cutting two sizes of the same design and sticking them together. Alternatively, gently bend the shape over soft paper or a corner of sponge and leave until dry. Paint or color shapes as required.

Coloring Carefully

Sugar paste takes color easily but some colors are stronger than others. When buying colors, remember that pastes and powders are easier to work with than liquids.

• Take a small amount of sugar paste and use a toothpick to add the color drop by drop, kneading in each addition until you achieve the desired color. Cover and set aside until required.

• There are two ways to marble paste. Either avoid working in the color thoroughly or make up batches of paste in two or more colors, and then gently knead the different pastes together to achieve the required effect.

• For topping a cake, roll out and use the paste immediately and allow it to dry before adding decorations.

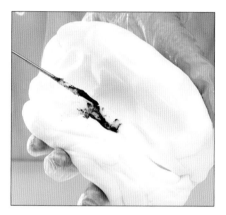

Delicate Designs

Pastillage and flower paste are used to make very delicate flowers or fine shapes, and for designs that need to be attached to wire. Roll out the pastillage on a surface lightly dusted with cornstarch and cut out using a template and a damp knife. If using a fine patchwork template, grease the edges with a little white fat to help the paste come off the template easily. Allow to dry for about 2 hours on a surface lightly dusted with cornstarch. Turn over and dry for a further 2 hours or until dry – larger or thicker pieces may need longer. Paint or decorate when absolutely dry. Assemble shapes, or attach plaques with royal icing. Handle with care, as they are very fragile. Make more shapes than you will need, to allow for breakages.

Roping and Plaiting

Rolling and twisting one, two or more colors of sugar paste or marzipan together produces exciting and varied rope effects.

Straight-edged rope: Roll the chosen colors out to the same thickness and cut even strips. Twist them together gently and evenly. For cake edging, attach strips to the dampened cake or board as you twist them so there is minimal movement of the rope.

Rounded roping or plaiting: Roll out the colors into long thin sausage shapes of the same length and thickness. Twist or plait colors together. Roll the rope together gently if you need to make it longer or want a flattened effect.

Note: For speed and ease use a sugar paste gun.

Coloring and Molding Tips

• Use fine plastic gloves when kneading in strong colors, such as black or Christmas green.

• Keep a tiny piece of colored paste as reference in case you need to match up colors later.

• Wrap in plastic wrap or place in a polythene bag immediately.

• Work delicate items between pieces of polythene or plastic wrap.

Flowers

Beautiful flowers and blossoms can be made using pastillage, flower paste, or marzipan. Use a flower cutter with a two-piece rubber mold to create the final shape and veining. Alternatively, use a simple blossom cutter with a plunger, and finish the blossoms by hand.

1 Roll out the paste quite thinly. When you are experienced you can use pastillage or flower paste very thinly to produce delicate results.

2 Cut out the flower or blossom shapes and press them between rubber molds lightly dusted with cornstarch. Tease the blooms out onto a gently curved surface so that they bend and curl like real flowers.

3 Leave the flowers to dry for several hours. To paint them, use a tiny brush dipped in edible color, and catch the edges of the petals or brush fine lines on the petals. Attach silver or pearl centers with a drop of royal icing. Dust with flower colors, silver, or pearl dusting powders.

Plunger Cutter: Alternatively, cut out blossoms with a plunger cutter. These may be small or very tiny. Using a toothpick or frilling tool, indent the middle of the blossom curve to give a petal effect.

Frilly Petals: For a floppy petal effect, gently run over the edges of each petal with a toothpick until it is frilled up.

Frills and Folds

Simple frills can be used to edge a cake or board. The same technique can be used to finish the centers of flowers or petal edges.

Frilled strip: Roll out a strip of paste or marzipan on a lightly sugared board. Roll a toothpick or friller tool firmly along one edge. Keep moving so that the paste does not stick to the board. Lift the frill carefully to put it in place. Or roll up into a tight carnation-style flower head. For a different effect fold or pleat the edge of the paste by pinching gently.

Frilled circle: Cut out a circle of paste. Roll a toothpick or friller tool at intervals around the edge.

Circular frill: Frill a circle of paste as above, then stamp out the middle with a cutter. A small circular frill can be applied to a figure model as a skirt.

Larger circular frills can be used as edging or top decoration on cakes.

Frilled or pleated covered board: Roll a toothpick over the paste covering a board to give a frilled or pleated effect.

Using Simple Tools

A crimper or embossing tool is quick and easy to use. The choice is huge. The paste or marzipan must be soft for this technique.

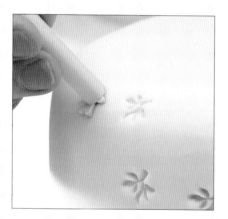

Embossing tools: Dip the tool into confectioners' sugar to prevent the paste from sticking. Gently press the tool into the paste to make regular or random patterns to suit your design. Dust or paint color over immediately and leave to dry.

Crimping tools: For top and bottom edges of a cake, or a board edge, pinch the crimper on the paste so that it is about 1/4 –1/3in thick.

Decorating with Chocolate

Chocolate is popular for all types of cakes, including more formal occasions such as weddings. It is generally easy to work with for both simple and stunning effects.

Mixed with butter, sugar, or cream in varying proportions, melted chocolate makes a variety of excellent coatings and fillings. Bitter, milk or white chocolate can all be used. Two different types of result can be achieved by working with the chocolate either warm or when cold and set. For the best flavor, use a good-quality chocolate with a high percentage of cocoa solids.

Ganache

8 squares bitter, milk or white chocolate,
   broken into pieces
$1/2$ cup whipping cream
$1/4$ cup dairy butter, softened

1 Put the chocolate in a bowl. Heat the cream in a small saucepan until it is almost boiling.

2 Pour the hot cream into the chocolate, stirring until the chocolate has melted, and blended with the cream.

3 While still warm, work in the butter, which should be almost runny but not translucent.

Flavoring ganache: Add any of the following before the ganache becomes firm.
- 1-2tsp finely grated orange or lemon zest
- $1/2$-1tsp grated nutmeg or ground cinnamon
- 2-3tbsp brandy, whisky, Cointreau or your favorite spirit
- 1-2tbsp strong black coffee or fresh orange juice

Coating with ganache: Allow the ganache to cool and thicken slightly. Pour it all over the top of the cake in one firm swift movement. Spread the ganache gently for an even covering, or if it is still very runny, tap the cake board gently on the surface so the coating runs evenly. Leave to cool and set.

Frosting or piping with ganache: Leave until cool but not set. Beat the ganache well with a wooden spoon and it will lighten into a fluffy frosting. Spread this evenly as a filling or over the top or sides of a cake. For piping, spoon into a medium piping bag fitted with a star nozzle and pipe rosettes or roping around the cake.

Melting Chocolate

Chocolate can be melted in a bowl over hot water or in the microwave. It is important to remember a few guidelines.
- When melting chocolate in a bowl over a saucepan of hot water, the water must not boil – it should barely simmer. The base of the bowl must be higher than the water level. If the bowl sits in the water the chocolate will overheat. It will thicken, become oily and/or separate slightly – it is said to 'seize'.
- If any water or moisture (including steam), comes into contact with the chocolate it will seize as above.
- Do not stir too much until the chocolate has fully melted.
- Microwave carefully and on medium, not a higher setting, and in short bursts of 30-50 seconds. When overcooked or burnt the chocolate is useless.

Chocolate Curls

Chocolate Curl Tips
• Do not work with too much chocolate.
It is easier to observe and control the
temperature of small quantities.
• Good-quality chocolate can be more
temperamental than less-expensive
products as it has a higher cocoa fat content.
• White chocolate cools and sets slower
than bitter chocolate.

Make curls in advance, not in a last-minute rush, and store them in an airtight container in a dry place. They will keep for a few days. Do not put them in the refrigerator, as condensation will form on them when you bring them back to room temperature.

Melt about 4 squares of chocolate until thoroughly melted and quite smooth. Spread out in two batches on clean flat trays or boards. Marble is ideal to work on as it is cool but other smooth surfaces are also good. Spread the chocolate smoothly and evenly but not too thinly. Let it cool or leave in a cool place briefly to set. The chocolate will lose its gloss when ready. Watch the chocolate closely – when it has become too set it will be brittle and will not roll. The atmosphere and heat of the kitchen will determine how quickly it sets. Transfer it to a cooler place, if necessary, for a few minutes. You can re-melt the chocolate leftovers and repeat the process until you have sufficient curls.

Curls, caraque, cigars or rolls are made from melted chocolate using different tools.
Caraque: This is the term for long thin spiky curls. Use a large blade or spatula, and pull it toward you at an acute angle over the surface of the chocolate. The chocolate will curl and roll for as long as you keep going at the same angle.
Rolls or cigars: Use a clean new paint stripper tool or scraper. Push it through the chocolate making a thicker, more even roll.
Thick curls: Use an ice cream scoop or the blunt edge of a round cutter to scrape off stubby, round curls.

Chocolate Leaves

Select firm fresh leaves – holly and bay are ideal as they have a well-defined shape. Wash and polish them well. Brush cooling chocolate quite thickly on the underside of each leaf. Place on wax paper or foil, and leave to set completely. When ready to use the leaves, gently peel the real leaves off the chocolate leaves.

 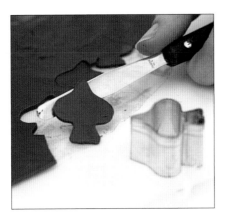

Marbling Chocolate

Marbled chocolate can be very effective for cake toppings or cut-out shapes and leaves. Melt contrasting types of chocolate separately. Pour some of one type onto a board or the top of a cake. Then add small spoonfuls of the contrasting chocolate. Use a small spoon or knife to swirl and pull the chocolates into an exciting marbled mixture. Leave to set. Marbled chocolate can also be used for cut-outs or curls.

Chocolate Shapes

Cut out shapes from thinly spread melted chocolate, prepared as for making curls. Be sure to spread the chocolate evenly and quite thinly. Carefully transfer cut-out shapes to a board or container, using a palette knife, and store them in a cool, dry place. Sharp, distinct and simple shapes such as squares, semi-circles, stars, or teddy bears, are more successful than fussy or intricate outlines that may not stamp out easily in chocolate.

Piping Chocolate

As it cools, chocolate develops a lovely flowing texture, but do not let it get too cool. Use a small paper piping bag without a nozzle so the chocolate can be softened in the bag in the microwave if necessary, if it should become too cool. Alternatively, use a small bag with a no.1 nozzle.

Simple piped shapes can be used to decorate cakes or desserts. Draw or trace the design onto wax paper. Place a sheet of cellophane over the top and pipe the chocolate over the design. Move the cellophane and pipe over the shape again. Repeat until you have made enough shapes. Cool until set.

Shapes or designs can also be piped straight onto a cake.

For a stunning result, use contrasting types of chocolate. Pipe or drizzle them alternately on the design. Paper can be shaped, for example over a rolling pin, before the chocolate sets. The chocolate will then harden in a curve.

 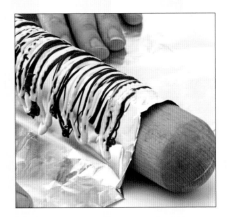

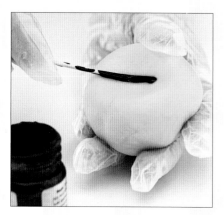

Decorating with Marzipan

Marzipan is similar to sugar paste to handle and it can be used for the same techniques. Besides covering fruit cakes it is mainly used for molding and modeling animals, baskets, flowers, and fruit.

Marzipan is more oily and moist than sugar paste therefore it needs to be left longer to dry out. A little sugar paste or pastillage can be added to marzipan to make it stronger. Marzipan can also become crumbly when dried but it can be softened by slowly kneading in a little glucose or white vegetable fat. Then allow the paste to stand for 24–48 hours before use. Your hands are the best tools for modeling, but you will also need shaped modeling tools. Remember to keep marzipan wrapped when it is not in use to prevent it from drying.

Coloring Marzipan

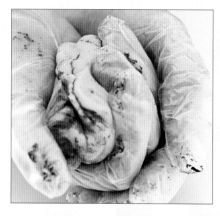

Use a natural marzipan base and make up light colors first. Powder and paste colors, made with alcohol or used dry are best. Water-based colors can make marzipan too moist. If you do use water-based color, add it drop by drop with a toothpick or the tip of a tiny knife.
• Knead the marzipan to work in the color. As the paste warms up in your hands, the color will begin to blend in more evenly.
• Add color gradually until you see how strong it is. Use fine plastic gloves when mixing in dark or strong colors.
• Chocolate marzipan, with unsweetened cocoa powder kneaded in, is very successful in color and flavor. You may want to add extra sugar or sugar syrup to large batches, to prevent the paste from drying out too much.

Marzipan Petit Fours

Marzipan can be used to make a variety of petit fours in many shapes, flavors and colors. A colorful box of marzipan fruits makes an attractive gift. They can look very realistic with a little time and patience. Use soft colors, as strong colors do not look as appetising. Dry them well to improve their keeping qualities. Simple shapes, such as carrots, apples, pears, and bananas, are the best to start with.

To make carrots, color the marzipan terracotta. Knead a small piece into a long, tapered carrot shape. With a skewer or toothpick, mark the characteristic indents around the carrot and mark a hole in the top for the stalks. Brush or scratch a little terracotta color into the indents and attach 2-3 small pieces of angelica or candied lime peel for the stalks.

Marzipan Roses

The size of the finished flower is determined by the initial cone and ball of paste. When the five basic petals are in place, any number can be added to create larger or floppier blooms. To shape the petals, wear fine plastic gloves or work the marzipan between pieces of polythene or plastic wrap with a little cornstarch. This way you can create really thin petals without the past sticking.

1 Mold a cone of paste. Take a tiny ball of paste and gently thin out one edge with your thumb to create a petal shape. Completely wrap this around the cone to form the bud, nipping in the paste at the middle to form a waist.

2 Make another two petals in the same way and wrap them around, overlapping each other at the middle. and gently nipping in again. This is a small rose or bud.

3 For a full rose, add another three petals and overlap them. You can add as many more petals as you wish. Gently pull or bend the edges of the petals outward to create the required realistic rose effect.

4 Check that the waist of the flower is tightly pinched and cut off the excess. Leave the finished roses on wax paper in a cool dry place to dry overnight.

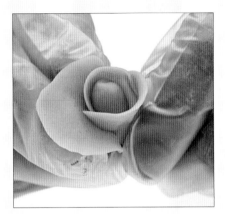

Coating Marzipan Shapes

Marzipan shapes can be dipped in melted chocolate. They can be sprayed with color diluted with alcohol, with confectioner's varnish, gum arabic solution, or melted cocoa butter to give a good glaze.

Marzipan Tips

• Thin plastic or rubber gloves prevent strong colors from staining your hands. You can shape petals or other fine shapes more easily wearing them than working between sheets of cellophane or plastic wrap.
• Keep marzipan wrapped tightly when not in use.
• Use natural marzipan for a better color.
• For long storage, paint the modeled item with confectioner's glaze.
• Read the manufacturer's instructions carefully when buying food glaze or varnishes.

Marzipan Flowers

Flowers that can be made in sugar paste or pastillage can also be made using marzipan. A little sugar paste or pastillage should be added to strengthen the marzipan. Use colored marzipan or paint the finished flowers. They may also be sugar glazed by dipping in syrup boiled to 150ºC/300ºF, the 'hard crack' stage. This should be done after the flowers have been dried out for at least 24 hours. Flowers to be dipped in syrup must be made a little thicker. Pierce a wire rod or fork into the base for dipping and place on an oiled tray to set.

Simple flowers can be quickly cut out with small cutters. Using colored marzipan – pale pink, yellow, or purple – cut with a small blossom cutter and place on sponge to dry. Cut a bought stamen with a round head to the length required and dip the head in edible glue. Push it through the center of the flower until secured and leave to set.

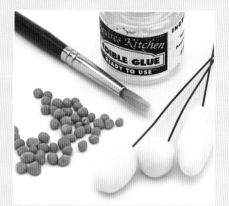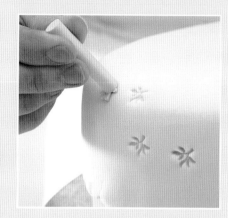

Cakes for All Occasions

This brilliant collection of decorated cakes has everything to offer – good looks, irresistible flavors, and contemporary styles. There are designs for every season and celebration, including favorite recipes, and classic finishes, as well as cakes with a distinctly modern appeal.

Decorating a cake is enjoyable and producing a party piece need not be daunting. This inspiring chapter will help you to create stunning centerpieces with confidence. Whether you are catering for a birthday, anniversary, formal occasion, or fun gathering, you will find just the right idea. Discover that making a stunning wedding cake is perfectly possible using a deceptively simple yet stylish design.

You can make a cake for the sheer fun of being creative and sharing something special. There is no need to wait for an annual event before trying many of these recipes – whip up an indulgent chocolate creation; bake a pyramid of fairy cakes; go retro with little fancies; or zest up the day with a glorious citrus gâteau.

Iced Cup Cakes

The great thing about making lots of little cakes is you can vary the toppings to suit your guests, your children, or your mood, and have fun with several different ideas at the same time.

Makes about 15

1 x 3-egg quantity Victoria Sponge Cake mixture (page 16)

1-2tsp unsweetened cocoa powder

2-3tsp milk

5 cherries with stalks

2 quantities Glacé Icing (page 24)

2tbsp Chocolate Buttercream (page 23)

5 chocolate shapes (page 43)

confectioners' sugar, sifted

red or blue edible food coloring

silver dragees

coloured stars

1 Preheat the oven to 180ºC/350ºF/gas mark 4. Prepare the sponge cake mixture. Prepare 15 paper cup cake cases in a muffin pan. Mix the unsweetened cocoa powder with the milk and use to flavor about one third of the mixture. Spoon the mixtures into the cake cases and bake for 15-20 minutes until evenly risen, lightly browned, and just firm to the touch. Transfer to a wire rack and leave until cold.

2 Set aside five plain cakes, selecting those that are more domed. Color 1tbsp of the glacé icing red or blue. Spoon white glacé icing over the remaining plain cup cakes. Add drops of colored icing and then swirl the colored icing into the white with a toothpick. Finish with silver dragees or colored stars.

3 Place a cherry on each of the reserved plain cakes, keeping them in place with a little glacé icing. Holding the cherry stalk to keep the fruit in place, pour about 1tbsp glacé icing over the cherry. Add extra icing if necessary, to coat the cake. Leave to set firm.

4 Cut a small lid off the top of each chocolate cake. Pipe a swirl of buttercream into the center of each. Replace the lid on top. Add a chocolate shape and sift a little confectioners' sugar over the top.

Frosted Fruits Gâteau

Most fruits take sugar frosting but the smaller fruit on stalks look the best. Autumn berries are good if they are still firm. Any very soft or slightly blemished fruit will not work well as they do not dry out fully. When well coated with sugar fruit will keep for several days in a dry atmosphere.

Serves 6-8

6oz mixed firm berries

4oz mixed fruits, such as cherries, redcurrants and physallis

1 small egg white

1/2 cup superfine sugar

7in Genoese Sponge Cake (page 17)

1 1/2 cups heavy cream

1 Set aside the softer and larger berries for the filling, cutting them in half if necessary. Dry the fruit thoroughly on paper towel.

2 Put the egg white in a small bowl and beat very slightly to loosen it. Put the sugar in a larger bowl. Cover a clean tray with wax paper.

3 Brush the fruit thinly with egg white, brushing the egg white into the cracks and crevices.

4 Then coat thoroughly in the sugar by dipping the fruit and sprinkling with sugar. Place on the wax paper. Leave in a warm dry place for several hours or until the sugar coating is completely dry and crisp.

5 Whisk the cream until it stands in soft peaks. Sandwich the sponge cake layers with about a third of the cream, and the reserved berries. Spread a little cream over the top and pipe the rest around the top edge of the cake.

6 Place the cake on a serving plate. Arrange the frosted fruits on top just before serving.

Sugar Coating Tips

• Fruit should be clean and dry.

• Repeat the coating process for the best result.

• For longer keeping, store the fruit in an airtight container. Add a little salt or silica crystals wrapped in a twist of cheesecloth to absorb any moisture.

Carrot Cake

This moist cake is covered in a rich and naughty topping. The decorative marzipan carrots and cinnamon sticks are fun to make, especially as they can be prepared well ahead and stored in an airtight container.

Serves 16

³/₄ cup sunflower oil

³/₄ cup soft light brown sugar

3 large eggs, beaten

finely grated zest of 1 orange and juice of ¹/₂ orange

1¹/₂ cups whole-wheat self-rising flour

1tsp baking powder

1 cup golden raisins

1¹/₂ cups finely grated carrots

Topping and decoration

1 quantity American Frosting (page 25)

3¹/₂oz Marzipan (page 26)

brown and terracotta edible food colorings

angelica or glacé lime peel

1 Make the decorations first. Color two-thirds of the marzipan terracotta and use to make carrots (see page 44). Use a toothpick to mark the characteristic indents and brush a little coloring into the cracks. Push tiny sticks of angelica or glacé lime peel into the tops for stalks.

2 Color the rest of the marzipan brown and roll out thinly. Roll tiny pieces into sticks to resemble cinnamon sticks, then cut or fray the edges. Leave to dry out.

3 Preheat the oven to 180°C/350°F/gas mark 4. Line and grease a 9in round pan. Blend all the cake ingredients in a bowl and beat thoroughly. Spoon the mixture into the prepared pan and smooth it evenly.

4 Bake for 40-50 minutes, until the cake is risen and firm to the touch. Leave to cool in the pan then transfer to a wire rack.

5 Prepare the American frosting. Spread the frosting all over the cake, peaking and swirling it attractively. Place on a serving dish. Arrange the carrots and cinnamon sticks on the cake shortly before serving.

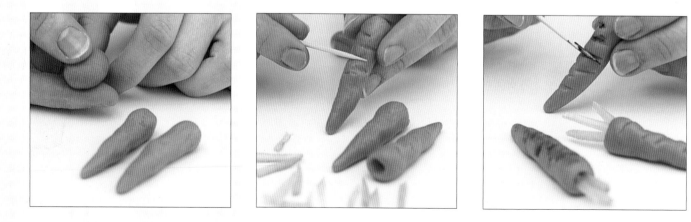

Tipsy Chocolate Treat

Serves 8-10

9 squares bitter chocolate

³/₄ cup dairy butter

6 eggs, separated

1 cup superfine sugar

¹/₂ cup self-rising flour

3-4tbsp rum

Icing and Decoration

1 quantity bitter chocolate Ganache
   (page 41)

3 squares white chocolate

4 squares bitter chocolate

This indulgent, grown-up chocolate cake is well laced with rum underneath the drizzled chocolate decoration.

1 Line and grease a deep 8in round loose-bottomed pan. Preheat the oven to 170°C/325°F/gas mark 3. Melt the chocolate and butter gently in a heatproof bowl over a saucepan of hot water. Alternatively, melt in the microwave for 30–50 seconds at a time on medium. Leave to cool slightly.

2 Whisk the egg yolks with ³/₄ cup of the sugar until pale, thick and creamy. Gently stir in the cooled chocolate. Then fold in the flour.

3 In a separate bowl, whisk the egg whites until stiff but not dry. Then gently whisk in the rest of the sugar. Fold the whites into the chocolate mixture and spoon the mixture into the prepared pan.

4 Bake for 1 hour 15 minutes, until the cake is well risen and springy to the touch. A knife should come out clean and free of sticky mixture. Leave to part-cool in the pan, then turn out onto a wire rack and leave until cold.

5 Invert the cake and sprinkle the rum over its base. Allow to soak in for a few minutes. Then turn the cake the right way up on the rack. Stand the rack over a tray or paper. Reserve a third of the ganache. Quickly pour the rest all over the cake. Make sure all the cake is covered, and save the drips of excess ganache that have fallen onto the tray or paper.

7 Cut a piece of foil and mark a rectangle about 10in x 3in on it. Have a rolling pin ready. Melt the white and bitter chocolate separately and spoon into small paper piping bags. Snip off the points for piping finely. Drizzle white chocolate in lines across the top of the cake.

8 Drizzle the bitter chocolate on the foil first, then the white chocolate, keeping within the marked rectangle. Reserve the unused chocolate. Carefully drape the foil over the rolling pin and leave to set. When firm, carefully remove pieces of the drizzled chocolate semi-circles and arrange several on top of the cake.

9 Transfer the cake to a serving plate. Re-melt the remaining ganache and chocolate together and allow to cool until thick enough to pipe. Then pipe around the base of the cake. Keep in a cool place until ready to serve.

Retro Iced Fancies

Originally called *fondant fancies,* and covered with a soft pouring fondant, these favorites of a bygone era seem to have taken on a new lease of life. Here they are coated with soft royal icing instead of the traditional fondant. Glacé icing will not do. They can be made in whatever shape and color you like, but look particularly attractive in soft pastel shades.

Makes 10-12

2-egg Victoria Sponge Cake baked in a
   6in square or a rectangular pan
   (page 16)
1/2 quantity Royal Icing (page 28)
edible food coloring
few blanched almonds or pieces of
   candied peel

1 Cut the cake into bite-size squares, circles, triangles, or other shapes, such as crescents, and diamonds. Place on a wire rack.

2 Divide the icing among three bowls. Keep one portion white and cover it closely with plastic wrap. Color the other two portions as you wish, then gently dilute them with a little water or lemon juice to a pouring consistency – just a little thicker than for run-outs.

3 Coat half the batch of cakes with one color and half with the other. If the coats are thin, repeat once the first coat has dried. Place a piece of peel or an almond on some of the cakes before you coat them.

4 Color the reserved white icing two or more different colors and use to pipe or drizzle designs on the cakes. Leave one color to set fully before adding another color. Leave to set before serving.

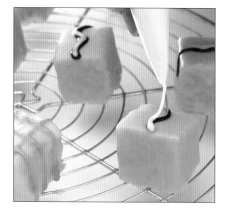

Fondant Tip
Fondant can be bought as a packet mix from specialty cake decorating suppliers. It can be made up as directed and used for these iced fancies for a truly authentic effect.

Orange and Lemon Gâteau

What can you do with a frozen sponge cake? Simple, slice the layers and sandwich them together with tangy lemon curd. Coat in a fruity buttercream and top with candied shreds of orange rind and shards of caramelized sugar. Nothing to it really!

Serves 10–12

5 or 6 thin layers lemon Victoria Sponge
  Cake (page 16) or Madeira Cake
  (page 18)
2 quantities lemon Buttercream (page 23)
  or Meringue Buttercream (page 24)
1 large orange
1/2 cup superfine sugar
2tbsp orange juice
6tbsp lemon curd
1/4 cup granulated sugar
10in round gold cake board

1 Chill the thin cake layers. Prepare the buttercream and leave to firm up.

2 Use a vegetable peeler to cut thin strips of orange rind, avoiding the white pith or trimming it off. Then cut into fine strips. Dissolve the caster sugar in the orange juice in a small saucepan. Add the strips of rind and simmer gently until the sugar has almost caramelized, and all the liquid has evaporated.

3 Tip the rinds onto a sheet of non-stick baking paper. Separate the strands and leave in an airy room that is not too cool or damp, until hardened.

4 Sandwich the sponge cake layers together alternately with lemon curd and a third of the buttercream. Lightly cover the top and sides with buttercream, finishing with a simple swirled or knife-mark pattern. Chill until ready to serve.

5 Meanwhile, sprinkle the granulated sugar on a small sheet of foil. Place under a hot grill until the sugar has dissolved and is bubbling and golden brown. Set aside to cool.

6 Place the cake on the board. Just before serving arrange the shreds of orange rind in a pile in the center of the cake. Break the caramel into shards or large pieces. Arrange some caramel pieces with the orange rind on top and some around the edge of the cake.

Battenberg Cake

This unique cake is ideal for lovers of marzipan. It was apparently named after the marriage of Queen Victoria's granddaughter to Prince Louis of Battenberg in 1884. Our recipe has a choice of three flavor combinations.

Serves 6-8

1 x 4-egg Victoria Sponge Cake mixture (page 16) flavored and colored with vanilla; orange and chocolate; or lemon and orange

2-3tbsp apricot jelly

10oz Marzipan (page 26), flavored with 3tbsp sifted unsweetened cocoa powder for the chocolate cake

pink and green edible food coloring if making the vanilla cake

1 Preheat the oven to 180°C/350°F/gas mark 4. Line and grease a 7in shallow square baking pan. Cut a strip of double wax paper and grease it. Use this to divide the pan in half.

2 Prepare the sponge cake mixture, flavor it with vanilla, if liked, and divide in half. Color the vanilla portions pink and green. Alternatively, instead of vanilla, use chocolate in one portion and orange in the other; or lemon in one portion and orange in the other. Color the orange portion with a little orange food coloring.

3 Spoon one mixture into half the prepared baking pan, keeping the paper in the middle, and the rest in the other side. Try to make the divide as straight as possible. Bake in the middle of the oven for 35-40 minutes. Turn out and cool on a wire rack.

4 When cool, trim the edges and cut the cake portions lengthwise in half, making four equal parts. Warm the jelly in a small saucepan. Brush two sides of each portion of cake with jelly and stick them together to give a effect.

5 Roll out the marzipan to a rectangle wide and long enough to wrap around the cake. Trim the edges neatly. Brush the outside of the cake with jelly. Place the cake on the marzipan and wrap the paste around the cake. Dampen the edges lightly to form a neat join at one of the corners of the cake.

6 Pinch the top and bottom edges of the paste into a pattern with crimpers. Use the extra marzipan to make marzipan flowers and leaves in various colors or other decorations of your choice.

Sunburst

Something to celebrate – a christening or a new house perhaps? Whatever the reason, bring some added sunshine to the occasion with this quick and simple, three-dimensional design with sparkle and silver shimmer.

Serves: 16-20

8in square Golden Fruit Cake (page 21)

2tbsp Apricot Glaze (page 26)

8oz Marzipan (optional, page 26)

1¹/₂lb Sugar Paste (page 30)

yellow and blue edible food colors

blue sequin ribbon

yellow sparkles

silver moon dust

turquoise balls

10in square cake board

1 Brush the cake with apricot glaze, then cover with the marzipan, if using, or cover with sugar paste alone. Use about two-thirds of the sugar paste to cover the cake, reserving the rest for decoration. Transfer the cake to the board.

2 Color two-thirds of the remaining sugar paste pale turquoise (using blue and yellow) and one-third pale yellow. Wrap in plastic wrap. Roll out a quarter of the turquoise paste and use to cover the board. Then frill the edge with a toothpick or frilling tool (page 40). Trim the base of the cake and the board with sequin ribbon.

3 Roll out the yellow paste quite thickly and cut a 1¹/₂-2in circle for the sun. Cut out 7-8 strips shaped from narrow to wide for the sun's rays. Attach the sun and the rays to the top of the cake with a little water.

4 Roll out the rest of the turquoise paste quite thickly and cut out a variety of cloud-like shapes. Use the blunt ends of different-sized round cutters and the wide ends of piping nozzles to make the shapes and cut a third of the circle. Use a fine, sharp, pointed knife to cut out the marked shapes of larger clouds. Cut away some of the centers to increase the curve. Layer the clouds over the sun's rays, raising some pieces for a three dimensional effect. Cut several tiny raindrops from the remaining blue paste.

5 Sprinkle the sun with yellow sparkles. Using a damp brush, brush the clouds with moon dust. Finally, place the turquoise balls on the board at the base of the cake with a little icing.

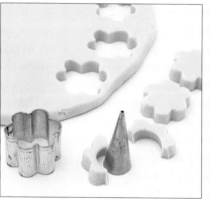

Chocolate Heaven

A glamorous casing of chocolate ganache and a topping of tiny alcoholic truffles transform a simple chocolate sponge cake into a stunning dinner party gâteau or centerpiece for almost any occasion.

Serves 8-12

1¼ cups heavy cream

2-4tbsp brandy, whisky or Courvoisier

7in chocolate Genoese Sponge Cake (page 17)

1 quantity Ganache (page 41)

¼ cup confectioners' sugar, sifted

¼ cup unsweetened cocoa powder, sifted

Chocolate Leaves (page 42)

1 Whip the cream lightly. Take a third of the cream and stir in half the brandy, whisky, or Courvoisier. Sandwich the sponge cake layers together with this and place on a serving plate.

2 Cut a strip of foil at least the length of the cake circumference, and twice the height of the side. Spread one third of the warm ganache over this, making the base edge straight along the foil, but the top edge attractively jagged. Leave to set but do not allow to become hard.

3 Divide the remaining ganache in half. Beat half the remaining cream into one portion of ganache and continue to beat lightly until it thickens to a spreading consistency. Swirl this over the top of the cake and spread it around the sides.

4 For the truffles, mix the remaining ganache with the remaining alcohol and cream, and the confectioners' sugar. Beat well, then place in the refrigerator to set.

5 Wrap the just-set chocolate case around the cake, jagged edge up, and gently peel off the foil as you press the chocolate onto the cake. Press the edges to seal. Chill the cake until the chocolate is firm.

6 Dust your hands with cocoa and roll small teaspoons of the truffle mixture into tiny balls. Chill again. When ready to serve, carefully arrange the truffles on the top of the cake, adding some on the serving plate. Dust with more cocoa powder and finish with a few chocolate leaves.

Berrytime

Realistic-looking three-dimensional raspberries, bramble berries and tayberries can all be made by hand with a little time and patience. Individual berries can be wired together with leaves. Flat, or bas relief, berries, to fit on the vertical sides of a cake, can be made in flexible plastic molds. Molds are also available for making detailed clusters of berries and leaves. A combination of molds and cutters works well.

Serves 10-12

8in round Golden Fruit Cake (page 21)

1lb Marzipan (page 26)

1¹/₂lb Sugar Paste (page 30)

Raspberry pink, blackberry and leaf green gel or dust colors

8oz bought flower paste mix

floristry wire (24-26 gauge)

green and brown floristry tape (known as gutta percha)

edible glue

10in square cake board

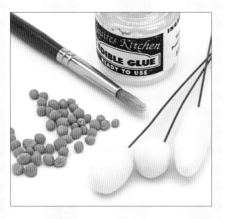

1 Cover the cake with marzipan. Color three quarters of the sugar paste a shade of raspberry pink and use to cover the cake. Cover the board with white sugar paste and top with sugar paste that you have colored grass green.

2 Make up the flower paste according to the packet instructions. Knead until thoroughly workable. Use about a quarter to fill individual berry molds lightly dusted with cornstarch, if using. Turn out and leave to harden in a warm dry place for at least 24 hours. Paint the shapes the colors of the berries and leaves using diluted gel or dry powders.

3 Color about a quarter of the remaining flower paste a shade of raspberry pink. Mold about 15 pea-sized round or pear-shaped white balls for cores and attach them to 6in lengths floristry wire. To do this, make a tiny hook at one end of the wire to hold paste and moisten the wire with glue. Leave to dry for 1-2 hours.

4 For each berry roll 20-30 tiny balls of pink paste and attach them to the cores with glue. Shape gently with your fingers and leave to dry for 1-2 hours. Support the wires in a block of floristry foam while the paste is drying.

5 For the calyx (the leafy cup which holds the berry), color the rest of the paste leaf green. Roll out a small piece of paste thinly and cut out a small calyx. Gently flatten out the points with a dog-bone tool. Place the paste on a piece of foam and then push in the center to give it a cup shape. Push a berry wire through the center, brush the paste with glue, and secure the calyx to the berry. Bend the points with a paintbrush to give a life-like shape.

6 Cut out several leaves from the green sugar paste. Vein them with a vein marker and shape them gently, then attach to wires with glue. Leave everything to set hard under a lamp for 24 hours.

7 Tint the berries and leaves with shades of purple and green-brown, respectively. Take 2-3 berries and 2-3 leaves, and wrap their wires together with green tape to make a small bunch.

8 Arrange the bunches and the molded fruits on and around the cake, attaching them with edible glue.

Petal Power Cake

This charming flower-covered creation is perfect for Mother's day instead of a bunch of flowers. Use freesias instead of roses, if you like, and color the cake to match the colors of the petals.

Serves 6-8

8in Madeira Cake or Golden Fruit Cake
(pages 18 or 21)

2tbsp Apricot Glaze (page 26)

12oz Marzipan (page 26)

1lb Sugar Paste (page 30)

3-4 roses in full bloom

1 small egg white, lightly beaten

2tbsp superfine sugar

edible food colors to match roses

edible leaf green dusting powder

10in round cake board

1 Using the template on page 96, cut the cake into a petal shape. Brush with apricot glaze and cover with marzipan. Set aside for several hours. Cover the board with colored paper to match the flowers if you wish.

2 Discard any blemished petals and put the best ones on a board covered with wax paper. Save the buds or centers of the roses to decorate the board.

3 Brush the petals thinly with egg white. Then sprinkle them with sugar to coat them evenly and fairly thickly. Leave on the paper for several hours to dry and harden.

4 Color the remaining sugar paste to match the petals, marbling the colors if you wish. Remove about a fifth of the paste, then cover the cake with the rest. Place the cake on the board.

5 Using a sugar paste gun and the reserved colored or white sugar paste, make sufficient rope to wrap around the edge of the cake. The white paste can be colored first, if liked. Twist two lengths of different-colored ropes together for an attractive effect.

6 Use a tiny flower embosser to mark a delicate pattern all over the cake. Brush a little dusting powder in a pale leaf green into these indents (page 40).

7 Arrange a selection of sugared petals on top of the cake and on the board. Add the reserved flower buds for a finishing touch.

Storing sugared roses

Sugared rose petals will keep well in an airtight container for a couple of weeks. To help keep them dry, add a little salt or silica crystals tied up in a small piece of cheesecloth to absorb moisture.

Butterfly Thank You Cake

Individual cakes make the perfect gift, particularly as a Thank You. Why not make one large square cake and cut it into four? Freeze the remaining sections so you always have a small cake ready to be transformed into an impromptu gift.

Serves 2-4

4in square Dark Rich Fruit Cake or
    Madeira Cake (pages 20 or 18)
1tbsp Apricot Glaze (page 26)
6oz Marzipan (page 26)
1/2 quantity Royal Icing (page 28) plus
    1 quantity Royal Icing without glycerine
pink and hyacinth edible food color
    powders
white stamens and colored stamens
2-3 prepared leaves

1 Brush the cake with apricot glaze and cover with marzipan. Leave to dry for 24 hours. Over the next couple of days give the cake one coat of white and two coats of lavender royal icing. Leave to dry thoroughly.

2 Meanwhile, make up the royal icing without glycerine. Color half pink and half a light lavender color. Use pink and hyacinth colors to achieve the right shades. Using the template on page 96 and run-out instructions on page 37, make 6-8 of the small flat run-out butterflies in lavender with pink dots. Leave to in a cool place to harden.

3 Make 3-4 medium-sized pink butterfly run-out pieces with lavender dots. Attach white stamens to the body while still wet. Leave to dry. Pipe a tiny amount of pink icing on either side of the body pieces and attach the wings. Raise the wings slightly and support them on a soft curved surface so they dry raised.

4 Use some of the remaining lavender icing to pipe tiny dots and lines around the top edge of the cake. Attach a small bunch of colored stamens and two leaves to the top of the cake. Position one butterfly on the bunch of stamens. Add as many more butterflies as you wish, attaching smaller ones around the sides. Butterflies can be attached to a gift box for the cake.

5 Support the cake on folds of matching tissue paper and place in a small cake box.

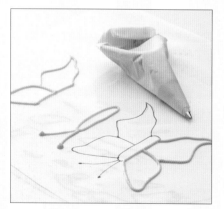

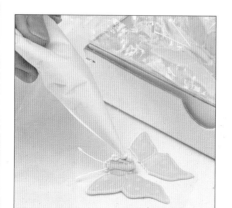

Spring is Here

This light, fresh design suits Easter or any spring event. If you like the classic simnel cake, use the dark fruit cake recipe and place a layer of marzipan in the middle of the mixture as you fill the pan before baking.

Serves 16-20

8in round Golden Fruit Cake (page 21)

3tbsp Apricot Glaze (page 26)

1lb Marzipan (page 26)

1 quantity Royal Icing (page 28)

6oz bought flower paste or pastillage mix

saffron yellow and leaf-green edible
  food colors

yellow ribbon

10in round cake board

1 Brush the cake with apricot glaze and cover with marzipan. Coat the cake and the board with royal icing and leave to dry. Reserve 1-2 tbsp royal icing if possible, for attaching the flowers.

2 Make up the flower paste or pastillage as directed on the packet. Color one third of the paste yellow and one third pale green. Use blossom cutters to to cut out 12 large blossoms and 12 small blossoms out of the white paste. Cut 12 small blossoms from the yellow paste. Shape the petals with a frilling tool.

3 Pipe white centers in the yellow blossoms with royal icing. Color a little royal icing pale yellow and pipe yellow centers in the white blossoms.

4 Use the green paste to make 26-30 leaves. Press between leaf veiners to shape and thin out. Curve the leaves slightly to give a natural effect. Set aside to dry.

5 Attach the small flowers, with leaves, around the base of the cake. Position an arrangement of the larger flowers, with leaves, on the top of the cake.

6 Tie a double yellow ribbon around the cake and add any remaining flowers or leaves around the base.

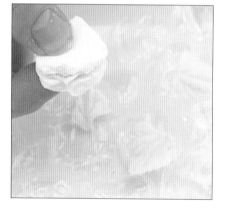

Birthday Bonanza

For some Birthday celebrations you just want to go a little crazy and this cake suits that mood perfectly. Whatever the age, candles, sparklers, streamers, and party poppers create the required sparkle and party impression.

Serves 16-18

¹/₂lb bought pastillage mix
orange, sunflower and terracotta edible
    paste colors
gold wires
edible glue
bronze or gold dusting powder
4-6 tiny polystyrene balls
9in round Madeira Cake (page 18)
4oz lemon-flavored Buttercream
    (page 23)
1¹/₄lb Sugar Paste (page 30)
party poppers, sparklers, long sparkly
    party candles, fine gold ribbon,
11in thin board covered with bronze
    wrapping paper

1 Make up the pastillage as directed on the packet and color it a strong sunflower yellow. Marble half the paste with orange and terracotta streaks. Wrap the rest tightly in plastic wrap and set aside.

2 Roll the marbled pastillage out thinly. Cut into about 20 long thin triangles to resemble flames for the central pieces of the explosion. Attach half to gold wires with glue and leave to set. Lay the rest over a rolling pin so they dry in a curved shape.

3 Attach polystyrene balls to wires with glue. Dust your hands with cornstarch, flatten hazelnut-sized pieces of yellow or marbled pastillage in the palm of your hands until thin enough to wrap around the wetted polystyrene balls (as for marzipan roses page 45). Shape these into balloons and leave to harden. Paint or dust with gold if you wish. Leave all decorations to dry for at least a day.

4 Reserve 1-2tbsp of the buttercream and use the rest to coat the cake. Mix any excess pastillage with a little sugar paste, flatten it to a thick domed round about 2in across and center it on top of the cake.

5 Color the sugar paste a rich burnt orange. Roll out to about 16in and lay carefully over the cake, making sure it is centered. From the center cut triangles over the dome and pull them out for explosive effect. Support these pieces on crumpled soft paper or absorbent cotton. Flatten the paste on the sides of the cake and trim. Gently brush the cake all over with bronze powder. Leave to set for about a day.

6 Attach the curved marbled orange flames to the center with buttercream. Push the wires of the remaining flames and balloons gently into the center of the cake. Add candles, sparklers, gold ribbons, party poppers, and streamers to create a party centerpiece. Light all the candles and sparklers just before serving.

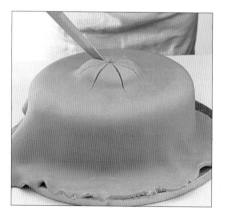

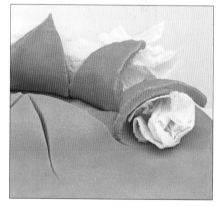

Birthday Surprises

These little boxes can be made in any mix of colors – all white and pearly would be very sophisticated for a 21st birthday or for a wedding cake for instance, or try a mix of candy colors for a little girl or boy's birthday. Work out your cake pan and box sizes before you start, allowing for the two larger sizes to be made up of two layers of sponge cake.

Serves 16-20

10-egg Madeira Cake mix (page 18) baked in either an 11in square or 8in x 10in rectangular pan
2 quantities Buttercream (page 23)
2¼lb Sugar Paste (page 30)
bluebell blue edible food coloring
white and blue sugar-coated chocolate candy such as M&Ms
8in square cake board

1 Thoroughly chill the cake. Cut out cubes of about the following sizes: 4½ in, 3½ in, 2½in, and 1in. The two larger cubes may have to be made from two stacked layers of cake sandwiched together with buttercream. Make as many of the small ones as you like to add around the base.

2 To create the tumbling effect, cut a corner wedge off the second and third boxes, making sure they stand securely on the cut corners. Wrap the sponge cakes individually in plastic wrap until required.

3 Color half the sugar past blue, wrap in plastic wrap and set aside. Roll out half the white sugar paste and cut four 4½in squares. Spread the cake sides with buttercream and carefully attach the paste sides one at a time, sealing the each of the corners neatly.

4 Measure the remaining two sides before you cut the paste, as they will now be slightly larger than first sides. Attach the paste in the same way.

5 Cover the remaining boxes, taking care at all the corners to keep them in a good sharp shape. Cover the board with the remaining sugar paste.

6 Stack all the boxes, attaching them with a little buttercream and set aside to firm up for a few hours. At the last minute, just before serving the cake, attach the color candy with buttercream.

21st Birthday

Everyone loves a cup cake and this impressive collection suits any age, and almost any occasion. A good strong color theme is important; matched with lots of ideas for the individual toppings and you have a fun recipe for success. Make plenty of cakes, as they are sure to go!

Makes about 30

1 quantity Carrot Cake mixture (page 52)
silver cup cake cases
1lb Royal Icing (page 28)
blue edible food coloring
2oz Sugar Paste (page 30)
silver candles, balls, ribbons and/or
    netting to decorate
edible blue or sliver glitter
blue and silver ribbon
two- or three-tier cake stand

1 Preheat the oven to 180°C/350°F/gas mark 4. Place 30 silver cake cases in small muffin pans. Make the carrot cake mixture and divide it among the cake cases. Bake for about 20 minutes, until evenly risen, lightly browned and springy to touch. Allow to cool on wire racks.

2 Color half the royal icing pale blue. Coat half the cakes with white icing and half with blue. Top some of the cakes with silver balls, arranged in '21' shapes, while the icing is wet. Leave to set for several hours or overnight.

3 Color or marble the sugar paste with blue. Roll out half thinly and cut out star or flower shapes. Roll the rest of the paste into ropes and shape into the numerals one and two, small enough to fit on the cakes. Leave these decorations to dry.

4 Color some of the royal icing a darker shade of blue. Choose a variety of piped designs, such as dots, lattice, diagonal lines, circles and flowers, and decorate five or more cakes in similar designs, using different colorways. Simple designs using contrasting colors are very effective. Add numbers, stars, candles, streamers and/or glitter, to some of the cakes. Use a limited number of different designs and make several cakes of each type. Leave to set.

5 To serve, arrange all the cakes in a pile on a two- or three-tiered cake stand. Make sure cakes with candles are stable and upright. Tie a big ribbon around the base of the stand and light the candles.

Cup cake tip

Bite-size cup cakes are stylish and fun. Make them in petit four cases, reducing the cooking time to 10-15 minutes. Keep all the decorations miniature in proportion with the tiny cakes.

Engagement Ring Cake

This ring theme is one that you can also adapt for weddings and anniversaries. Try covering the cake with edible gold for a very special celebration.

Serves 16-20

3¹/₂oz bought petal paste or
    pastillage mix
blue edible food coloring
6-8tbsp Royal Icing (page 28)
silver or pearl balls
silver snowflake dusting powder
3-egg Madeira Cake mixture (page 18)
2oz Buttercream (page 23)
2¹/₄lb Sugar Paste (page 30)
11in square cake board
fresh flowers

1 Before starting the cake, make up the petal paste or pastillage. Make a selection of blossoms and flowers in white and blue. Cut out the flower and blossom shapes and press them between rubber molds lightly dusted with cornstarch. With a spot of icing, fix pearl or silver balls in the flower centers. Make a selection of rose leaves and dust them with silver snowflake dust. Leave to dry.

2 Preheat the oven to180°C/350°F/gas mark 4. Grease and flour a 9in savarin pan or ring mold. Fill with the cake mixture, rounding the top, and bake for 40-50 minutes, until a skewer comes out free of sticky mixture. Leave in the pan to cool.

3 Remove the cake from the pan and freeze for 1-2 hours before covering. Coat the board with royal icing. When the cake is part-frozen, trim off the flat edge around the top rim and round it into a smooth and evenly-domed shape.

4 Coat the cake with buttercream. Roll out the sugar paste into a circle 2-3in larger than the ring. Allow plenty of paste to cover the underneath of the cake. Lift the paste carefully using a rolling pin and place it carefully over the ring, letting as much as possible fall into the hole in the center. Smooth the paste over the top and sides.

5 Turn the cake over. Make one slit in the center of the excess paste and carefully pull the pieces through to cover the inside rim. Gently work the paste up to cover the rest of the cake and smooth out any joins.

6 Turn the cake back over, correct way up and, with your hands or smoothers, ease out any creases in the paste. Dust all over with snowflake dust. Place on the board.

7 Use a little royal icing to attach the large flowers to the cake and smaller flowers around them. Arrange the remaining paste flowers on the board together with some fresh flowers.

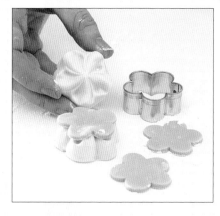

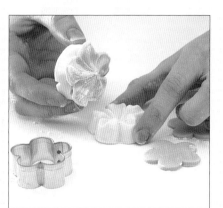

Checkmate

Lashings of chocolate and a tempting challenge especially for the man in your life! If you want to make a real game, buy a full set of chocolate chessmen... but this does mean that the cake cannot be eaten until the game is over.

Serves 18-20

1lb Sugar Paste (page 30) blended
   with 2oz melted bitter or white
   chocolate (see step 1) or
   1lb chocolate modeling paste
Double quantity of Madeira Cake mixture
   (page 18), flavored with 1tbsp instant
   coffee dissolved in 2tsp boiling water,
   baked in a 9in square cake pan
½ quantity Buttercream (page 23)
   flavored with coffee or chocolate
3 squares each white and bitter chocolate
½ quantity each of white and bitter
   chocolate Ganache (page 41), cooled
   to a piping consistency
gold rope
thin brown ribbon
11in square gold board

1 Work the sugar paste until soft and smooth. Then gradually work in the cooled melted chocolate, kneading it on a clean work surface until thoroughly blended. Add sifted confectioners' sugar if necessary.

2 Coat the cake with buttercream. Roll out a third of the chocolate paste to a square the size of the top of the cake and lay it on neatly. Roll out four pieces to fit the sides. Attach them and then gently mold the corners together. Smooth over the sides and top to get neat square corners.

3 Place the cake on the gold board. Trim the base and top edges with twisted gold rope and brown ribbon. Leave until firm.

4 Melt the white and bitter chocolates separately and spread out smoothly and evenly on sheets of foil. Leave to cool. Before the chocolate sets too hard, cut out small squares, making at least 20 of each type to allow for breakages.

5 Make the ganache and allow to cool to piping consistency. On wax paper or non-stick backing parchment, pipe 10-12 or more rosettes in each color, making them as tall or pointed as you can. Make the white a different shape from the dark shapes if you wish. Leave the shapes to set firmly in the refrigerator.

6 Attach the chocolate squares to the top of the cake, using any remaining buttercream or melted chocolate to keep them in place. Add the chocolate rosettes.

Winter Blues

This jolly scene makes a delightful Christmas cake with plenty of fun modeling and challenging finger work for young cooks. The penguins are, in fact, quite simple to make but you may end up with black fingers!

Serves 10-12

1 quantity Dark Rich Fruit Cake mixture (page 20) baked in an oval cake pan 8in x 6in

Apricot Glaze (page 26)

1lb Marzipan (page 26)

1 quantity Royal Icing (page 28)

bluebell blue and orange berberis edible food color

4oz Sugar Paste (page 30)

4oz bought black sugar paste

daffodil dusting powder

clear snowflake sparkles

edible glue

10in silver oval cake board

1 Brush the cake with apricot glaze and cover with marzipan. Coat the top with white royal icing. Color the rest pale blue and ice the side of the cake. Leave to dry. Place the cake on the board.

2 Prepare the penguins: for each one, shape a small ball of black paste for the head and equal-sized pieces of white and black paste for the body. Color a little white paste orange for the feet.

3 Lightly moisten one side of each of the two body pieces with glue and squash them together. Wipe off excess glue to avoid making a mess. Shape the body into a fat pear shape. Flatten the top and bottom. With tiny scissors, snip wing shapes in to the black paste and gently pull them into shape. Attach the head with a little water. Leave to dry for as long as possible.

4 Roll out the orange sugar paste and cut tiny circles for feet. Flatten one side and cut in half to make two webbed feet. Attach the feet with a little glue. Pipe white eyes and paint on black pupils. Make or pipe an orange beak. Attach the beak if necessary. Leave to set. Finally, dust yellow powder onto the breast – take care as it is very bright!

5 On the top of the cake, mark out an oval shape to make a run-out pond (page 37). Pipe the outline with slightly softened blue icing. When set, soften the royal icing to a flooding consistency and flood in the pond. Leave to set.

6 Gently add and rough up a little icing all around the top edge of the cake, allowing some to drip down the sides. Sprinkle with clear snowflake sparkles. Spread rough icing around the base of the cake on the board and add sparkles. Use a little white royal icing in a tiny bag to pipe fine lines of snow around the edges of the pond.

7 Attach the penguins on top and around the cake with royal icing. Trim the board with a ribbon.

Christmas by Starlight

This stunning design is simple and quick to make. The cut-outs and stars need a day or more to dry out, so do this before you cover the cake with marzipan and sugar paste. Add candles to the table for a really star-lit effect.

Serves 10-12

6oz bought flower paste mix

medium and small star cutters

gold cake wires

edible gold paint

snowflake and shooting star cutter or ruler

1¼lb Sugar Paste (page 30)

10in round board

pale green edible food colouring

green sparkles

2in Christmas tree cutter

Apricot Glaze (page 26)

1lb Marzipan (page 26)

8in round Dark Rich Fruit Cake (page 20)

sparkly green ribbon

1 celpick (cake insert to hold stems
 or wires)

1 Make up the flower paste according to the instructions on the packet. Roll out a little of the paste very thinly and cut out 30-40 stars of different sizes. Glue these on to gold wires, three to a wire and leave to set. Paint some of the stars gold.

2 Roll out a strip of flower paste. Emboss it with a snowflake or shooting star design and then use a small paintbrush to remove carefully. Attach some of these with glue to wires.

3 Use 4oz of the sugar paste for the trees: color half with pale green coloring and green sparkles. Roll out to ⅛in thick and cut out several Christmas trees in white and green. Leave to harden.

4 Brush the cake with apricot glaze. Cover with marzipan and then with sugar paste. Cover the board with sugar paste. While soft, emboss the cake sides and top with stars and snowflake patterns. Emboss the board. Paint some of the shooting stars, or the larger designs, with gold paint. Place the cake and board on a colorful base board or platter.

5 Tie a sparkly green ribbon around the cake. Attach the green trees over the ribbon, attaching them with glue or royal icing. Stand 3-4 white trees on the top of the cake and support them with icing.

6 Make a small hole in the top of the cake behind the trees and insert the celpick in this. Arrange the wires with flying stars attached in the celpick, taking care to ensure that the stars don't all fall off. If necessary, place a small piece of paste in the celpick to keep the wires in place.

Yule Log

This is an excellent last-minute cake for Christmas. The jelly roll can be made with any of the suggested flavors – chocolate is traditional but often just a bit too rich for some – a whole-wheat sponge cake with nuts added makes a change. Make the sponge cake well in advance if you like, fill it with buttercream and freeze. Allow an hour for the cake to defrost before decorating.

Serves 8

3-egg Jelly Roll (page 17) made with whole-wheat flour

$^1/_4$ cup flaked almonds (or chopped mixed nuts)

1 quantity Buttercream (page 23)

4-6 squares bitter chocolate

1tbsp unsweetened cocoa powder

a little sifted confectioners' sugar

1-2tsp boiled water

1 Make and bake the jelly roll, adding the flaked almonds with the flour. Roll up, cool, and un-roll. Then fill with half the buttercream and re-roll.

2 Melt the chocolate until smooth. Spread out in two or more batches on trays, a marble board, or a clean work surface, and flatten it evenly with a spatula. If your kitchen is warm, spread the chocolate on trays that can be moved to a cooler place.

3 Allow the chocolate to cool until it loses its shine. Keep testing the edges to check for setting so it does not cool too much and set hard. When it has set too much you will have to melt it again.

4 Use a clean paint stripper or wide metal spatula to push through the chocolate, making thick curls or cigar-type rolls, or thinner curls if you prefer. Put the curls in a cool place until required.

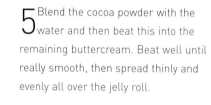

5 Blend the cocoa powder with the water and then beat this into the remaining buttercream. Beat well until really smooth, then spread thinly and evenly all over the jelly roll.

6 Immediately arrange the chocolate curls neatly all over the cake to resemble a pile of logs. Dust with a little confectioners' sugar if you wish and keep in a cool place until ready to serve.

Happiness and Harmony Wedding Cake

Serves 20-30

9in square Dark Rich Fruit Cake
  (page 20)

Apricot Glaze (page 26)

1^1/$_2$ lb Marzipan (page 26)

1^1/$_2$ lb Royal Icing (page 28)

cream edible food coloring (or mix tiny
  amounts of sunflower, chestnut and
  tangerine)

snowflake sparkle dust

bright pink carnations and greenery

gold and bright pink ribbons

11in square board

The decoration on this cake is influenced by feng shui. The intertwined fishes represent harmony and peace, while fresh flowers add a splash of color.

1 Brush the cake with apricot glaze and cover with marzipan. Coat with pale ivory cream colored royal icing. Lightly ice the board. When all icing is dry, fix the cake in place on the board with royal icing.

2 Use the small template (page 96) to make four pairs of run-out fish in white royal icing and leave to set. When completely dry, dust with snowflake sparkle. Attach a gold ribbon and a thinner pink ribbon around the base of the cake.

3 Mark the top and sides in half, into triangles. With a no.1 nozzle, pipe fine snail piping along the base of the cake and up the sides at the corners. Outline the upper triangle with snail or zig-zag piping. Fill the triangle with cornelli piping (page 36).

4 Outline each triangle on the top of the cake with snail or zig-zag piping. Mark and pipe a large fish run-out directly onto the cake using the larger template (page 96). Fill in the second triangle with cornelli piping. Leave to dry.

5 Attach the small fish to the sides with royal icing. Leave to set thoroughly, then dust with a little more snowflake sparkle. Attach fresh flowers at the last moment.

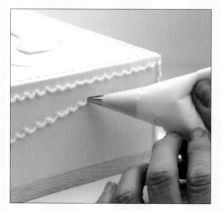

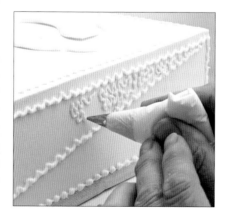

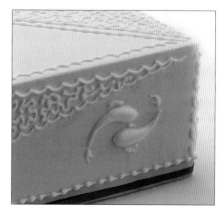

Love Birds Wedding Cake

Stunning birds in white and bronze make the perfect wedding cake top piece. Clever cutters are used to make the dove shapes and surprisingly simple piping with dramatic use of ribbons and bows completes the decoration.

Serves 100

6in, 8in, and 12in round Dark Rich Fruit
    Cakes (page 20)
Apricot Glaze (page 26)
2¹/₂lb Marzipan (page 26)
2¹/₂lb Sugar Paste (page 30)
¹/₂lb pastillage or flower paste mix
¹/₂lb Royal Icing (page 28)
apricot or skin-tone edible food color
copper and white satin lustre dust
    powders
dove patchwork cutters
Gildesol edible gilding medium
edible glue
floristry wire
white tape
bronze, apricot, and white ribbons
14in round cake board

Making Favors

To make favors, wrap apricot and bronzed sugared almonds in fine white netting and tie with very fine ribbon. To bronze the almonds, brush with Gildesol and bronze dust.

1 Brush all three cakes with apricot glaze and cover with marzipan. Cover them with varying shades of apricot sugar paste. Leave to firm up. Cover at least 2in of the edge of the cake board with sugar paste and frill it with a fine toothpick or frilling tool.

2 Prepare the pastillage according to the packet instructions. Roll it out very thinly and cut out as many doves as possible – they are very fragile so it is a good idea to allow for breakages. Follow the instructions with the dove cutters to get good shape definition. Use a paintbrush to carefully remove the shapes from the cutters.

3 Cover wires with white tape and then carefully attach them to the backs of the doves with glue. Leave to set for several hours. Brush half the dove shapes with Gildesol and then brush with bronze satin dust. Brush the remaining dove shapes with Gildesol and white dust. Leave to set for several hours.

4 Cut a piece of fine graph paper long enough to go around the largest cake. Place this around the cake. Pin prick fine marks as a guide for the top and bottom of each line of dots. Mark the sides of the other cakes in the same way. Then pipe fine dots in rows around the sides of all three cakes. Leave to set.

5 Trim the edges of the cakes and the base board with bronze ribbon. Make two or three large ribbon bows and attach them to pieces of covered floristry wire.

6 Place the cakes on top of each other, set back, not centered. Very carefully place a bow on each side of the assembled cakes. Place two, four, or more doves facing each other on the top cake. Add extra doves with the bows on either side of the lower tiers if you wish.

Templates

Piped Chocolate Decoration
(page 43)
Cup Cakes (page 48)

Petal Power Cake (page 68)
Enlarge to 200% size for
8in cake

Butterfly Thank You Cake
(page 70)

Simple Decoration for
Sponge Cake (page 18)
Enlarge to 200% size
for 8in cake

Happiness and Harmony
Wedding Cake
(page 92)